# THE NEW
# KILLING
# FIELDS

# THE NEW KILLING FIELDS

## Massacre and the Politics of Intervention

**NICOLAUS MILLS** and
**KIRA BRUNNER, editors**

*Bill Berkeley   Kira Brunner   Michael Ignatieff
Darryl Li   Peter Maass   Nicolaus Mills   George Packer
Richard Lloyd Parry   Samantha Power   David Rieff
Geoffrey Robinson   William Shawcross
Erin Trowbridge   Michael Walzer*

BASIC
BOOKS

A Member of the Perseus Books Group

"Justice on a Hill: Genocide Trials in Rwanda" reprinted by permission of George Packer.
Testimony from Bernardine Niyirora reprinted by permission from *Le Génocide au centre du Rwanda: Quelques témoignages des rescapés de Kabgayi* (Genocide in the Center of Rwanda: Testimonies from Survivors of Kabgayi), ed. Abbé Hidebrand Karangwa, published in Kigali by Kinyamateka, October 2001.

Published by Basic Books,
A Member of the Perseus Books Group

Set in 11.5-point Dante MT by the Perseus Books Group

A CIP catalog record for this book is available from the Library of Congress.
ISBN 0-465-00803-8

02 03 04 05 / 10 9 8 7 6 5 4 3 2 1

*In memory of*
*Irving Howe and Simone Plastrik*

# CONTENTS

# PREFACE

On the afternoon of September 11, I borrowed a friend's bicycle and pedaled the five miles from my apartment on Riverside Drive to Lower Manhattan, where the World Trade Center was still burning. It was an eerie trip. The West Side Highway, normally choked with automobiles, was almost empty. Only police cars and ambulances were being allowed on it. Even eerier was the quiet. At the piers along the Hudson River, commuters were already lining up to catch the ferries going to New Jersey. But despite facing a long wait on an unusually hot fall day, nobody was complaining or even speaking. I could only think of the newsreels I had seen of Londoners during the blitz steadily going about their business in the midst of chaos.

I knew I would be writing a story for the New York paper at which I often freelance. But as I watched people walk home from work in the middle of the day, it was difficult for me to shake my sense of guilt. I felt like a voyeur. It was a feeling that did not go away two days later when I went to work as a volunteer at the emergency headquarters the Red Cross set up in Brooklyn.

Such doubts about being a writer or bearing witness in a time of crisis are even more central to *The New Killing Fields*. There is no way for us to report on and analyze the man-made catastrophes that over the last decade consumed Yugoslavia, Rwanda, and East Timor without also asking ourselves if we are not exploiting these catastrophes. It is only when we think of the alternative—remaining silent—that an undertaking like this book make sense. Failing to write with accuracy and insight about the killing fields of the 1990s is bad enough. Allowing them to fade from memory with the passage of time is unforgivable.

In the aftermath of September 11, it has become the conventional wisdom to say that in the foreseeable future America and the West will care only about protecting themselves from terrorism. We believe the opposite should be the case. If America and the West are to achieve safety for themselves in the coming years, they will have to show that they care about more than just their own suffering. The war against terrorism cannot be won without allies, especially in the countries in which terrorists are most likely to hide. Our new vulnerability increases the need for greater moral and political imagination on the part of policy makers precisely because conventional military superiority no longer guarantees safety in a world in which a terrorist can turn the openness and technical savvy of a nation into liabilities.

There is a telling parallel between what happened in America on September 11 and what happened in the killing fields of the 1990s over a longer period of time. As Samantha Power writes in the essay that concludes this book, "The hope is that the attack will make Americans inside and outside government more capable of imagining evil committed against innocent civilians." In the nineties, it was enough to be a Croat or a Tutsi or an East Timorese to be targeted for death. After September 11, being an American was also enough.

What we do with such knowledge of ourselves and others is the question this book addresses by looking at three very different killing fields. It is all well and good to provide aid to a country after it has been torn apart, but as we begin a new century, it is crucial for us to reach beyond rescue and find ways of preventing a country from being torn apart in the first place. The slaughter in the killing fields we describe (and they are far from being the only killing fields of the nineties) occurred in real time and presented nations with a chance to respond in real time. Nobody could look back and say, "If only we had known." In an age of globalization and twenty-four-hour television coverage, the world knew very quickly what was happening in Yugoslavia, Rwanda, and East Timor.

In justifying America's decision to provide Lend-Lease aid to Great Britain at the start of World War II, Franklin Roosevelt used the analogy of helping to put out a fire in a neighbor's house. Roosevelt's point was that what needed to be done immediately was fight the fire at hand. It made no sense to wait and see the damage the fire might cause or worry over the expense of fighting it. In the 1990s the same imperatives applied in Yugoslavia, Rwanda, and East Timor, but America and the West, which had, as no one else did, the power to intervene, did not treat the slaughter that occurred in these countries like fire that needed to be put out as soon as it arose.

It is not difficult to understand America's reluctance to act. Ever since Vietnam, Americans on both the left and right have been wary of intervening in the affairs of other nations. We worry about being accused of playing the role of world policeman. We worry about being stretched beyond our resources. We worry about being thought arrogant. These are understandable fears, rooted in a history of terrible hubris. The trouble is that these are also fears that, if accepted uncritically, make America, along with its allies, spectators to slaughter, willing at most to finger-point and scold.

In this book, which covers too large a sweep of territory to have been reported on by a single author, we do not speak with one voice, but we do consistently make the argument that humanitarian intervention, however difficult it may be to engage in consistently, is required when hundreds of thousands of people are trapped in the killing fields of a country and saving them is possible. The order of this book reflects this conviction. At the start we look back on Cambodia, which more than two decades ago was described as a killing field as the result of the genocide committed there by the Khmer Rouge. Then we report on three contemporary killing fields, and finally we conclude with analyses that detail how nations need not be bystanders to atrocity.

In giving such paramount importance to the question of humanitarian intervention, we are aware of the rocky ground on which we have chosen to stand and the burden we are placing on America and the West at a time when their power is immense but in many ways they no longer control global affairs as they once did. Good intentions and endless calls "to do something" when they are not backed by the will to see them through can only make life worse for those trapped in the world's killing fields. But there is also—as we think events in Yugoslavia, Rwanda, and East Timor show—reason for believing that far more often than the world's political leaders currently acknowledge, humanitarian intervention can work, can save lives, can overcome the political obstacles it inevitably faces.

NICOLAUS MILLS
*New York, N.Y.*

# PART ONE
# Accountability

# 1

# The Language of Slaughter

Nicolaus Mills

In the midst of his speech at the 1993 dedication of the United States Holocaust Memorial Museum in Washington, Nobel Peace Prize winner Elie Wiesel shocked President Bill Clinton and the audience by departing from his prepared remarks to observe, "Mr. President, I cannot not tell you something. I have been in the former Yugoslavia. I cannot sleep for what I have seen. As a Jew, I am saying that we must do something to stop the bloodshed in that country."

Behind Wiesel's remarks was not only a call for action but an equally far-reaching assertion: fifty years later we were not applying the lessons of the Holocaust to the mass killing going on in Europe close to where the Nazi death camps had been.

In *The New Killing Fields* we have taken Wiesel's remarks to heart and tried to come to terms with the moral and political issues raised by the widespread mass killing and ethnic cleansing that have occurred since the start of the 1990s. In any number of ways, this combination of mass killing and ethnic cleansing does not equal the genocide of the Nazi era. It has been anything but a model of high tech efficiency and planning. Its perpetrators have contented themselves with using murder and intimidation to revenge themselves or drive their enemies from the land they want. The Nazis' desire to exterminate every Jew on the planet does not have a parallel in the nineties.

These differences do not, however, make the forces behind the new killing fields less worthy of condemnation or less necessary to prevent in the future. What the killing fields of the nineties have in common is that they are lands in which life was made intolerable through deliberate campaigns of murder and terror. This is true whether we are talking about the former Yugoslavia, where two hundred thousand Bosnian Muslims were slaughtered while troops from the North Atlantic Treaty Organization stood by; Rwanda, where in a hundred days eight hundred thousand Tutsis met the same fate, butchered largely by machete; or East Timor, where, according to a United Nations assessment, a quarter of the country fled or was pushed across the border into refugee camps in West Timor and twelve hundred more victims were added to a death list that totaled two hundred thousand since Indonesian occupation began in 1975.

The nightmare these contemporary killing fields embody is one that, to paraphrase Wiesel, calls for action, not comparison. Yet for the West, and particularly for America, confronting this new mass killing and its cleansing of civilian populations unable and unequipped to defend themselves has consistently been a matter of doing too little too late. In an era of twenty-four-hour television coverage of the world, it has not been possible to say of the new killing fields, "We did not know." But time and again those countries and institutions most able to help have found reasons for ignoring the new killing fields, failing to act when the chances for saving life were greatest or taking refuge in meaningless distinctions, as the Clinton State Department did in 1994, when it insisted that what was going on in Rwanda were "acts of genocide" rather than genocide.

Given the longstanding preoccupation in America and Europe with enemies who could be labeled communists, it is not surprising that the men responsible over the course of the nineties for the terror and mass murder in Yugoslavia, Rwanda, and East Timor did not draw the attention they would have if the cold war had still been going on and they had been viewed as surrogates for Moscow. Indeed, unlike Saddam Hussein and Iraq, these new killers and their followers did not even threaten American and European oil interests. In the pre-September 11 world, it was necessary for America and the West to deal with them primarily on the basis of humanitarian concerns rather than those of political self-interest.

Why were these concerns not enough to cause the West and the rest of the world to act in ways that would have minimized and, where possible, prevented the bloodshed of the new killing fields? To those of us whose essays make up *The New Killing Fields*, this question will not go away. But it is also, we realize, a question that requires us to go beyond finger-pointing and ask, how should the international community act when governments massacre their own people? What are the tactical and moral criteria for humanitarian intervention, especially for nations that were once colonial powers? When do human rights supersede those of sovereignty, and how do we move from generalized compassion for the victims of mass slaughter and terror to concrete action that saves lives?

The aim of *The New Killing Fields* is to try, as much as possible, to answer these questions by looking closely at what has happened over recent years in Yugoslavia, Rwanda, and East Timor. In focusing on these three countries, we do not mean to minimize the terrible brutality that went on elsewhere during the nineties. Our point is rather that the lessons that can be drawn from Yugoslavia, Rwanda, and East Timor—so different from each other in history and geography—reach far beyond their borders and allow us to talk about the killing fields of the post–cold war world without making this book simply a catalog of horrors.

In an address he delivered to the Canadian House and Senate in 1999, Czech president Vaclav Havel observed that one of the few bright spots in the West's intervention in the Yugoslavia was that it dealt a severe blow to the notion that what a government did to the people within its borders was not grounds for action by the international community. Havel's remarks point up how difficult it has been to find signs of positive change or progress emerging from the new killing fields. Our hope is that the essays that make up this book can, if only in a small way, help to reverse this trend.

We believe that any serious discussion of the new killing fields must acknowledge how rapidly the world has changed since the end of the cold war. The twelve-year period between the fall of the Berlin Wall in 1989 and the fall of the World Trade Center in 2001, the era of the new killing fields we write about, has already yielded to a time in which the developed nations of the world see themselves as vulnerable to terrorism in a way they never did. In the near future calls by government officials for humanitarian intervention are going to be scrutinized more closely than ever. With the emergence of smart bombs and computerized battlefields, the most militarily sophisticated countries will be increasingly reluctant to put troops in harm's way unless their own safety is at stake. Given these pressures, any serious discussion of the new killing fields of the nineties must be rooted in an abiding sense of the toll they took in human life and suffering. Detail, not hearsay or guesswork, is crucial in this regard, and it is for this reason that so many of the writers who appear in this book are men and women who went to Yugoslavia, Rwanda, and East Timor as reporters.

The dangers of writing either melodramatically or reductively about the slaughter and terror at the center of these new killing fields are all too real. Three years after the end of World War I, the Austrian writer Karl Kraus described problems like those we face today in a satire he called "Promotional Trips to Hell." Kraus told the story of an imaginary Swiss tourist agency that took the curious to the battlefield of Verdun, where from the comfort of their cars they might view "the quintessence of the horrors of modern warfare." Today that same impulse to exploit atrocity may be seen in Cambodia, where, the government of Hun Sen is trying to make Anlong Veng, the killing-fields stronghold of the Khmer Rouge, into a tourist attraction. So far, nobody is talking about converting the former Yugoslavia, Rwanda, and East Timor into historical tourist spots, but what remains an issue in this era of media culture is the ease with which the atrocities that occurred in these countries over the last decade can be turned, if a writer is not careful, into nothing more than serious-sounding entertainment.

Fortunately, there is an alternative. Since the end of the nineteenth century, a small but distinct group of writers, linked primarily by their willingness to bear witness, has developed a language of slaughter that in its descriptive simplicity and freedom from easy moralizing, portrays the mass suffering it describes unblinkingly while simultaneously making the point that governments and individuals have the power—if they will only use it—to stop this mass suffering.

Joseph Conrad laid the modern foundations for this language of slaughter, in which the focus is invariably on the individual as a victim of forces he cannot cope with by himself, in 1899, with the publication of *Heart of Darkness* in *Blackwood's Magazine*. The Polish-born Conrad went to the Congo in 1890 with the expectation of working as a captain on a river steamship. But the command he was promised never materialized, and appalled by what he saw—"Everything here is repellant to me," he wrote—Conrad returned to Europe six months later. What he could not shed, however, were the sights in Africa that had sickened him.

In writing about them, Conrad was not raising issues that were new to his European readers, as Sven Lindquist pointed out in his 1996 book *Exterminate All the Brutes: One Man's Odyssey into the Heart of Darkness and the Origins of European Genocide*. Since the Berlin Conference of 1884, the Congo had been the personal property of King Leopold II of Belgium, and throughout the 1890s reports of the atrocities committed there had been filtering back to Europe. In the mid–1890s the Baptist missionary Edward Wilhelm Sjöblom began sending back personal accounts that were published in Sweden and England. In 1896 Sir Charles Dilke, an ex-British government cabinet secretary and a member of the Aborigines Protection Society who had read Sjöblom's accounts, published a critical piece in the new magazine *Cosmopolis* attacking the "flogging and shooting that are going on in the heart of Africa." In 1897 the *Century Magazine* published the diary of the missionary E. J. Glave, in which he described the beatings he had observed as part of a "fiendish policy" that was depopulating the Congo in order to extract rubber from it, and in 1898 the *Saturday Review*, Conrad's favorite paper, published the story of Captain Leon Rom, "who ornamented his flower beds with heads of twenty-one natives killed in a punitive expedition."

Conrad's revulsion at the slaughter he saw in the Congo was no greater than that of men like Dilke and Glave. His genius was in giving the source of the slaughter a human face and allowing his readers to grasp the numbing regularity with which the slaughter was carried out.

The figure who is the greatest single source of violence in *Heart of Darkness* is the chief of the Inner Station, a man known only as Kurtz. Like the fabled Captain Rom, Kurtz has a fondness for shrunken heads. The fence posts around his house are ornamented with them. And like King Leopold II, who described his Belgian agents as "all-powerful protectors" and "benevolent teachers" engaged in "the work of material and moral regeneration," Kurtz sees himself as a defender of "higher principles." He is the author of a report on "The Suppression of Savage Customs."

Conrad will not, however, let Kurtz, who concludes his report with the postscript, "Exterminate all the brutes!" avoid political judgment by writing him off as simply pathological. Kurtz is an imperial everyman. "All Europe contributed to the making of Kurtz," Conrad tells us after noting that Kurtz's mother was half-English and his father was half-French. Even more important, Kurtz's excesses are portrayed as the natural extension of a system of extracting ivory at any cost. It is the voice of Charlie Marlow, who, like Conrad, came to the Congo to captain a riverboat, that dominates *Heart of Darkness*, and what Marlow captures with his painstakingly detailed narrative is a panorama of brutality. We see emaciated black prisoners, each with an iron collar around his neck, being marched to work. We see a "middle-aged Negro with a bullet hole in his head" lying beside the road. We see a black worker "screeching horribly" from a beating he is given for accidentally causing a fire.

Marlow has no illusions about why this brutality is tolerated. He describes European imperialism as the conquest of "those who have a different complexion or slightly flatter noses than ourselves," and he sneers at the "philanthropic pretense" that is used to justify it. He even asks his readers to imagine what would happen to the English countryside if it were suddenly subjected to African imperialism. "I fancy every farm and cottage thereabouts would get empty very soon," he writes, "if a lot of mysterious niggers armed with all kinds of fearful weapons suddenly took to traveling on the road between Deal and Gravesend, catching the yokels right and left to carry heavy loads for them." But what dominates Marlow's language is a matter-of-factness that rarely calls attention to his inner feelings and avoids moralizing about how imperialism might be reformed. It is the contrast between the horrors that Marlow describes and the neutral tone of his language that makes him believable, and it is this same contrast that invites the reader of Conrad's story to make the larger political and moral judgments Marlow will not volunteer.

A quarter century later, with the outbreak of World War I and the initiation of modern warfare—which at battles such as Ypres and the Somme left, on the British side alone, more than three hundred thousand dead and wounded—the language of slaughter was expanded to cover new horrors. In addition to Conrad, Thomas Hardy and Henry James were both alive at the start of World War I, but their generation of novelists would not be the ones to bring the language of slaughter into the twentieth century. That task would fall to a new generation of writers who believed the war was, as James wrote, "a nightmare from which there is no waking save by sleep," but who, in contrast to James, experienced combat firsthand.

In England this new generation of writers was made up of classically educated men who quickly found that nothing they had read about war as an occasion for heroism and sacrifice applied. In their writing the butchery of war crowds out all else. Carnage, not battle strategy or feats of daring, was their real subject. In Robert Graves's *Goodbye to All That* the battlefield is "the continual experience of death." In Edmund Blunden's *Undertones of War* it is a place "cancerous with bodies." In Siegfried Sassoon's *The Memoirs of George Sherston* it is "slaughter" that leaves the dead "grotesque and undignified."

It was, however, an American writer, Ernest Hemingway, whose formal education stopped with the end of high school and whose literary values were initially shaped by working as a reporter for the *Kansas City Star*, who, with more depth than any other writer of his generation, extended the language of slaughter that Conrad had developed.

The classic Hemingway passage—and arguably the single piece of writing that best describes modern warfare as slaughter rather than glorious combat—occurs in the middle of his 1929 novel, *A Farewell to Arms*, when the narrator, Lieutenant Frederic Henry, an American serving as an ambulance driver in the Italian Army, observes of the work he is engaged in, "I was always embarrassed by the words sacred, glorious, and sacrifice and the expression in vain. We had heard them, sometimes standing in the rain almost out of earshot, so that only the shouted words came through, and had read them on proclamations that were slapped up by billposters over other proclamations, now for a long time, and I had seen nothing sacred, and the things that were glorious had no glory and the sacrifices were like the stockyards of Chicago if nothing was done with the meat except to bury it. Abstract words such as glory, honor, courage, or hallow were obscene beside the concrete names of villages, the numbers of roads, the names of rivers, the numbers of regiments, and the dates."

There is an unbridgeable gap between the rhetorical simplicity of Hemingway's prose and the flowery language President Woodrow Wilson used in 1917 when, in a speech that blended the idea of banking and Christian sacrifice, he declared war on Germany by announcing, "The day has come when America is privileged to spend her blood and her might for the principles that gave her birth and happiness and the peace she has treasured." But what is equally striking about the Hemingway passage is how the already stripped-down language Conrad used to describe slaughter has been pared even further.

Lieutenant Henry has, in the course of the war, been wounded, as was Hemingway, who served as an ambulance driver for the American Red Cross in Italy, and so unlike Conrad's Marlow, Henry is as much a victim as a firsthand observer of the carnage around him. But Henry, who eventually deserts the Italian army and flees to Switzerland, refuses to dwell on his own wounding or to portray it as anything more than the result of random violence. "I was blown up while eating cheese," he sardonically observes when he learns that he may be in line for a medal. The result, as with Conrad, is that the reader is again invited to fill in the blanks, to go beyond the deliberately understated prose put before him.

In extending this invitation, Hemingway offers far more guidance than Conrad, a figure he came to admire in the twenties at a time when Conrad was falling out of literary favor. In disdaining words such as *sacred* and *glorious*, Lieutenant Henry explicitly dismisses the language that from Homer to Napoleon was used to describe war at its most heroic. Such language had become deceptive for Hemingway, and so, too, had the process of talking abstractly about war or constantly using metaphors to describe it. The only analogy that Hemingway will allow his narrator to use is one that reduces the sacrifice of war to slaughter in the Chicago stockyards and suggests that the soldiers are being treated as if they were cattle. The real lack of feeling in this passage is that of those leaders, in and out of the military, who try to prettify battlefield slaughter. Lieutenant Henry's seeming lack of feeling, his refusal to speak of war as if its sacrifices will make transcendence possible, is by contrast the response that makes most sense in this context. By his literalism—by employing a language that focuses on the names of villages and the numbers of regiments—Henry turns his back on euphemism and allows the details of the carnage he has experienced to define its significance.

For the better part of three decades, Hemingway's barebones style remained the gold standard for writers seeking to describe the slaughter that the modern state was capable of unleashing. But with the end of the Second World War and the liberation of the Nazi concentration camps by the Allies, it became necessary to account for a new set of realities. There was still room for irony and understatement, but in the years after the war, it was nausea, stemming from a numbing horror, that gave the new language of slaughter its most characteristic quality.

Martha Gellhorn, Hemingway's third wife and a distinguished war correspondent in her own right, reflected this change in a story she wrote for *Collier's* in 1945 about her visit to the Dachau concentration camp on the day Germany surrendered. Looking back on that day fifty years later, Gellhorn remembered, "Years of war had taught me a great deal, but war was nothing like Dachau. Compared to Dachau, war was clean." The same appalled sensibility was part of Gellhorn's 1945 reportage on Dachau. Her minimalist prose was designed to describe how the concentration camps had stripped the men and women in them of recognizable life. They appear as living corpses in Gellhorn's eyes. "Behind the barbed wires and electric fence, the skeletons sat in the sun and searched themselves for lice," she writes of the prisoners. "They have no age and no faces; they all look alike and like nothing you will see if you are lucky." It is an insight Gellhorn is embarrassed to witness from the perspective of someone personally undamaged by the war, and later on in her article, she goes on to explain, "Aside from the terrible anger you feel, you are ashamed." But Gellhorn will not let her shame silence her. The key for Gellhorn is to capture a world that she and the troops with her fear others will never believe existed, and she closes her *Collier's* story by turning away from the Nazis to talk about America and the Allies. "It took us twelve years to open the gates of Dachau," she writes. "We were blind and unbelieving and slow, and that we can never be again."

The most important writing on the concentration camps of World War II came, however, not from those who reported on them after they were liberated, but from those who had spent years in them before the rest of the world had a true picture of them. It was these men and women who for the second time in the twentieth century extended the language of slaughter so that it could reach a new audience.

What distinguished these writers was their personal vulnerability to the events they described. Conrad's Charlie Marlow saw the slaughter of the Congo from the vantage point of a skeptical European working there. Hemingway's Lieutenant Frederic Henry saw the slaughter of World War I from the perspective of someone who was wounded. But concentration camp survivors saw the slaughter of the Holocaust from the perspective of its intended victims. When they wrote about a "queue of human skeletons" or the humiliation of being tattooed with an identification number, they were describing themselves down to the last detail.

As such, the Holocaust survivors brought a unique ethic with them. In a world in which they were expected to die—and take to the grave the victim's experience of Nazi genocide—they triumphed by living and in turn felt compelled to make sure future generations learned of their experiences. They had to defy the kind of cynicism that famed Nazi hunter Simon Wiesenthal records in *The Murderers Are Among Us* when he tells the story of an SS officer boasting, "Even if some proof should remain and some of you survive, people will say that the events you describe are too monstrous to be believed: they will say they are the exaggerations of Allied propaganda and will believe us."

For the survivor-writers of the Holocaust, the result was a world in which bearing witness gave them purpose. It was a purpose that virtually all Holocaust writers talked about, but none more eloquently than Primo Levi, whose Holocaust writings from 1947 until his suicide forty years later in 1987 were crucial in making the Holocaust accessible to a worldwide audience. Early in his first memoir, *Survival in Auschwitz*, Levi makes the link between surviving and writing. "Because the Lager was a great machine to reduce us to beasts, we must not become beasts," he writes. "Even in this place one can survive, and therefore one must want to survive in order to tell the story, to bear witness."

But for Levi and the other Holocaust writers, bearing witness was only the beginning. How they bore witness took a very definite literary form. "Terse documents. Precisely kept ledgers of horrors. Accounts told with childlike artlessness," Elie Wiesel observed years later in *One Generation After*, and in a 1986 conversation with novelist Philip Roth, Levi went even further in discussing the economy of style he strove for. "My model (or, if you prefer, my style) was that of the weekly report commonly used in factories," Levi observed. "It must be precise, concise, and written in a style comprehensible to everybody." For Levi and the Holocaust writers, the idea of allowing an elaborate prose, let alone a prose that was hard to follow by virtue of its shifting perspectives, to divert attention from the events they wanted to record was anathema. They wished to remain believable at all costs. "When describing the tragic world of Auschwitz, I have deliberately assumed the calm, sober language of the witness, neither the lamenting tones of the victim nor the irate voice of someone who seeks revenge," Levi insisted. "I thought that my account would be all the more credible and useful the more it appeared objective and the less it sounded overly emotional."

In this concern for being believed, Levi was again far from alone. As the late Terrence Des Pres pointed out in *The Survivor*, his study of the writing from the Nazi death camps, in the overwhelming number of Holocaust memoirs, the writers say "we" rather than "I" and offer what is in essence a group portrait. There is a sense on their parts that they not only went through a collective experience in the camps, but that they are speaking for the dead as well as the living. "He bears witness through these words of mine," Levi wrote of an Auschwitz friend, and for survivor after survivor, this tie with those who died is one they feel shaping their prose. All remember the role that luck and friendship played in their survival and know they might just as easily have been killed as survived.

In this same spirit the Holocaust writers also tended to adopt what Levi called in *The Drowned and the Saved* the "humility of the good chronicler." They made sure their narratives did not get sidetracked with flights of fancy or unneeded moralizing. James Agee's plea in *Let Us Now Praise Famous Men*, "In God's name don't think of it as art," echoes throughout their work in their desire to have their readers remain unconcerned with the problems of literary construction. In the vast majority of Holocaust memoirs, the brutal repetitiveness of daily life in the camps sets the tone, and it is this brutal repetitiveness the memoirists seek to capture. Their ideal reader, a figure Levi refers to as "the judge," will, they conclude, have the best chance of understanding the slaughterhouse world the Nazis created if he or she is given concrete information in the order it happened with only minimal hindsight to soften the shock of it.

Fifty years later these same beliefs animate the language of slaughter that has focused our attention on the killing fields of the former Yugoslavia, Rwanda, and East Timor. What has changed, however, is the way people now get their news. In describing the world they knew first-hand, Joseph Conrad and Ernest Hemingway were in a position to write about events for which the visual record was crude and incomplete. Their competition with pictures was minimal, as was their fear of being thought redundant. As Holocaust survivors, Wiesel and Levi were in a similar position in relation to their readers. They were able to write personally about events that the newsreels and still photography of the 1940s never showed while they were happening.

Today, thanks to the electronic media and twenty-four-hour news cycle, writers do not have such leeway. Just as Vietnam was turned into a living-room war by the television networks, so Yugoslavia, Rwanda, and East Timor were turned into living-room killing fields that television watchers could view any hour of the day or night. Even when the media were kicked out of a country in which mass killing was going on, they were never gone for long. As David Rieff observed in *Slaughter-*

*house*, his account of diplomacy and ethnic cleansing in the former Yugoslavia, "Two hundred thousand Muslims died, in full view of the world's television cameras, and more than two million other people were forcibly displaced." In addition, Yugoslavia, Rwanda, and East Timor were places in which the writers who went there had options those they described did not. This is not to say that the writers who covered the killing fields of these countries did not act bravely and encounter unforeseen dangers that put them in jeopardy, but as professional observers rather than participants, they could always opt to leave. They carried with them passports, money, and credit cards. When they put themselves at risk, it was in most cases because they wanted to get closer to the story they were working on.

As a result one characteristic of the first wave of writing on the killing fields of the nineties is a self-conscious humility on the part of those who reported on them. Nobody, no matter how brave he or she was, feels qualified to write as a "we" rather than an "I," and in book after book authors make a point of informing the reader just how unaccustomed they are to the level of terror and murder they encounter. "With one exception . . . I had never interviewed a rape victim before," Roy Gutman writes in *A Witness to Genocide*, his Pulitzer Prize-winning collection of essays on Bosnia. "We were like aliens," Peter Maass observes in *Love Thy Neighbor* of himself and a group of journalists reporting on how Serb atrocities have affected a nursing home. "How many hacks to dismember a person?" Philip Gourevitch asks in *We Wish to Inform You that Tomorrow We Will Be Killed with Our Families*, his account of genocide in Rwanda.

What follows from this self-questioning are not, however, accounts of the killing fields of the nineties that end as self-indulgent apologies but accounts that transcend their authors' fears about their qualifications and their ability to find the right words for the horrors they report on. "Imagine, talking to skeletons! As I spoke to one of them, I looked at his arm and realized that I could grab hold of it and snap it in two places like a brittle twig. I could do the same with his legs. I saw dozens of other walking skeletons of that sort," Peter Maass writes after a trip to the Serbian prison camp at Trnopolje. Like Philip Gourevitch's description of the "macheted skulls" that "had rolled here and there" in a Rwandan school he was taken to or correspondent Cameron Barr's report in the *Christian Science Monitor* of Indonesian soldiers cutting off the ear of an East Timorese man they have just shot, what characterizes the most revealing accounts of the killing fields of the nineties is a prose that in its tautness and candor allows us to speak of the language of slaughter that has its roots in Conrad and Hemingway continuing into the present.

Equally significant, the writers who since the start of the nineties have made Yugoslavia, Rwanda, and East Timor their focus have not allowed themselves to become political agnostics. They are never so naïve as to argue that in the conflicts they describe only one side was guilty of atrocities. But they are not so overwhelmed by what they have seen that they cannot distinguish the worst perpetrators of violence, cannot give proper weight to the slaughter that at its most extreme was done by Serbs to Muslims, by the Hutu majority to the Tutsi minority, by Indonesian army and paramilitary units to the people of East Timor.

It is the continuation of this story that is the subject of *The New Killing Fields*. We would not be able to write as we do about what has happened in Yugoslavia, Rwanda, and East Timor if the groundwork for understanding them had not already been laid. But we would also not need to write as we do if these were areas in which a peaceful future were assured. What worries us is that when the television cameras are pulled out of such trouble spots, the world quickly loses interest in them and acts as though they can heal themselves.

In this present period, when the slaughter that in the nineties reached such a frenzy in Yugoslavia, Rwanda, and East Timor has stopped, we have a chance to do there what was not possible earlier: see if a permanent stability can be achieved so that a new cycle of killing and ethnic cleansing does not start up again. It is a tall order but hardly an impossible one, especially if it can be fulfilled with the help of an increasingly broad coalition of nations. In the aftermath of September 11, America and the West, which have, to a degree that nobody else does, the resources for dealing with the new killing fields, will, however, have to believe that their own struggles with terrorism and their need for allies are helped, not hindered, by battling the forces that brought such chaos to Yugoslavia, Rwanda, and East Timor. They will also have to fight being paralyzed into inaction by the knowledge that nothing they do in the future can ever make up for the enormity of suffering they have witnessed during the past decade from the comfort of their living rooms.

# 2

# Arguing for Humanitarian Intervention

Michael Walzer

There is nothing new about human disasters caused by human beings. We have always been, if not our own, certainly each other's worst enemies. From the Assyrians in ancient Israel and the Romans in Carthage to the Belgians in the Congo and the Turks in Armenia, history is a bloody and barbaric tale. Still, in this regard, the twentieth century was an age of innovation, first—and most important—in the way disasters were planned and organized and then, more recently, in the way they were publicized. I want to begin with the second of these innovations—the product of an extraordinary speedup in both travel and communication. It may be possible to kill people on a very large scale more efficiently than ever before, but it is much harder to kill them in secret. In the contemporary world there is very little that happens far away, out of sight, or behind the scenes; the camera crews arrive faster than rigor mortis. We are instant spectators of every atrocity; we sit in our living rooms and see the murdered children, the desperate refugees. Perhaps horrific crimes are still committed in dark places, but not many; contemporary horrors are well-lit. And so a question is posed that has never been posed before—at least never with such immediacy, never so inescapably: What is our responsibility? What should we do?

In the old days, "humanitarian intervention" was a lawyer's doctrine, a way of justifying a very limited set of exceptions to the principles of national sovereignty and territorial integrity. It is a good doctrine, because exceptions are always necessary, principles are never absolute. But we need to rethink it today, as the exceptions become less and less exceptional. The "acts that shock the conscience of humankind"—and, according to the nineteenth-century law books, justify humanitarian intervention—are probably no more frequent these days than they were in the past, but they are more shocking, because we are more intimately engaged by them and with them. Cases multiply in the world and in the media: Somalia, Bosnia, Rwanda, East Timor, Liberia, Sierra Leone, and Kosovo in only the past decade. The last of these has dominated recent political debates, but it isn't the most illuminating case. I want to step back a bit, reach for a wider range of examples, and try to answer four questions about humanitarian intervention: First, what are its occasions? Second, who are its preferred agents? Third, how should the agents act to meet the occasions? And fourth, when is it time to end the intervention?

## Occasions

The occasions have to be extreme if they are to justify, perhaps even require, the use of force across an international boundary. Every violation of human rights isn't a justification. The common brutalities of authoritarian politics, the daily oppressiveness of traditional social practices—these are not occasions for intervention; they have to be dealt with locally, by the people who know the politics, who enact or resist the practices. The fact that these people can't easily or quickly reduce the incidence of brutality and oppression isn't a sufficient reason for foreigners to invade their country. Foreign politicians and soldiers are too likely to misread the situation, or to underestimate the force required to change it, or to stimulate a "patriotic" reaction in defense of the brutal politics and the oppressive practices. Social change is best achieved from within.

I want to insist on this point; I don't mean to describe a continuum that begins with common nastiness and ends with genocide, but rather a radical break, a chasm, with nastiness on one side and genocide on the other. We should not allow ourselves to approach genocide by degrees.

Still, on this side of the chasm, we can mark out a continuum of brutality and oppression, and somewhere along this continuum an international response (short of military force) is necessary. Diplomatic
pressure and economic sanctions, for example, are useful means of
engagement with tyrannical regimes. The sanctions might be imposed
by some free-form coalition of interested states. Or perhaps we should
work toward a more established regional or global authority that could
regulate the imposition, carefully matching the severity of the sanctions
to the severity of the oppression. But these are still external acts; they
are efforts to prompt *but not to preempt* an internal response. They still
assume the value, and hold open the possibility, of domestic politics.
The interested states or the regional or global authorities bring pressure
to bear, so to speak, at the border; and then they wait for something to
happen on the other side.

But when what is going on is the "ethnic cleansing" of a province or
country or the systematic massacre of a religious or national community, it doesn't seem possible to wait for a local response. Now we are on
the other side of the chasm. The stakes are too high, the suffering
already too great. Perhaps there is no capacity to respond among the
people directly at risk and no will to respond among their fellow citizens. The victims are weak and vulnerable; their enemies are cruel;
their neighbors indifferent. The rest of us watch and are shocked. This
is the occasion for intervention.

We will need to argue, of course, about each case, but the list I've
already provided seems a fairly obvious one. These days the intervening
army will claim to be enforcing human rights, and that was a plausible
and fully comprehensible claim in each of the cases on my list (or would
have been, since interventions weren't attempted in all of them). We are
best served, I think, by a stark and minimalist version of human rights
here: it is life and liberty that are at stake. With regard to these two, the
language of rights is readily available and sufficiently understood across
the globe. Still, we could as easily say that what is being enforced, and
what should be enforced, is simple decency.

In practice, even with a minimalist understanding of human rights,
even with a commitment to nothing more than decency, there are more
occasions for intervention than there are actual interventions. When the

oppressors are too powerful, they are rarely challenged, however shock-ing the oppression. This obvious truth about international society is often used as an argument against the interventions that do take place. It is hypocritical, critics say to the "humanitarian" politicians or soldiers, to intervene in this case when you didn't intervene in that one—as if, having declined to challenge China in Tibet, say, the United Nations should have stayed out of East Timor for the sake of moral consistency. But consistency isn't an issue here. We can't meet all our occasions; we rightly calculate the risks in each one. We need to ask what the costs of intervention will be for the people being rescued, for the rescuers, and for everyone else. And then, we can only do what we can do.

The standard cases have a standard form: a government, an army, a police force, tyrannically controlled, attacks its own people or some sub-set of its own people, a vulnerable minority, say, territorially based or dispersed throughout the country. (We might think of these attacks as examples of state terrorism and then consider forceful humanitarian responses, such as the NATO campaign in Kosovo, as instances of the "war against terrorism," *avant la lettre*. But I won't pursue this line of argument here.) The attack takes place within the country's borders; it doesn't require any boundary crossings; it is an exercise of sovereign power. There is no aggression, no invading army to resist and beat back. Instead, the rescuing forces are the invaders; they are the ones who, in the strict sense of international law, begin the war. But they come into a situation where the moral stakes are clear: the oppressors or, better, the state agents of oppression are readily identifiable; their victims are plain to see.

Even in the list with which I started, however, there are some non-standard cases—Sierra Leone is the clearest example—where the state apparatus isn't the villain, where what we might think of as the admin-istration of brutality is decentralized, anarchic, almost random. It isn't the power of the oppressors that interventionists have to worry about, but the amorphousness of the oppression. I won't have much to say about cases like this. Intervention is clearly justifiable but, right now at least, it's radically unclear how it should be undertaken. Perhaps there is not much to do beyond what the Nigerians did in Sierra Leone: they reduced the number of killings, the scope of the barbarism.

## Agents

"We can only do what we can do." Who is this "we"? The Kosovo debate focused on the United States, NATO, and the UN as agents of military intervention. These are indeed three political collectives capable of agency, but by no means the only three. The United States and NATO generate suspicion among the sorts of people who are called "idealists" because of their readiness to act unilaterally and their presumed imperial ambitions; the UN generates skepticism among the sorts of people who are called "realists" because of its political weakness and military ineffectiveness. The arguments here are overdetermined; I am not going to join them. We are more likely to understand the problem of agency if we start with other agents. The most successful interventions in the last thirty years have been acts of war by neighboring states: Vietnam in Cambodia, India in East Pakistan (now Bangladesh), Tanzania in Uganda. These are useful examples for testing our ideas about intervention because they don't involve extraneous issues such as the new (or old) world order; they don't require us to consult Lenin's, or anyone else's, theory of imperialism. In each of these cases, there were horrifying acts that should have been stopped and agents who succeeded, more or less, in stopping them. So let's use these cases to address the two questions most commonly posed by critics of the Kosovo war: Does it matter that the agents acted alone? Does it matter that their motives were not wholly (or even chiefly) altruistic?

In the history of humanitarian intervention, unilateralism is far more common than its opposite. One reason for this is obvious: the great reluctance of most states to cede the direction of their armed forces to an organization they don't control. But unilateralism may also follow from the need for an immediate response to "acts that shock." Imagine a case where the shock doesn't have anything to do with human evildoing: a fire in a neighbor's house in a new town where there is no fire department. It wouldn't make much sense to call a meeting of the block association, while the house is burning, and vote on whether or not to help (and it would make even less sense to give a veto on helping to the three richest families on the block). I don't think that the case would be all that different if, instead of a fire, there was a brutal husband, no police department, and screams for help in the night. Here too, the block association is of little use; neighborly unilateralism seems entirely justified. In cases like these, anyone who can help should help. And that sounds like a plausible maxim for humanitarian intervention also: who can, should.

But now let's imagine a block association or an international organization that planned in advance for the fire, or the scream in the night, or the mass murder. Then there would be particular people or specially recruited military forces delegated to act in a crisis, and the definition of "crisis" could be determined—as best it can be—in advance, in exactly the kind of meeting that seems so implausible, so morally inappropriate, at the moment when immediate action is necessary. The person who rushes into a neighbor's house in my domestic example and the political or military commanders of the invading forces in the international cases would still have to act on their own understanding of the events unfolding in front of them and on their own interpretation of the responsibility they have been given. But now they act under specified constraints, and they can call on the help of those in whose name they are acting. This is the form that multilateral intervention is most likely to take, if the UN, say, were ever to authorize it in advance of a particular crisis. It seems preferable to the different unilateral alternatives, because it involves some kind of prior warning, an agreed-upon description of the occasions for intervention, and the prospect of overwhelming force.

But is it preferable in fact, right now, given the UN as it actually is? What makes police forces effective in domestic society, when they are effective, is their commitment to the entire body of citizens from which they are drawn and the (relative) trust of the citizens in that commitment. But the UN's General Assembly and Security Council, so far, give very little evidence of being so committed, and there can't be many people in the world today who would willingly entrust their lives to UN police. So if, in any of my examples, the UN's authorized agents or their domestic equivalents decide not to intervene, and the fire is still burning, the screams can still be heard, the murders go on—then unilateralist rights and obligations are instantly restored. Collective decisions to act may well exclude unilateral action, but collective decisions not to act don't have the same effect. In this sense, unilateralism is the dominant response when the common conscience is shocked. If there is no collective response, anyone can respond. If no one is acting, act.

In the Cambodia, East Pakistan, and Uganda cases, there were no prior arrangements and no authorized agents. Had the UN's Security Council or General Assembly been called into session, it would almost certainly have decided against intervention, probably by majority vote, in any case because of great-power opposition. So, anyone acting to shut down the Khmer Rouge killing fields or to stem the tide of Bengalese refugees or to stop Idi Amin's butchery would have to act unilaterally. Everything depended on the political decision of a single state.

Do these singular agents have a right to act or do they have an obligation? I have been using both words, but they don't always go together: there can be rights where there are no obligations. In "good Samaritan" cases in domestic society, we commonly say that passersby are bound to respond (to the injured stranger by the side of the road, to the cry of a child drowning in the lake); they are not, however, bound to risk their lives. If the risks are clear, they have a right to respond; responding is certainly a good thing and possibly the right thing to do; still, they are not morally bound to do it. But military interventions across international boundaries always impose risks on the intervening forces. So perhaps there is no obligation here either; perhaps there is a right to intervene but also a right to refuse the risks, to maintain a kind of neutrality—even between murderers and their victims. Or perhaps humanitarian intervention is an example of what philosophers call an "imperfect" duty: someone should stop the awfulness, but it isn't possible to give that someone a proper name, to point a finger, say, at a particular country. The problem of imperfect duty yields best to multilateral solutions; we simply assign responsibility in advance through some commonly accepted decision procedure.

But perhaps, again, these descriptions are too weak: I am inclined to say that intervention is more than a right and more than an imperfect duty. After all, the survival of the intervening state is not at risk. And then why shouldn't the obligation simply fall on the most capable state, the nearest or the strongest, as in the maxim I have already suggested: Who can, should? Nonintervention in the face of mass murder or ethnic cleansing is not the same as neutrality in time of war. The moral urgencies are different; we are usually unsure of the consequences of a war, but we know very well the consequences of a massacre. Still, if we follow the logic of the argument so far, it will be necessary to recruit volunteers for humanitarian interventions; the "who" who can and should is only the state, not any particular man or woman; for individuals the duty remains imperfect. Deciding whether to volunteer, they may choose to apply the same test to themselves—who can, should— but the choice is theirs.

The dominance that I have ascribed to unilateralism might be questioned—commonly is questioned—because of a fear of the motives of single states acting alone. Won't they act in their own interests rather than in the interests of humanity? Yes, they probably will or, better, they will act in their own interests as well as in the interests of humanity; I don't think that it is particularly insightful, merely cynical, to suggest that those larger interests have no hold at all (surely the balance of interest and morality among interventionists is no different than it is among noninterventionists). In any case, how would humanity be better served by multilateral decision-making? Wouldn't each state involved in the decision process also act in its own interests? And then the outcome would be determined by bargaining among the interested parties—and humanity, obviously, would not be one of the parties. We might hope that particular interests would cancel each other out, leaving some kind of general interest (this is in fact Rousseau's account, or one of his accounts, of how citizens arrive at a "general will"). But it is equally possible that the bargain will reflect only a mix of particular interests, which may or may not be better for humanity than the interests of a single party. Anyway, political motivations are always mixed, whether the actors are one or many. A pure moral will doesn't exist in political life, and it shouldn't be necessary to pretend to that kind of purity. The leaders of states have a right, indeed, they have an obligation, to consider the interests of their own people, even when they are acting to help other people. We should assume, then, that the Indians acted in their national interest when they assisted the secession of East Pakistan, and that Tanzania acted in its own interests when it moved troops into Idi Amin's Uganda. But these interventions also served humanitarian purposes, and presumably were intended to do that too. The victims of massacre or "ethnic cleansing" are very lucky if a neighboring state, or a coalition of states, has more than one reason to rescue them. It would be foolish to declare the multiplicity morally disabling. If the intervention is expanded beyond its necessary bounds because of some "ulterior" motive, then it should be criticized; within those bounds, mixed motives are a practical advantage.

## Means

When the agents act, how should they act? Humanitarian intervention involves the use of force, and it is crucial to its success that it be pursued forcefully; the aim is the defeat of the people, whoever they are, who are carrying out the massacres or the ethnic cleansing. If what is going on is awful enough to justify going in, then it is awful enough to justify the pursuit of military victory. But this simple proposition hasn't found ready acceptance in international society. Most clearly in the Bosnian case, repeated efforts were made to deal with the disaster without fighting against its perpetrators. Force was taken, indeed, to be a "last" resort, but in an ongoing political conflict "lastness" never arrives; there is always something to be done before doing whatever it is that comes last. So military observers were sent into Bosnia to report on what was happening; and then UN forces brought humanitarian relief to the victims, and then they provided some degree of military protection for relief workers, and then they sought (unsuccessfully) to create a few "safe zones" for the Bosnians. But if soldiers do nothing more than these things, they are hardly an impediment to further killing; they may even be said to provide a kind of background support for it. They guard roads, defend doctors and nurses, deliver medical supplies and food to a growing number of victims and refugees—and the number keeps growing. Sometimes it is helpful to interpose soldiers as "peacekeepers" between the killers and their victims. But though that may work for a time, it doesn't reduce the power of the killers, and so it is a formula for trouble later on. Peacekeeping is an honorable activity, but not if there is no peace. Sometimes, unhappily, it is better to make war.

In Cambodia, East Pakistan, and Uganda, the interventions were carried out on the ground; this was old-fashioned war-making. The Kosovo war provides an alternative model: a war fought from the air, with technologies designed to reduce (almost to zero!) the risk of casualties to the intervening army. I won't stop here to consider at any length the reasons for the alternative model, which have to do with the increasing inability of modern democracies to use the armies they recruit in ways that put soldiers at risk. There are no "lower orders," no invisible, expendable citizens in democratic states today. And in the absence of a clear threat to the community itself, there is little willingness even among political elites to sacrifice for the sake of global law and order or, more particularly, for the sake of Rwandans or Kosovars. But the inability and the unwillingness, whatever their sources, make for moral problems. A war fought entirely from the air, and from far away, probably can't be won without attacking civilian targets. These can be bridges and television stations, electric generators and water purification plants, rather than residential areas, but the attacks will endanger the lives of innocent men, women, and children nonetheless. The aim is to bring pressure to bear on a government acting barbarically toward a minority of its citizens by threatening to harm, or actually harming, the majority to which, presumably, the government is still committed. Obviously this isn't a strategy that would have worked against the Khmer Rouge in Cambodia, but it's probably not legitimate even where it might work—so long as there is the possibility of a more precise intervention against the forces actually engaged in the barbarous acts. The same rules apply here as in war generally: noncombatants are immune from direct attack and have to be protected as far as possible from "collateral damage"; soldiers have to accept risks to themselves in order to avoid imposing risks on the civilian population.

Any country considering military intervention would obviously embrace technologies that were said to be risk-free for its own soldiers, and the embrace would be entirely justified so long as the same technologies were also risk-free for civilians on the other side. This is precisely the claim made on behalf of "smart bombs": they can be delivered from great distances (safely), and they never miss. But the claim is, for the moment at least, greatly exaggerated. There is no technological fix currently available, and therefore no way of avoiding this simple truth: from the standpoint of justice, you cannot invade a foreign country, with all the consequences that has for other people, while insisting that your own soldiers can never be put at risk. Once the intervention has begun, it may become morally, even if it is not yet militarily, necessary to fight on the ground—in order to win more quickly and save many lives, for example, or to stop some particularly barbarous response to the intervention.

That's the moral argument against no-risk interventions, but there is also a prudential argument. Interventions will rarely be successful unless there is a visible willingness to fight and to take casualties. In the Kosovo case, if a NATO army had been in sight, so to speak, before the bombing of Serbia began, it is unlikely that the bombing would have been necessary; nor would there ever have been the tide of desperate and embittered refugees. Postwar Kosovo would look very different; the tasks of policing and reconstruction would be easier than they have been; the odds on success much better.

## Endings

Imagine the intervening army fully engaged. How should it understand the victory that it is aiming at? When is it time to go home? Should the army aim only at stopping the killings, or at destroying the military or paramilitary forces carrying them out, or at replacing the regime that employs these forces, or at punishing the leaders of the regime? Is intervention only a war or also an occupation? These are hard questions, and I want to begin my own response by acknowledging that I have answered them differently at different times.

The answer that best fits the original legal doctrine of humanitarian intervention, and that I defended in *Just and Unjust Wars* (1977), is that the aim of the intervening army is simply to stop the killing. Its leaders prove that their motives are primarily humanitarian, that they are not driven by imperial ambition, by moving in as quickly as possible to defeat the killers and rescue their victims and then by leaving as quickly as possible. Sorting things out afterward, dealing with the consequences of the awfulness, deciding what to do with its agents—that is not properly the work of foreigners. The people who have always lived there, wherever "there" is, have to be given a chance to reconstruct their common life. The crisis that they have just been through should not become an occasion for foreign domination. The principles of political sovereignty and territorial integrity require the "in and quickly out" rule.

But there are three sorts of occasions when this rule seems impossible to apply. The first is perhaps best exemplified by the Cambodian killing fields, which were so extensive as to leave, at the end, no institutional base, and perhaps no human base, for reconstruction. I don't say this to justify the Vietnamese establishment of a satellite regime, but rather to explain the need, years later, for the UN's effort to create, from the outside, a locally legitimate political system. The UN couldn't or wouldn't stop the killing when it was actually taking place, but had it done so, the "in and quickly out" test would not have provided a plausible measure of its success; it would have had to deal, somehow, with the aftermath of the killing.

The second occasion is exemplified by all those countries—Uganda, Rwanda, Kosovo, and others—where the extent and depth of the ethnic divisions make it likely that the killings will resume as soon as the intervening forces withdraw. If the original killers don't return to their work, then the revenge of their victims will prove equally deadly. Now "in and quickly out" is a kind of bad faith, a choice of legal virtue at the expense of political and moral effectiveness. If one accepts the risks of intervention in countries like these, one had better accept also the risks of occupation.

The third occasion is the one I called nonstandard earlier on: where the state has simply disintegrated. It's not that its army or police have been defeated; they simply don't exist. The country is in the hand of paramilitary forces and warlords—gangs, really—who have been, let's say, temporarily subdued. What is necessary now is to create a state, and the creation will have to be virtually *ex nihilo*. And that is not work for the short term.

In 1995, in an article called "The Politics of Rescue," published in *Dissent*, I argued that leftist critics of protectorates and trusteeships needed to rethink their position, for arrangements of this sort might sometimes be the best outcome of a humanitarian intervention. The historical record makes it clear enough that protectors and trustees, under the old League of Nations, for example, again and again failed to fulfill their obligations; nor have these arrangements been as temporary as they were supposed to be. Still, their purpose can sometimes be a legitimate one: to open a span of time and to authorize a kind of political work between the "in" and the "out" of a humanitarian intervention. This purpose doesn't cancel the requirement that the intervening forces get out. We need to think about better ways of making sure that the purpose is actually realized and the requirement finally met. Perhaps this is a place where multilateralism can play a more central role than it does, or has done, in the original interventions. For multilateral occupations are unlikely to serve the interests of any single state and so are unlikely to be sustained any longer than necessary. The greater danger is that they won't be sustained long enough: each participating state will look for an excuse to pull its own forces out. An independent UN force, not bound or hindered by the political decisions of individual states, might be the most reliable protector and trustee— if we could be sure that it would protect the right people, in a timely way. Whenever that assurance doesn't exist, unilateralism returns, again, as a justifiable option.

Either way, we still need an equivalent of the "in and out" rule, a way of recognizing when these longstanding interventions reach their endpoint. The appropriate rule is best expressed by a phrase that I have already used: "local legitimacy." The intervening forces should aim at finding or establishing a form of authority that fits or at least accommodates the local political culture, and a set of authorities, independent of themselves, who are capable of governing the country and who command sufficient popular support so that their government won't be massively coercive. Once such authorities are in place, the intervening forces should withdraw: "in and finally out."

But this formula may be as quixotic as "in and quickly out." Perhaps foreign forces can't do the work that I've just described; they will only be dragged deeper and deeper into a conflict they will never be able to control, gradually becoming indistinguishable from the other parties. That prospect is surely a great disincentive to intervention; it will often override not only the benign intentions but even the imperial ambitions of potential interveners. In fact, most of the countries whose inhabitants (or some of them) desperately need to be rescued offer precious little political or economic reward to the states that attempt the rescue. One almost wishes that the impure motivations of such states had more plausible objects, the pursuit of which might hold them to their task. At the same time, however, it's important to insist that the task is limited: once the massacres and ethnic cleansing are really over and the people in command are committed to avoiding their return, the intervention is finished. The new regime doesn't have to be democratic or liberal or pluralist or (even) capitalist. It doesn't have to be anything, except non-murderous. When intervention is understood in this minimalist fashion, it may be a little easier to see it through.

As in the argument about occasions, minimalism in endings suggests that we should be careful in our use of human rights language. For if we pursue the legal logic of rights (at least as that logic is understood in the United States), it will be very difficult for the intervening forces to get out before they have brought the people who organized the massacres or the ethnic cleansing to trial and established a new regime committed to enforcing the full set of human rights. If those goals are actually within reach, then, of course, it is right to reach for them. But intervention is a political and military process, not a legal one, and it is subject to the compromises and tactical shifts that politics and war require. So we will often need to accept more minimal goals, in order to minimize the use of force and the time span over which it is used. I want to stress, however, that we need, and haven't yet come close to, a clear understanding of what "minimum" really means. The intervening forces have to be prepared to use the weapons they carry, and they have to be prepared to stay what may be a long course. The international community needs to find ways of supporting these forces—and also, since what they are doing is dangerous and won't always be done well, of supervising, regulating, and criticizing them.

## Conclusion

I have tried to answer possible objections to my argument as I went along, but there are a couple of common criticisms of the contemporary practice of humanitarian intervention that I want to single out and address more explicitly, even at the cost of repeating myself. A few repetitions, on key points, will make my conclusion. I am going to take Edward Luttwak's critical review in the July 14, 2000, *Times Literary Supplement* of Michael Ignatieff's *Virtual War* as a useful summary of the arguments to which I need to respond, since it is short, sharp, cogent, and typical. Ignatieff offers a stronger human rights justification of humanitarian warfare than I have provided, though he would certainly agree that not every rights violation "shocks the conscience of humankind" and justifies military intervention. In any case, Luttwak's objections apply (or fail to apply) across the board—that is, to the arguments I've made here as well as to Ignatieff's book.

First objection: the "prescription that X should fight Y whenever Y egregiously violates X's moral and juridical norms would legitimize eternal war." This claim seems somewhat inconsistent with Luttwak's further claim (see below) that the necessity of fighting not only forever but everywhere follows from the fact that there are so many violations of commonly recognized norms. But leave that aside for now. If we intervene only in extremity, only in order to stop mass murder and mass deportation, the idea that we are defending X's norms and not Y's is simply wrong. Possessive nouns don't modify morality in such cases, and there isn't a series of different moralities—the proof of this is the standard and singular lie told by all the killers and "cleansers": they deny what they are doing; they don't try to justify it by reference to a set of private norms.

Second objection: "Even without civil wars, massacres, or mutilations, the perfectly normal, everyday, functioning of armies, police forces, and bureaucracies entails constant extortion, frequent robbery and rape, and pervasive oppression"—all of which, Luttwak claims, is ignored by the humanitarian interveners. So it is, and should be, or else we would indeed be fighting all the time and everywhere. But note that Luttwak assumes now that the wrongness of the extortion, robbery, rape, and oppression is not a matter of X's or Y's private norms but can be recognized by anyone. Maybe he goes too far here, because bureaucratic extortion, at least, has different meaning and valence in different times and places. But the main actions on his list are indeed awful, and commonly known to be awful; they just aren't awful enough to justify a military invasion. I don't think the point is all that difficult, even if we disagree about exactly where the line should be drawn. Pol Pot's killing fields had to be shut down—and by a foreign army if necessary. The prisons of all the more ordinary dictators in the modern world should also be shut down—emptied and closed. But that is properly the work of their own subjects.

Third objection: "What does it mean," Luttwak asks, "for the morality of a supposedly moral rule when it is applied arbitrarily, against some but not others?" The answer to this question depends on what the word "arbitrarily" means here. Consider a domestic example. The police can't stop every speeding car. If they go after only the ones they think they will be able to catch without endangering themselves or anyone else, their arrests will be "determined by choice or discretion," which is one of the meanings of "arbitrary," but surely that determination doesn't undermine the justice of enforcing the speeding laws. On the other hand, if they only go after cars that have bumper stickers they don't like, if they treat traffic control as nothing more than an opportunity to harass political "enemies," then their actions "arise from will or caprice," another definition of "arbitrary," and are indeed unjust. It's the first kind of "arbitrariness" that ought to qualify humanitarian interventions (and often does). They are indeed discretionary, and we have to hope that prudential calculations shape the decision to intervene or not. Hence, as I have already acknowledged, there won't be an actual intervention every time the justifying conditions for it exist. But, to answer Luttwak's question, that acknowledgment doesn't do anything to the morality of the justifying rule. It's not immoral to act, or decline to act, for prudential reasons.

These three objections relate to the occasions for intervention, and rightly so. If no coherent account of the occasions is possible, then it isn't necessary to answer the other questions that I have addressed. My own answers to those other questions can certainly be contested. But the main point that I want to make is that the questions themselves cannot be avoided. Since there are in fact legitimate occasions for humanitarian intervention, since we know, roughly, what ought to be done, we have to argue about how to do it; we have to argue about agents, means, and endings. There are a lot of people around today who want to avoid these arguments and postpone indefinitely the kinds of action they might require. These people have all sorts of reasons, but none of them, it seems to me, are good or moral reasons.

# 3

# Lessons of Cambodia

WILLIAM SHAWCROSS

Since September 11, no question has been more urgent for America and the West than how to combat terrorism. The danger of this dramatic and necessary change is, however, that it threatens to obscure the problem of humanitarian intervention—the need for it and its limits. This is no small matter, for even in these dangerous times, it remains crucial for America and the West to establish that in international affairs they care about more than just their own self-interest.

The 1999 war in Kosovo was defined by British Prime Minister Tony Blair as the world's first humanitarian war. The war was followed by international intervention in East Timor—first by Australia and then by the United Nations—to end Indonesia's brutal twenty-four-year occupation of the island. At the end of the old millennium, the world seemed to be changing the way it thought about humanitarian intervention. On September 20, 1999, UN Secretary-General Kofi Annan spoke to this subject in his address to the last UN General Assembly session of the twentieth century. He pointed out that the notion of state sovereignty, central to the concept of the United Nations, is being redefined by the forces of globalization and international cooperation. Individual rights, Annan went on to argue, were now seen as more important than in the past, and the international community was searching (at least rhetorically) for new ways to intervene effectively and to limit the impunity of dictators.

The reports that Annan commissioned at the end of the nineties on the 1994 genocide in Rwanda and the 1995 massacre of civilians at Srebrenica revealed in painful detail how very hard it is, for both organizational and political reasons, for the international community to respond with necessary speed to unfolding humanitarian disasters. The bottom line in both crises was that major governments did not want to do more. They did not keep their promises to protect people. Annan was correct in his assertion that when the international community promises to protect citizens, "It must be willing to back its promises with the necessary means. Otherwise it is surely better not to raise hopes in the first place." Others went even further in pointing up the perils of humanitarian intervention. Edward Luttwak argued that humanitarian intervention can be counterproductive and that the international imposition of cease-fires often ignores the underlying problems that led to war in the first place. In an essay in the July/August 1999 *Foreign Affairs* entitled "Give War A Chance," published at the time of the Kosovo War, Luttwak argued that sometimes only the evil of war can resolve a political conflict and bring about peace.

What is certainly true is that the history of interventions in the last decade shows how immensely difficult it is for the world to impose the solutions it seeks on recalcitrant regimes. Slobodan Milosevic ruled Serbia throughout the 1990s until NATO's intervention in Kosovo in 1999 led, with the help of the Serbian people, to the collapse of his regime, and he was finally turned over to the International Tribunal in The Hague to face trial for war crimes. Saddam Hussein, on the other hand, is still in power, and the Taliban were removed from power in Afghanistan only because the United States, after the atrocity of September 11, was willing to assault them with full military force. Before then, the chronic crisis in Afghanistan had been ignored by the international community for more than a decade. In his 1999 speech, Kofi Annan criticized this partial vision, which is often governed by something as capricious as the access of television cameras. He decried "our willingness to act in some areas of conflict, while limiting ourselves to humanitarian palliatives in many other crises whose daily toll of death and suffering ought to shame us into action."

The ultimate consequences of the humanitarian interventions that took place in the former Yugoslavia and East Timor are still unclear. In the short term, conditions for the vast majority of people in both crises have improved immeasurably, as have those of the people of Afghanistan with the fall of the Taliban. There is reason to hope that such improvements will be sustained. But if we want historical perspective on the long-term difficulties we face in these countries—and on how whatever happens in them is bound to reach beyond their borders—it is instructive to look at some aspects of the story of Cambodia over the last twenty years. What happened after Cambodia became a vast killing field?

It was clear from the moment the Khmer Rouge won victory in April 1975 that it was intent on creating a radical revolution of extraordinary brutality. But the outside world paid very little attention. The regime immediately drove the population of Phnom Penh into the countryside, expelled almost all foreigners, and closed off the country from the outside world. Its intention was to create an autarchic agrarian dictatorship. Over the next three and a half years, refugees were the main witnesses to what was occurring within, and they brought with them consistent stories of horror. They told of mass starvation and disease in the work camps created by the Khmer Rouge leaders and the systematic murder of people linked to the old regime, as well as those who questioned the wisdom of the revolution.

Before the Khmer Rouge victory, reports of its atrocious rule had filtered out of the areas it controlled. But few people listened. Even after April 1975, it took a long time for the world to accept the reality of the horror within Cambodia. Western intellectuals, many of whom had been opposed to the U.S. war effort in Indochina and tended to see Washington's enemies as courageous freedom fighters, were slow to accept that the refugees were telling the truth. Some even argued that their reports were CIA propaganda, designed to justify the claim that a communist victory would lead to a "bloodbath." But in March 1977, the French socialist and expert on Indochina Jean Lacouture denounced the Khmer Rouge for practicing what he called "auto genocide." Lacouture wrote, "After Auschwitz and the gulag, we might have thought this century had produced the ultimate in horror, but we are seeing the suicide of a people in the name of revolution—worse, in the name of socialism."

In 1978, the continued refugee tales of atrocities drove Senator George McGovern to ask, "Do we sit on the sidelines and watch a population slaughtered or do we marshal military force and put an end to it?" "One would think," he went on, "the international community would at least condemn the situation and move to stop what appears like genocide." McGovern was making serious points, but he was dismissed by both right and left.

At the end of 1978, Vietnam, for its own strategic reasons, invaded Cambodia to overthrow its former Khmer Rouge allies. For the Cambodian people this was a liberation; by then an estimated 1.7 million of Cambodia's seven million people had died from starvation, forced labor, and mass execution during the Khmer Rouge period. But Vietnam's intervention, which Hanoi declared was "irreversible," quickly became an occupation that lasted until the early nineties. Hanoi created a client regime largely out of defectors from the Khmer Rouge, including a young man named Hun Sen, who became the dominant figure in Phnom Penh. For more than ten years, this government ruled Cambodia, isolated from most of the world.

Even though the new regime ended mass killings and forced starvation, impunity remained complete. No effort was made to punish the authors of the genocide. The puppet Communist Party installed by Vietnam set up nationwide secret police structures and used systematic torture as one of its primary tools to combat Khmer Rouge guerrillas and other enemies of the regime. The director of the T3 prison, Sin Sen, infamous even in a closed regime for ordering the torture and deaths of real and perceived political opponents (not just Khmer Rouge), was rewarded for his work by a steady series of promotions, until he became the national chief of police. Throughout the eighties, Vietnam's dictatorship held on to power.

Loath to tolerate the notion that states may conquer weaker neighbors for any reason, the United Nations voted overwhelmingly not to recognize the Vietnamese-controlled regime in Phnom Penh. Instead, it ousted the representative of the old Khmer Rouge government and allowed a coalition that included the Khmer Rouge—and was led by Cambodia's former ruler, Prince Sihanouk—to hold Cambodia's UN seat.

Meanwhile up to half a million refugees fleeing first from the Khmer Rouge, then from the Vietnamese, and finally from famine, camped along the Thai–Cambodian border. Some of the camps were controlled by the Khmer Rouge, who were armed with Chinese weapons supplied through Thailand. Most of the refugees were in camps controlled by non-communist groups, including the royalists led by Prince Sihanouk's son Prince Ranariddh. The most fortunate were in refugee camps just inside Thailand run by the United Nations High Commissioner on Refugees.

The world's continued support for the remnants of the Khmer Rouge regime provided Vietnam and its supporters with an effective propaganda weapon. But in truth the autocratic and brutal regime they controlled in Cambodia showed little sign of seeking either the truth about the Khmer Rouge period or justice for its victims.

Throughout that period, humanitarian aid was the only intervention allowed by the Vietnamese and their client regime. Both in Phnom Penh and along the Thai–Cambodian border, food provision undoubtedly saved lives but, as it had done since the first great international human-itarian intervention in Biafra, it also fed and fueled the continuing war.

By 1983, the Cambodian relief effort was already one of the largest the world had ever mounted in terms of dollars spent per head of the population. In the Bangladesh crisis of 1971–1973, about thirteen hun-dred million dollars were spent on behalf of a population of seventy-five million. For Cambodia, close to a thousand million dollars were spent over three years on a population of seven million. Much of the money was ill spent, because the Western donors and agencies wanted to act as quickly as possible, without the necessary preparation, and because the Vietnamese imposed political rather than strictly humani-tarian priorities on the aid program inside Cambodia. The same factors were at work in the camps along the border controlled by the Khmer Rouge, but fortunately most of the border refugee population was out-side Khmer Rouge control. These were the Cambodians who benefited most from international concern. The relief agencies, despite their many failings, were at least able to educate children and teach skills to the adults in a way that was impossible under Vietnamese rule inside Cambodia.

Only the collapse of the Soviet Union—Vietnam's principal patron—and the conclusion of the cold war, ended Cambodia's limbo. As a result of efforts led by the Australian foreign minister, Gareth Evans, and Steven Solarz, a veteran member of the U.S. Congress, a plan was produced to bring Cambodia back into the international community. In October 1991, the Paris Peace Agreement created a virtual UN Trusteeship. The agreement was signed by the four main parties to the conflict: the Vietnamese client government in Phnom Penh under Prime Minister Hun Sen, two noncommunist opposition groups, and the Khmer Rouge. Including the Khmer Rouge, rather than attempting to put its leaders on trial, was distasteful to say the least, but it was essential for getting China, still the Khmer Rouge's principal sponsor, to agree to the peace process and to stop arming the Khmer Rouge. Many of those who argued for such a compromise believed, correctly it turned out, that the Khmer Rouge would wither once forced to come in from the cold. But in any case, they had few options. The alternative in the early nineties was a continuation of the war, no international recognition for Cambodia, and no chance for peace.

This is not the place to retell the story of the efforts of the UN Transitional Authority in Cambodia (UNTAC). It did have considerable successes, but it also created huge expectations that it was only partly able to fulfill. The UN was unable to take control of ministries in the government of Hun Sen as the Paris Agreement proposed. The Khmer Rouge withdrew from the process and then attacked it.

The Hun Sen regime also did everything it could to undermine the attempt to enforce democratic political and judicial norms. The national police chief, Sin Sen, created a network, known as the "A teams," which was responsible for the murder of political opponents in the run-up to the 1993 elections sponsored by the UN. In spite of the presence of about 16,000 UN blue helmets and 3,600 CivPol (UN civilian police), more than a hundred opposition party members were killed by these forces. Members of the network have acknowledged the crimes to the American writer Brad Adams. But they maintain that they would have been killed themselves if they had not followed orders and that they had been brainwashed into believing their victims were actually Khmer Rouge operatives.

UNTAC officials gathered some information about the operations and personnel of these forces, but fearful that the Cambodian People's Party would withdraw from the elections if confronted directly, they made only token efforts to disrupt the network. For the most part the UN chose to work quietly behind the scenes, releasing only one report on political violence during its eighteen-month tenure. When UNTAC demanded the resignation of one particularly brutal provincial governor, Ung Samy of Battambang province, Hun Sen said that if Ung Samy went, he would go too. The UN backed off.

In principle, UNTAC offered the best opportunity in modern Cambodian history to address the question of justice and begin to hold perpetrators accountable. Many Cambodians saw this development as one of the primary purposes of the UN "occupation"—even more important than the election, which became the centerpiece of what is better described as the UN's trusteeship. Nonetheless, the Cambodian courts, firmly under the control of Hun Sen's People's Party, steadfastly refused to investigate even the clumsiest political murder, and without the backing of most of its member states, UNTAC was reduced to belatedly setting up a special prosecutor's office that in the end ordered the arrest of only four alleged murderers and was unable to bring even one of them to trial. One of the accused died in custody, and the other three were released after the UN left. Sin Sen later said that he was amused at watching the UN spin its wheels while his operatives continued their work.

Violence did not stop the well-managed elections held in May 1993. These elections returned a majority for the royalist party (FUNCIN-PEC) led by Prince Ranariddh against Hun Sen's People's Party. But Hun Sen and his communist cadre would not accept the result; they threatened war with the UN and the secession of the eastern half of the country if the UN tried to impose the choice the people had made. The UN had neither the mandate nor the muscle to challenge them. As a result UNTAC presided over the creation of an unhappy coalition between royalists and communists. Ranariddh and Hun Sen became co-prime ministers. But Hun Sen's Communists, with their entrenched organization, dominated the new regime until, eventually, they destroyed it and resumed sole power again. The new government urged the UN to leave quickly, and the vast army of men and women in their white cars departed in summer 1993. Only a new and important UN human rights office remained.

The first year of the new regime was relatively free of gross human rights abuses. It even seemed at first that it might take action against those accused by the UN human rights investigators of political murders in Battambang. It did not. In 1994, the government enshrined impunity in the law by prohibiting government employees, including soldiers and police, from being charged or arrested without the permission of the relevant minister. Unsurprisingly, that permission was rarely given. Thus, while the prisons overflowed with ordinary citizens, the most dangerous and violent elements of society—soldiers and police—were virtually never prosecuted. Instead, Hun Sen built up a new security network. In 1994, he was able to wrestle the national police chief job away from party rivals and appoint his own man, someone with a reputation for brutality. Overt political violence returned, with the killing of three journalists, threats to members of opposition members of parliament, and a grenade attack on an opposition party—the Buddhist Liberal Democratic Party. This attack was even publicly announced in advance by Hun Sen, who said that if the party congress went ahead, grenades might be thrown at it. While pro forma denunciations were issued by some donor governments, little pressure was put on the new rulers in Phnom Penh to bring the perpetrators to justice.

The single worst case of impunity was the attack on a legal, peaceful political rally by the Khmer Nation Party led by Sam Rainsy, a popular former minister of finance who had been dismissed from the government in 1994 after organizing a campaign against official corruption. On March 30, 1997, Rainsy led a protest against the corruption and lack of independence of the Cambodian judiciary in a park across from the National Assembly. Four grenades were hurled into the middle of the crowd, killing sixteen and injuring more than a hundred. Rainsy was saved by his bodyguard, who acted as a human shield, dying in the process. Witnesses chased the grenade throwers toward the People's Party compound, but were stopped at gunpoint by Hun Sen's bodyguards.

The FBI was called in because an American was injured in what was considered a "terrorist attack." The FBI quickly concluded that Hun Sen was the only person who could have given the order for the grenade attack. Virtually everyone in Cambodia saw this incident as an attempted assassination of the leader of the opposition designed to send a message to Cambodians to avoid oppositional politics. Worried that the investigation was moving too close to Hun Sen and would further destabilize Cambodia, the U.S. ambassador ordered the FBI out of the country, and the investigation ground to a halt.

Many senior Cambodian officials, even in the People's Party, hoped that the FBI would publicly announce its findings, believing such action would force Hun Sen from power. But this did not happen. Although the identities of at least some of the perpetrators are known to the police, no one has been arrested. Hun Sen attempted to blame Sam Rainsy for the attack, suggesting he organized it to discredit the government.

Later that year Hun Sen staged a bloody coup d'etat against Ranariddh, his co-prime minister. The UN human rights office confirmed more than ninety extra-judicial executions after the coup, most of them of senior members of FUNCINPEC's military organization; Ho Sok, FUNCINPEC's deputy minister of the interior, was murdered in the office of a police general on the day after the coup. The murder was not even investigated.

Since the UN left in 1993, the impunity of murderers, old and new, has become standard in Cambodia. The UN human rights office and the UN special representatives for human rights have each produced extensive reports on the subject of impunity and on individual cases. Local human rights organizations have also written extensive reports on the subject, taking great risks to document case after case of violence that has led neither to investigations nor prosecutions.

Even senior military and police officials admit to the problem and complain about it, although when specific cases are raised they often go into denial. Freedom from punishment extends, too, to lower levels of government. Everyone in Cambodia is familiar with drunken soldiers refusing to pay their bills at restaurants, or illegal military and police checkpoints where one must pay a bribe to pass, or ordinary citizens having to move out of a line when a man in uniform arrives. Everyone knows who these people are, but no one dares to touch them.

Something of the same attitude applies to the Khmer Rouge. They had been weakened by the UN intervention, but Hun Sen has since been more interested in embracing than prosecuting them. In August 1996, to the dismay of King Sihanouk, the government rushed through an amnesty for a Khmer Rouge leader, Ieng Sary—who was now a warlord controlling the gem mines on the Thai–Cambodian border—to detach him from the rump of the Khmer Rouge still controlled by Pol Pot. Amnesty International complained that "amnesties which have the effect of preventing the emergence of the truth and subsequent accountability before the law should not be acceptable." The king agreed. As Amnesty International pointed out in its letter to the king, "Impunity is one of the main contributing factors to continuing cycles of human rights violations worldwide."

In 1997 Hun Sen requested an international tribunal to try the Khmer Rouge, but it is now clear that he did so only as part of a strategy for defeating them politically and strengthening his own hand. He was not interested in seeking justice for Cambodians or in trying to figure out, as Cambodians wanted, why the Khmer Rouge had killed so many of its own people. By the time the international Commission of Experts published its report in February 1999, Pol Pot was dead, the Khmer Rouge had collapsed, and Hun Sen had shared a champagne toast at his house with two of the most notorious Khmer Rouge leaders, Nuon Chea—"Brother Number Two"—and Khieu Samphan. The two apparently negotiated their defection to the government in return for a promise that no charges would be brought against them. Both live in quiet liberty in the former Khmer Rouge stronghold of Pailin on the Thai–Cambodian border, receiving guests and traveling freely.

A few weeks after the Commission of Experts report was issued, the last senior Khmer Rouge holdout, Ta Mok, was handed over to Cambodia by the Thai Army, which decided finally to wash its hands of the Khmer Rouge problem. Mok has been held since at the military prison in Phnom Penh with Duch, the former chief interrogator at the Khmer Rouge's notorious Tuol Sleng prison. These two are the only people ever arrested for the crimes of the Khmer Rouge. Mok and Duch receive deluxe treatment: Mok is the only prisoner in Cambodia to have a private bathroom. Duch has air conditioning.

For Hun Sen, a former Khmer Rouge battalion commander himself, the Khmer Rouge problem had been solved. Trials for the Khmer Rouge were no longer politically useful, given the many deals he had struck with people like Ieng Sary, Nuon Chea, Khieu Samphan, and lower ranking Khmer Rouge commanders—and they could cause trouble with his new ally China, which vehemently opposed a tribunal given its close ties to the Khmer Rouge while it was in power.

Instead, Hun Sen began to throw up obstacles to a tribunal at every opportunity. But when he announced to Cambodians that they should "bury the past," the public response was negative; even some elements of the Cambodian People's Party protested. Hun Sen then shifted gears, announcing his support for a Cambodian tribunal with international participation. Under intense pressure from the United States, which had been a staunch supporter of an international tribunal, the UN reluctantly agreed to a "mixed tribunal." In a February 2000 letter, Kofi Annan established four principles for its operation: The tribunal must, Annan argued, contain a majority of foreign judges in order to address the question of judicial independence, have an independent international prosecutor so as to ensure the power to indict, receive a commitment from the Cambodian government to arrest any person indicted by the tribunal, and agree that the amnesty granted to Ieng Sary would not be a bar to prosecution.

Hun Sen rejected these conditions. Instead, he demanded a domestic tribunal with the involvement of judges from friendly states willing to supply them. The Clinton administration, which appeared to want a tribunal at any cost, then announced its support for a complicated arrangement in which there would be a majority of Cambodian judges and no independent international prosecutor, but where a "super major-ity" of judges would be required for any acquittal and an appeals panel would be created to break any deadlocks between the Cambodian and international co-prosecutors.

This new arrangement was a dangerous precedent for international justice, but the UN accepted it. Still, this capitulation was not enough for Hun Sen. He imposed new conditions and raised new objections. He frequently raised the specter of renewed civil war if Ieng Sary or others were arrested and pushed through a law that conflicted with commit-ments he had made to the UN.

He then delayed final passage of the law creating the tribunal for almost a year and failed to respond to UN concerns over the operating agreement governing the relationship between the UN and the Cambo-dian government.

Senior UN officials became increasingly frustrated and concerned about Hun Sen's apparent lack of good faith and "lack of urgency" in concluding negotiations. In February 2002, the UN announced its with-drawal from the process. The UN said it had concluded that as currently envisaged the mixed tribunal "would not guarantee the independence, objectivity and impartiality that a court established with the support of the United Nations must have." The UN was particularly worried that Cambodia had refused to sign a legally binding agreement specifying the rules by which the UN would participate. Instead, Cambodia insisted that only its own rules would govern UN assistance. The delay in the creation of the tribunal allowed one of the most murderous Khmer Rouge leaders, Ke Pauk, member of the standing committee and the military commander perhaps most responsible for mass purges, to die in February of natural causes without having spent a day in jail. One by one, Khmer Rouge leaders are taking their secrets to their graves.

Astonishingly, several Western countries, including the United States, France, and Australia, responded to the UN's decision by criti-cizing the organization publicly and insisting that it continue negotia-tions. This criticism reflected the fact that these governments were less interested in credible or substantial justice than in staging a trial—any sort of trial—in order to close the book on the dark Cambodian past and to improve relations with the Hun Sen regime. The UN has resisted this pressure and has continued to insist that its decision is final. That is undoubtedly the correct decision in the circumstances.

Given Hun Sen's record, it seems unlikely that the UN and Cambodia will be able to reach an agreement for a tribunal that protects the sorts of judicial standards that the UN has tried to uphold in the war crimes tribunals in The Hague and Arusha. If no agreement is reached, then the Cambodian government will be in charge of any trials that do take place. In that case there is little prospect for anything more than a show trial of Mok and Duch.

It now seems probable that no judicial accounting of the Khmer Rouge period will take place. Even if the UN and Hun Sen had reached a satisfactory agreement, only a handful of people would have faced trial, whereas in both former Yugoslavia and Rwanda minor figures as well as major have been prosecuted. Many Cambodians still live in villages with their former tormentors and, with the exception of a spate of revenge killings in 1979, have waited patiently for the killers of their relatives to be brought to justice.

In short, the story of the world and Cambodia since the mid–1970s shows the immense difficulty that the international community has in intervening effectively to judge—much less to stop—massive abuses of human rights. Today the notion that there is a right or even a duty of humanitarian intervention is much more widely accepted than when Senator George McGovern first proposed it against the Khmer Rouge in the late 1970s. But it is still hard, verging on impossible, for the UN or other global bodies to make progress against the obduracy of autocrats, let alone of tyrants and mass murderers. The failure of the world to change the policies of Slobodan Milosevic, Saddam Hussein, Robert Mugabe, or Hun Sen without resorting to military force shows that, despite the end of the cold war, the advantage still lies with those who abuse rather than respect the law.

# PART TWO
# Yugoslavia

# BEARING WITNESS

## Lejla Sabic

I WAS ALMOST FOURTEEN YEARS OLD when things became a mess. My school was half Serbian, half Muslim, but no one recognized the difference, and we were all together. My best friend was a Serbian girl named Boriana. One day, she told me as we were coming back from school, "Lejla, fill buckets or whatever you have in the house with water. If you have food, put it in the house." I said, "Why?" She said, "I cannot tell you." But she knew it, they knew it, that it was going to start. Serbians knew it, but we didn't. I didn't see Boriana again after that day.

In the beginning they were shooting, shooting, shooting, but they hadn't begun to kill yet. They were only in the sky, and it was like that for two or three days. My sister and I went to my aunt's house, and one night we heard people outside the buildings. It was Serbs who called themselves "White Eagles." They were the worst, they were not like regular soldiers. They walked around the building cursing as they called for us to "come outside!" We waited in the house. I was scared. I moved from window to window. I just wanted to find a place to hide.

My aunt's husband didn't have a gun, nothing, no weapon. Because there were three of us girls, he said, "If they come inside"—they didn't, thank God—"If they come in, I have only gasoline, and I will use it to burn all three of you." He knew that they would rape us, and he said he don't want to watch them doing that to us.

As the war went on there was food, then no food. The electricity was gone, there was no gas, and no water. We were happy when we had bread, but we had nothing to put on it. We received beans, rice, and sometimes cheese, but that wasn't enough, and it was dangerous to bring food in. When we finally got some potatoes and canned beef from the humanitarian aid, we prepared a special lunch. I said, "Thanks to God, I'm going to eat now." But just as we sat down to eat, I heard someone screaming from the street, "Oh, Mother, Mother!" I went to the window and saw a man picking up his leg that had been blown off. I saw others coming to drag him away from the snipers. But we called from the window, "Please don't go yet, stay there," because the snipers always tried to get the first one, then they would wait for people to come and save him, and then they would send another shot. Finally they removed him and put him in an ambulance. I couldn't eat lunch after that.

It's disgusting, you know, war is disgusting. At night it's dark, it's so dark, and you just feel something bad in the air coming at you.

# 4

# Murder in the Neighborhood

DAVID RIEFF

Early on the first evening I spent in Sarajevo during the siege, I took a walk from my hotel to Marshal Tito Street in the center of town. The electricity was off, as it usually was in those days, but more luckily, the night was foggy. Luckily, because that meant it was relatively safe to move around. Snipers are not much of a danger except when it's clear, even when they have infrared night scopes. Having not yet learned to appreciate the literally life-giving gift that no sniper fire represented, I moved about a bit like a tourist. I had not yet learned to be afraid. What I remember most is how dark the streets were and how I felt as if I had moved from the world of color to a world of black and white. As an old man in high boots and a ragged coat passed by me, dragging a bundle of roped-together staves behind him, and then, a few meters along, as I passed an old woman begging, I thought that I had somehow landed in a Roman Vishniak photograph of one of the Jewish ghettoes in Poland in the 1920s.

Outside the former Soviet Union and a few impoverished pockets of Slovakia and Romania, Europe was not supposed to look like this anymore. And it didn't. In Berlin, or Amsterdam, or Paris, old beggar women were Gypsies or recent immigrants from the non-white world, and if an elderly white man passed dragging an incongruous bundle, he was in all likelihood a released mental patient or a drunk. Sarajevo had been rich, pampered even, at least by Yugoslav standards. It had a Volkswagen factory and Italian tourists by the busload, local rock and roll, avant-garde theater, and its own Gypsies to do the begging.

To walk along a street in a European city and have every ingrained assumption about what could reasonably be expected contradicted in almost every particular, to look at the marble of a historic Corso and see fresh mortar splashes that look like bear tracks, to catch glimpses in the dark of people's faces and clothes and not be able to situate them at all—this in a place where the social markers should have been familiar, and would have been, even a year earlier. But a year earlier meant before the war had begun and the siege ring had tightened like a noose around the city, like a noose around a throat. I might as well have been alluding to a previous geological era, so little relevance did that past have on this present.

Instead of being able to see everything and to find cognitive room for it, I could barely see anything and understood still less. It was not that there were no familiar reference points. It was rather that enough of what was recognizable had been taken away, and enough of what remained had been so altered that it was easy to become disoriented. And that can get you killed in wartime. Even in the protected environs of Marshal Tito Street, far from the front line, there were no cars, only the sounds of talk and footfalls and, in the distance, the whistle, screech, thump, and thud, and the light flashes on the horizon that are the *son et lumière* of war at a safe distance.

I was not afraid. What I felt was intense surprise. "This is a siege," I kept thinking, "a siege in Europe in 1992." Of course, there were other sieges going on or just ended while I walked the streets of Sarajevo. There was Kuito in Angola, and Kabul, Afghanistan, which seemed as if it had been under murderous bombardment for decades. But this knowledge did nothing to mitigate my confusion. This siege was taking place an hour's plane ride from Vienna, which was another way of saying that this was a siege that was not supposed to be happening. Unbidden, the deadliest of all modern European historical analogies— Leningrad in 1942; the Warsaw Ghetto—rushed into my head. Throughout the Bosnian War, they were never to leave me. Perhaps, though I have since been to Kuito and have returned to Kabul—which I knew as an adolescent, when it was still intact—they never will.

I will not defend these analogies, at least if their validity depends on body counts. Sarajevo survived, unlike the Warsaw Ghetto, and though it suffered horribly, those sufferings pale next to those of Leningrad. But neither will I put up my own identity as collateral and pretend that I did not and do not feel more empathy for the people of Sarajevo than I did, than I do, for the people of Kabul, or that the analogy of the Warsaw Ghetto does not have more historical resonance for me, the comfortably deracinated descendant of Lithuanian and Galician Jews—who, with one exception, either came to America or were murdered by Germans—than that of, say, the Cambodian killing fields.

Note that I say empathy, not sympathy, let alone the palpably false and morally intolerable claim that under any circumstances a Bosnian life could be worth more than a Rwandan or a Kashmiri life. I do not think it wrong that the Western reporters who covered the war in Bosnia understood themselves to be documenting a slaughter in the neighborhood, and that this sense of connection gave the reporting we did a special urgency and perhaps elicited from many, though certainly not all of us, an especially passionate commitment as well—one that far transcended professional interest.

Of course, there were some reporters for whom Bosnia was too close to home. I am thinking here of journalists, but more commonly of activists for whom the European or North American identity he or she was born with is a burden if not a curse. These are people who, a generation ago, used to say they felt more at home in revolutionary Cuba or revolutionary Vietnam than they did in Dortmund, or Barcelona, or Chicago—the people whom Hans Magnus Enzensberger lampooned in his essay "Tourists of the Revolution." Today, all revolutionary utopias having been closed indefinitely for repairs, such people tend to content themselves with saying how uncomfortable they feel except in a few cosmopolitan Western cities and university towns and trying to live as best they can in a kind of internal exile within their own societies. For such people—and during the Balkan wars they were more commonly encountered amid the ranks of humanitarian aid agencies than among journalists—Bosnia was almost too familiar.

For the rest of us, whether we felt guilty or had an easy conscience about the matter, the profound empathy we felt for Bosnia made it seem like the center of the world. Now that the city has returned to its "normal" size, that is, now that it has been shorn of its symbolic significance and is a somewhat reduced version of what it was before the war—a smallish provincial city in southeastern Europe with a brighter past than future—it may even be impossible for anyone who was not there between 1992 and 1995 to understand what all that fuss, commitment, and passion on the part of outsiders was all about. If so, all I can say is that on a very basic level, while those of us who kept going back there could have fielded a host of explanations at the time, I'm not sure that we fully understood our own indissoluble connection to the place.

We were not, after all, the Balkan equivalents of those foreign sympathizers who, in the heady days of Nicaraguan *Sandinismo*, were known as "sandalistas." Far from being subjects of emulation, to a considerable extent the Bosnians seemed like oafish relatives. Before the war, it was they who had imitated us. Even during the war, one sat so often in living rooms under posters—depending on the social milieu and age of the people in question—of David Bowie, an S-Class Mercedes Benz, or a Wim Wenders movie. But these cultural affinities, when combined with the sound of the shelling outside, and the realization that the child who wanted to prattle on about Lippizaner horses might get her head blown off by a sniper the next morning, made for a compelling mix. It was a combination of family obligation in the broad cultural and historical sense—that was where the empathy came in— and the imperative of solidarity for what were people's very real sufferings—that was where the sympathy came in—that made Sarajevo a cause and not just a story for so many of us.

Of course, it was a great story as well. Even those most heartbroken by what they saw knew that in their bones. In any case, to be a good journalist, as to be a good doctor, one needs that sliver of ice in the heart. The Balkan wars, after all, were the ultimate "man bites dog" stories. War was supposed to happen "out there," in the poor world, not in Bosnia-Herzegovina, which, before 1992, had been one of the most industrialized corners of the southeastern corner of Europe. Remember, this was in the early 1990s, before most people in the West became almost accustomed once more to thinking about the Balkans as their great-grandparents had done—that is, as a war zone. And, of course, it was also long before the destruction of the World Trade Center, which symbolically ushered in the twenty-first century, much as the assassination of the archduke in Sarajevo in 1914 had symbolically ushered in the twentieth.

It would be silly to deny that an indefensible racism—as well as what I insist was an utterly defensible and appropriate neighborliness—lay behind at least some of the sympathy so many of us felt for the Bosnians. To say this is not to let the reverse racists, those who care far more for the places that feel least like home to them, off the hook. But it is to concede that most of us have not progressed beyond tribal allegiance or, at the time the Bosnian War started, beyond what turned out to be the mistaken belief that Europe would no longer be a theater of war and atrocity.

There, in retrospect, was a foolish, complacent thought. And yet part of this cognitive dissonance that was such an essential part of going to Sarajevo for the journalists and the aid workers was this blurring of the familiar with the unfamiliar, this sense that one was going to a place where everything one expected to happen was not happening and everything one imagined could never happen again was happening again. The American reporters who used to joke, to the slight mystification of their European colleagues, that going to Sarajevo was like taking a trip into the Twilight Zone were not wrong. Because, all 1950s U.S. television references aside, in the Balkans the irreducibly heartbreaking was heralded, for most of us, by the irreducibly odd.

There was the oddity of being able to leave some comfortable hotel in an attractive, modern European city—usually it was Zagreb, in Croatia, whose charms, albeit mostly of the Hapsburg, *kaffee mit schlag* variety, are considerable—and, after an hour's plane ride, finding oneself in a place that only a few years before had had many of the same charms but now had nothing. And there was the oddity of reporters in Sarajevo being able to find their level—that is, a milieu not that different from the one they frequented at home—whether it was among fans of Michael Schumacher or Robert Wilson—but at the same time functioning professionally as they would in Africa or Central Asia—that is, in a context of war and privation that was utterly unlike home.

This simultaneous sense of displacement and familiarity was not restricted to the reporters. Many seasoned aid workers—whose professional deformation it is to ally themselves solely with victims in wars, and who tend to view the wars that cause the sufferings they try to address with utter skepticism and disenchantment, if not outright cynicism—were moved by Bosnia in ways that confused them. Like journalists, they too had grown accustomed to working far from home in places where the fundamentally impartial nature of their commitment was easier to sustain. But in Bosnia, it was hard for relief workers not to choose sides. Not just hard, but inappropriate—as inappropriate as it would have been had they been working at home, which, after all, at least for the Europeans, was on a certain level precisely what they were doing.

The sense that so many of us had that the war in Bosnia was not just monstrous, but shouldn't have been happening at all—an attitude that human rights activists may have entertained about a Rwanda or an Afghanistan but reporters rarely did—was certainly accentuated by the fact that so many Bosnians felt that way as well. They constantly talked about how what was happening to them should not be happening. More often than not, they did not mean this in the irrefutable sense that what was happening was terrible or should not happen to anyone anywhere in the world. That feeling is one that is both shared and frequently expressed by any victim of any war or humanitarian disaster, from East Timor to Angola and Afghanistan to Burundi. But what the Bosnians often had in mind when they talked about their situation was that it should not be happening to *them*. And what they meant by that— some even came out and said so explicitly—was that they should not be suffering what they were suffering because they were Europeans.

"This is not Somalia," was the way more than one Bosnian acquaintance of mine put it. The assumptions that lay behind this were not hard to parse. Because the Bosnian middle classes, for all their Western European attitudes, had not experienced the sea-change of mass immigration from the poor world and the multiculturalist reorientation that it produced, at least among *bien-pensant* Europeans and North Americans, people in Sarajevo were more forthright about expressing such views. But had we who reported on the war been more honest about this to ourselves, we would have had to concede that we, and the audiences we wrote for, mostly shared the Bosnians' sense that being European should have immunized them from the rigors of war that they were undergoing.

It was not that the difference between Bosnia and some conflict in the poor world concerned the degree of suffering involved, despite what then-United Nations Secretary-General Boutros Boutros-Ghali claimed when, at the end of 1992, he lectured Sarajevans who had jeered him that he knew of ten places where people were worse off than they were. All attempts to create hierarchies of suffering in war are both ignorant and morally obscene. Rather, what distinguished the Bosnians' experience of what had befallen them and that of Rwandans, say, or Timorese, was their sense that it should not be happening to Europeans. Like all Europeans, they believed they had been manumitted by history from a past that was, unquestionably, as tragic, cruel, and sanguinary as any in the world. They had assumed that the Second World War—the war of their parents and grandparents—had been the last war, the last field of horror that their country would experience.

Of course, the fact that history—that Satan with a sense of humor—had something else in store for them was something that, understandably, for the first couple of years of the war they were unable to take in. But it was this tropism toward indignation over their fate (it had dissipated by the third year of the conflict, replaced by a bitter and perhaps all too rational combination of resignation, anger, and despair) that made Bosnia a unique experience among the wars of ethnic cleansing of the first post–cold war decade. Even the Kosovars took the hatred the Serbs bore for them (and which they repaid in kind) for granted. No Kosovar, apart, perhaps, from a few upper-middle-class intellectuals in Pristina, was surprised. Angry, yes; bereft, yes; but not surprised. In this, Kosovo, though it was so close to Bosnia geographically, was more like a war in the poor world.

What distinguished the Bosnians was that they kept asking why it had happened to them. It was almost as if they thought they had a contract with the zeitgeist that said otherwise. Again, the contrast with Kosovo or with Africa or Asia could not have been more stark. Plenty of people in Somalia, or Afghanistan, or East Timor will ask why they lost a child, or a friend, or their property. But few will ask why bad things happened to Somalia, or Afghanistan, or East Timor. Unlike the Bosnians, people in those countries aren't under any illusion that they live in a place where history or, to put it more accurately, tragedy, has come to its end.

If they complain at all, they do so in the same terms that the great Renaissance historian and politician Guicciardini did more than half a millennium ago, when he enjoined his readers not to bemoan the fact that their city had fallen, because all cities fall, but rather to bemoan the fact that they had had the bad fortune to live at the precise time when their city fell.

To point this out is not to condescend to the Bosnians, as so many UN officials—living tax-free and (from the point of view of those who came from the poor world) blessedly far from their own home countries—did with such contemptible and predictable regularity. Before the collapse of Yugoslavia, the Bosnians had had no reason to think otherwise. It would be the worst kind of vulgar utopian solecism to imagine that, as their children's heads were being blown off by snipers and all the future seemed to hold was want, fear, indifference, and pain, Sarajevians should have said, "Well, you know, people in Angola and Afghanistan are actually having a far rougher time than we are, and, now that I think about it, the world is really paying a disproportionate amount of attention to us and not nearly enough to them."

No, if anyone deserves to be judged on this score—or interrogated about their motives and their moral bona fides—it is not the Bosnians. Attaching the label of selfishness, if one even wants to call it that, is another way of describing their humanness. But those of us who covered the war—above all, those of us for whom Bosnia transcended being a story and became a cause—are in a very different position. Unlike the humanitarian aid workers, for whom Sarajevo—no matter how tragic—was one tragedy on a long continuum of such horror that they had pledged their lives to alleviating, the journalists' identification with Sarajevo, and with the Bosnian cause generally, was unique. For better and for worse, I doubt that it will be repeated again in my lifetime.

Here again, the Kosovo case is instructive. For although many of us sympathized with the Kosovars, we were under no illusion that we were in Sarajevo. By this I mean that in Bosnia, despite everything that happened, and despite the hate that eventually grew so strong in people's hearts that even the very loving were at least momentarily consumed by it, the comity that had existed between Serbs, Croats, and Bosnian Muslims was real—at least in the cities. The statistics to back this will be familiar to anyone who has ever paid attention to Bosnia: an intermarriage rate of more than 35 percent in Sarajevo in the year before the war; a common language; a common secular culture that looked toward Western Europe. These are the clichés of "multi-culti" Bosnia. But they also have the singular virtue of being true. In contrast, relations between Serbs and Kosovars were always a zero-sum game. Despite the fact that there have always been individual Serbs and individual Kosovars who felt (and feel) differently, the formula was simple: Albanians on top, Serbs get the chop, and vice versa. The fact that the Serbs were usually on top throughout the course of Yugoslav history, and that the "ethnic cleansing" of Albanians from the province has had an imaginative and emotional hold on Serb intellectuals dating back at least to the nineteenth century and probably much earlier, does little, alas, to alter this.

And what the journalists encountered in Kosovo, they had encountered in Sierra Leone, where the conflict so often seemed to consist of the Krio elite versus the rest; or in Liberia, where it was the Krahn people versus the Americo-Liberians; or Pashtun versus Tajik and Uzbek in Afghanistan. This sickening list, an inventory of human beings behaving at their collective worst, which in the long run drives any journalist of feeling either to alcoholism and the deepest misanthropy or to another beat, seemed to many of us to have a sole redeeming exception: Bosnia.

So perhaps this empathy that the journalists felt for the Bosnians was not just Eurocentric self-love after all. I use the equivocal "perhaps" before of course Bosnia affected us as Europeans and Euro-Americans in the sense that it seemed like an affront not just to our values but our expectations. Before Bosnia, journalists, most of whom are at least somewhat left wing, imagined that whatever horrors the future held in

store, fascism was not one of them. Then there came Slobodan Milosevic. When my colleague Ed Vulliamy, the first journalist to penetrate
the Serb gulag in northern Bosnia, entered the Omarska concentration
camp, one of his first reactions was to despair. This could not be happening again, forty-seven years after the liberation of Auschwitz and
Dachau.

Like the aid workers, many of us had not simply spent a great deal
of our professional lives away from Europe and North America, but had
devoted our careers to trying to make those who read our work or
looked at our pictures care about non-European, non-North American
tragedies. But we were certainly Eurocentric in the negative sense that
we had imagined that after the Holocaust Europe had learned its lesson.
Was this a species of vanity or self-love? I suppose it was. Nonetheless, I
am not prepared to repudiate it. For it was this sense that what was
going on in Bosnia should not have been happening that gave us our
energy—our willingness to expose ourselves to the risks we took, year
after dispiriting year.

The journalist's credo is one of passionate noninvolvement. At their
best, journalists make assumptions about the proper stances they
should take and the attributes they should embody that are not only
humanly over-ambitious, but also largely contradictory. Most journalists
aspire to be both professional insiders and professional outsiders at the
same time. They fancy that they know how to be comfortable in any
milieu from an ambassador's dinner table to the communal feeding station in a refugee camp, and from Friday prayers in Cairo to a meeting of
Lacanian analysts in Berkeley. And yet, at the same time, they usually
pretend to themselves and to others that they belong nowhere, have
long ago severed their ties with their origins, whether ethnic, religious,
or racial, and, more convincingly, that they have grown accustomed to
viewing the world with a certain distance. They do not claim to be
objective, of course, because they know that real objectivity is impossible, nor do they confuse distance with detachment. How could they,
since their stock-in-trade is storytelling?

But it would be idle to pretend that any of us feel equally engaged in
every story. To talk autobiographically, I took a great many risks in

Bosnia that I would not have been willing to take in a conflict where I was indifferent to the outcome. In the breakaway Georgian province of Abkhazia, shortly before the capital, Sukhumi, fell to the rebels, I was briefly trapped in the presidency building. The rebels had Sukhoi jets whose bunker-busting bombs were rumored to be able to penetrate nine stories below ground level. I remember thinking, "I don't give a fuck who wins this damn war. They're all a bunch of swine. All I want to do is get out of this place in one piece."

Luckily, I did. Alexandra Tuttle, the extraordinary *Wall Street Journal* correspondent, did not. She died when the last plane out of Sukhumi was shot down by rebel Triple-A. Every time I think of Abkhazia, I think of her. But dozens of foreign correspondents were killed during the Bosnian War, and hundreds hurt, either through wounds or the road accidents that were one of the stranger subplots of the war. I knew a number of them, and think of them often. But when I think of Bosnia, I do not think of my dead colleagues; I think of Bosnia. And when I think of the risks I took (risks that, at their most extreme, pale into insignificance compared with what others did), I think, without any hyperbole, that it was the least I should have done.

The reason for this is simple: I believed then, and I believe now, that Bosnia was worth dying for. In affirming this, I think I am simply stating openly what most of us who covered the war believed, and what drew us back to Sarajevo, or Travnik, or Tuzla, or Mostar, month after month and year after year. I do not want to exaggerate the quality of our conduct, let alone the effect we had, because although we did manage to keep the story alive, we did not manage to provoke the intervention most of us yearned for.

But at least for many of us, Bosnia was our generation's Spanish Civil War. Like our predecessors, who sided with the Republic in 1936, we thought our obligations went far beyond telling stories or reporting the news.

I do not want to tell war stories, and I won't. What is obvious is that what seemed like a moral imperative to those of us who felt this way about Bosnia must have seemed like prejudice to those who did not take the Bosnian side. I am not referring to the pro-Serb groups in Western

Europe and North America. They were either Serb nationalists or extreme leftists like Noam Chomsky, whose worldview could be summed up as "There is no wickedness in the world greater than the wickedness of the United States" and whose view about the Bosnian War could be summed up as "Better a Serb victory than a NATO victory." Unsurprisingly, these same fools are peddling a remarkably similar line about Osama bin Laden.

But there were many people, particularly within the United Nations and the European policy establishment, who took a "plague on all their houses" view of the Bosnian War. For them, pro-Bosnian journalists like me had simply been unwilling to hear the bad news that there was no right side to the conflict, only degrees of wickedness on the part of the political leadership of the Serbs, the Croats, and the Bosnian government and civilian victims who needed aid. I will go to my grave not simply believing that these people were wrong, but that their commitment to this brand of impartiality was a species of appeasement that cost eight thousand men and boys in Srebrenica their lives and led ineluctably to the Kosovo crisis. Again, the comparison to the conduct of the League of Nations and the so-called Sanctions Committee during the Spanish Civil War that, in the name of impartiality, denied the Spanish Republic the means to defend itself while weapons and troops were pouring into the Fascist side from Italy and Germany seems all too appropriate. As a result, for me, Kofi Annan, Nobel Peace Prize or no Nobel Prize, is and always will be the Pontius Pilate of our age. But in fairness, people who thought like Annan were right to believe that the press in Bosnia was not objective.

For me that lack of objectivity is a badge of honor. I do not think that we had the obligation to be objective about the Bosnian War any more than a journalist in 1940 would have had the obligation to be objective about the Second World War. Journalists were not permitted into the Warsaw Ghetto, but one would hope that had a reporter managed to get in, he or she would not have written a piece that tried to present the German and the Jewish points of view as if they were morally of equal weight. That I immediately gravitate to this analogy makes it clear how clear I believe the issues were in Bosnia. Because of course a journalism that was always partial, that gave up all pretense to objectivity, would soon deteriorate into polemic and advocacy. By definition, what my colleagues and I practiced in Bosnia has to be the exception rather than the rule. Just as every first-year philosophy student learns about limiting cases, why shouldn't there be limiting cases in journalistic practice—that is, events that demand that one no longer even pretend to be objective?

Were there pitfalls to this approach, moral hazards that we navigated with difficulty and, at times, failed to address? Absolutely. Those of us who were convinced of the rightness of the Bosnian cause tended to underplay the corruption of Bosnian political elites, who, throughout the war, even in Sarajevo, were making fortunes off the conflict, doing private deals with the Serbs, and placing family members, friends, and mistresses in cushy jobs abroad. We also wrote less than we should have about the relation between war and crime on the front line, where the black market flourished even in the worst moments of fighting, and about the cruelty of combat and the fact that torture was practiced routinely and prisoners taken only when the possibility of ransom existed. If I am making an inventory of what we should have written about, I would add that while we wrote about the way the Serbs used rape as a weapon of war, we did not write about the ubiquity of "nonpolitical" rape on all sides of the line.

But again, I would insist that an analogous list of subjects could have been made up during the Spanish Civil War. Did Ernest Hemingway write enough about the murder of priests by the militia of the Workers Party of Marxist Unity (POUM)? Of course, he didn't. Did Martha Gellhorn sufficiently understand the degree to which the Soviet Union was using the Spanish Republic for its own ends? From my small knowledge of her, even at the end of her life, I doubt she took in that piece of bad news completely. But do these and the many other sins of omission committed by journalists who sided with the Republic change the fact that by, in a certain sense, betraying their canon of impartiality, they did or at least tried to do the right thing? I don't believe so. And that justification—not a journalistic one, but a moral one—both accounts for what we did in the Bosnian War and may excuse what we did not do.

Again, I do not want to minimize the hazards of the decisions we took. The famous story about Jean-Paul Sartre at the end of his life telling an interviewer that he had known about the Gulag all along but that he had said nothing because he did not want to demoralize the French working class should be a cautionary tale to anyone who believes that the truth may be sacrificed for a good cause. But while we were partial, I do not believe that any of us ever lied for Bosnia. That obligation to tell the truth, whether it aids the cause of justice or retards it, is, I believe, the irreducible obligation of the writer, the reporter, and the photographer. Beyond that, morally speaking, we're on our own—as we should be.

I have written about the challenges that Bosnia posed to the journalists' approach, and though I have defended what we did, I will always wonder if we could have done it better. When all is said and done, what I really regret is not that there was a Bosnia to challenge all the received wisdom about impartiality or to pose the problem of Eurocentrism, no matter how reluctant, but rather that there are so few Bosnias. By "coming home" to Europe, Western journalists found their moral center again, however briefly. Anyone doubting this has only to look at the quality of the work that was produced during the Bosnian War. Has any press corps written or photographed better? I doubt it. And if the work was real, it was because the commitment was absolute.

Will it be reproduced? Someday, doubtless it will be. But for now, the model is Afghanistan, not Bosnia. In this new crisis, the journalists are back on familiar ground. At best, like me, they will reluctantly support the war, knowing full well how filthily it will be waged and how shabby the political compromises involved will be. Or, alternatively, they will find themselves seeing the conflict as one in which they are forced to move across frontlines between militarism and fundamentalism. Certainly, no journalists will go back to Kabul, or Quetta, or Herat because they believe Afghanistan is worth dying for on moral grounds. They, we, will go because the story is important, because someone must give voice to the refugees, because one has a professional obligation, or because that is what one is paid to do. Unlike in Bosnia, there will be little confusion of roles, no worries about whether one is behaving too much like an activist and not enough like a journalist, and no need to wear one's heart on one's sleeve. We will be back in the world of old habits, modes of feeling, and complaint.

# 5

# Paying for the
# Powell Doctrine

Peter Maass

In the early days of the Bosnian War, Colin Powell, who at the time chaired the Joint Chiefs of Staff, came to the conclusion that stopping the fighting would require the use of 250,000 troops. President George Bush took his advice to heart and, fearing another Vietnam, opted to keep U.S. troops at home, safe and sound. Powell's estimate seemed reasonable because the fighting in Bosnia was vicious, and under the Powell Doctrine, the U.S. government, when intervening abroad, would rely on the military equivalent of a sledgehammer, never a chisel. You can't miss with a sledgehammer, Powell believed.

In Washington, few politicians challenged Powell's judgment. The headlines from Bosnia told stark tales of torture, executions, concentration camps, and sieges. Bosnia was in the grip of genocide, and genocide, as everyone knows, is a massive and infernal machine—Evil and Apocalypse entwined—and it cannot be defeated on the cheap. Americans tend to equate the face of genocide with Adolf Hitler, not Radovan Karadzic. If you want to defeat Hitlerian evil, you must, it follows, amass the forces of D-Day and have a great generation on hand to storm the beaches (or mountains or deserts or jungles, as the case may be). Understandably, few politicians wished to send untold numbers of GIs to an obscure and violent country where it was hard to figure out who was committing genocide against whom and where American blood would seep into soil that contained no oil.

If you were in Bosnia at the time, as I was, the situation would not have appeared so fuzzy. You might have wondered, as I did, where Powell was planning to put all those troops, and what they would do. Genocide is a strange animal; it is monstrous, but not a monster. I met and occasionally shared a glass of brandy with more than a few war criminals in Bosnia, and I learned that these were not brave men and women, and that their numbers were not so immense. Many of the atrocities in the war were committed by paramilitary squads drawn heavily from Serbia's underworld; these soldiers—I use the word with great caution—were excellent killers of civilians and takers of whatever loot they could find, but they would not have fared well against an army, which, at the beginning of the war, the newly independent Bosnian government did not have. That is why the Serbs were able to seize so much territory at the start—they faced no organized opposition. Once it took shape, Bosnia's army found itself fighting an uphill battle and suffering from an international arms embargo that starved it of the weapons it needed to mount offensives (or defensives).

The siege of Sarajevo was maintained by heavy weapons and lazy soldiers like Dragisa, who made a point of not volunteering his last name when I visited him in the fall of 1992 at his place of work, a fortified machine-gun nest in the hills above the Bosnian capital. His job, and the job of the three soldiers he worked with, was to fire occasionally at the Sarajevans below them. Their aim was to terrify as much as kill. Return fire was infrequent, more a nuisance than a threat. Dragisa, who had a middle-aged paunch, possessed the high ground as well as a big gun and was surrounded by folded coils of ammunition that evoked the image of a pit of lazy snakes. He made himself comfortable in a cozy bunker with a stove. He was a bully, not a fighter. A few miles up the road from his lair, I visited one of his leaders, Biljana Plavsic. Plavsic is now on trial at The Hague as an architect of Bosnia's genocide, but in 1992 she operated out of a hotel at the Jahorina ski resort, which was closed for business because of the war. After walking down a maze of empty corridors, I found her alone in a small office, shivering in a winter jacket. There was no heat, no electricity. This was no Berchtesgaden.

That is what Bosnia's genocide looked like from the inside—cowardly and pathetic. This truth had the misfortune of going against conventional wisdom and political convenience, and so it was ignored or disbelieved for far too long. "The Serbs are not ten-foot-tall headhunters who would fight to the last drop of blood," an American diplomat in Zagreb told me one day. "Why don't we bomb targets in Bosnia and Serbia? My God, what are we paying $200 billion a year for—what is our military for? If you define our army as a force that won't risk taking casualties, then we don't have an army. We have Boy Scouts." A few hours later, the diplomat called and asked that I not use the quote, even though, as he knew, I would not cite his name. He was afraid that Powell would figure out who was behind the swipe and exact some form of bureaucratic revenge. It was dangerous for American officials in the Balkans to bring inconvenient facts to the attention of their superiors back home.

Genocide is a fearsome word, evoking a phenomenon nearly biblical in its fury; we should not be surprised that politicians retreat in its presence. How can a few thousand GIs defeat it? Would not their weapons be like spears against a tidal wave? But we should not feel helpless in the search for the DNA of genocide and ways to defeat it. Genocide is a policy, not a monster. It is implemented, often imperfectly, by men and women, not Goliaths. With skill and luck, it can be defeated by military intervention. Not always, but sometimes. The genocides of the 1990s in Bosnia and Rwanda succeeded not because they were unstoppable, but because international opposition was almost nonexistent. In Washington, defeating genocide was less important than getting it off the front page, even if that meant letting genocide succeed.

There was another route. The conflict in Afghanistan presented American policymakers with all of the obstacles that stopped them in their tracks in Bosnia: an apparently fearsome opponent (the Taliban, which wasn't so fearsome once the fighting began); a potentially slippery slope beginning with limited intervention (which wasn't so slippery in Afghanistan, because the Taliban were ousted swiftly and what has followed are low-intensity, mop-up operations); and geographical terrain that was unfavorable to the weapons and warriors of a superpower (yet the rugged Afghan mountains did not protect the Taliban from destruction). If we could crush the Taliban in Afghanistan, we could have crushed the Serbs in Bosnia. The missing factor, in the Balkans, was simply the desire to fight that war.

Among soldiers, defeat lingers longer than victory because it involves a loss of pride and a loss of lives on a mission that failed. These failures stain the mind forever, like dye on a shroud. That has been the case with the generation of officers who fought in Vietnam and who decided that the next time they were called upon to do violence in a distant land, they would make sure they had all the resources needed to win. Colin Powell, an Army major in Vietnam during the heaviest fighting there, turned those sentiments into national policy when, as chair of the Joint Chiefs of Staff from 1989 to 1993, he formulated his eponymous doctrine. Distilled to its essence, the Powell Doctrine calls on civilian leaders to do two things in considering war—provide the military with a clear mission and give the military whatever resources it deems necessary to carry it out. Here is how, in a PBS interview that aired in January 1996, Powell described his preference for "decisive force" in a foreign engagement: "If this is important enough to go to war for, we're going to do it in a way that there's no question what the outcome will be, and we're going to do it by [using] the force necessary to take the initiative away from [the] enemy and impose [our] will upon him. If you're not serious enough to do that, then you ought to think twice about going to war."

In the winter of 1992, as he fended off demands for U.S. military action in Bosnia, Powell described the flip side of his doctrine. "If force is used imprecisely or out of frustration rather than clear analysis, the situation can be made worse," he wrote in a *Foreign Affairs* article entitled "U.S. Forces: Challenges Ahead." "We should always be skeptical," he continued, "when so-called experts suggest that all a particular crisis calls for is a little surgical bombing or a limited attack. When the 'surgery' is over and the desired result is not obtained, a new set of experts then comes forward with talk of just a little escalation—more bombs, more men and women, more force. History has not been kind to this approach to war-making. In fact, this approach has been tragic."

In the war on Iraq, Bush the Elder's administration provided a clear mission—liberate Kuwait—and authorized the decisive force requested by the Pentagon. Powell was thus able to stand before journalists on January 23, 1991, and announce with the confidence of a general who had a half-million troops preparing to attack, "Here's our plan for the Iraqi Army: We're going to cut it off, then we're going to kill it." When the dust settled after the hundred-hour ground war, the Iraqi Army had not been killed. Enough of it remained to keep Saddam Hussein in power. But the Iraqi Army had been forced from Kuwait, and the loss of American life was slight. Powell was a hero, hailed as a visionary who knew when and how to fight.

Bosnia was everything Iraq was not, or so it seemed. The threat to U.S. security was not apparent. How could a country that most Americans had never heard of become, all of a sudden, so important that we should shed blood for it? In Washington, Slobodan Milosevic was not viewed as a Balkan Saddam or even a Balkan Mussolini. In fact, there was no shortage of American officials treating him as a respectable statesman. Even if Milosevic was guilty of war crimes that threatened our national interest—a big "if" at the time—what should our intervention seek to achieve: a cessation of fighting, a withdrawal of Serb forces from Bosnia, or the downfall of Milosevic? Powell sensed a quagmire. In an October 8, 1992 *New York Times* opinion piece entitled "Why Generals Get Nervous," he did not hide his disdain for reporters whose dispatches indicated a need for American action. "We have learned the lessons of history," he wrote, "even if some journalists have not."

But journalists were not the only ones who failed to genuflect before the lessons of history that Powell worshipped. In the crucial first year of the Bosnian War, Madeleine Albright, U.S. ambassador to the United Nations, was the principal advocate for intervention within the Clinton administration. She was not afraid to speak her mind to Powell, asking him, during one contentious meeting, "What's the point in having this superb military you are always talking about if we can't use it?" This was an accusation, and as Powell recalled in his 1995 autobiography, "I thought I would have an aneurysm."

Powell cherished the warning from George Santayana that those who cannot remember the past are condemned to repeat it. But Powell turned the warning into dogma, failing to realize that the future may not resemble the past, and yesterday's lessons may not solve tomorrow's problems. Albright realized this. The daughter of a Czech diplomat who fled to America as the Second World War began, she knew a genocide when she saw it, and she knew the genocide in Bosnia could be stopped, if only the men with stars on their shoulders could look at Bosnia without seeing Vietnam.

The Bosnian Serb Army consisted of approximately fifty thousand soldiers, according to most estimates. They were a less-than-awesome force, not for any lack of armaments—they had adequate stocks of small weapons, mortars, artillery and tanks—but for their training and morale. The army was an ad hoc collection of new conscripts and veterans of the Yugoslav National Army. For the most part, they had not fought to capture the territory they held in Bosnia. They pretty much took what they wanted in the first weeks of the war, when there was no organized opposition to the paramilitary death squads that were the shock troops of genocide. Until the final months of the war, little territory changed hands. Serbs held about 70 percent of the country almost from start to finish. Their principal strategy was not to attack, but to bomb and besiege and wait for the other side to surrender. It was an effective strategy.

General Ratko Mladic, the Bosnian Serb military leader who has since been indicted for war crimes, had a sufficient number of loyalists to lead his troops, but the troops themselves were reluctant to stick their necks out. Except for the early days of the war, there were no queues at recruiting outposts in Serb-held territory; instead, there were roadside checkpoints to prevent fighting-age males from escaping to Serbia. Although the vast majority of Serbs in Bosnia supported the war, few wanted to die for the cause; they had no stomach for close combat against people who could defend themselves.

I learned this lesson in Banja Luka, the largest city under Serb control. On a hot afternoon in the summer of 1992, I came across a teenager named Boris. His blond hair was tied into a ponytail, and he wore the sort of small-lensed glasses worn by John Lennon; for all I knew, Boris was a Beatles fan, too. The war was not six months old, but already Boris had no appetite for it. "The Serb people are being seduced," he told me. "They don't know what is happening. They see what they want to see, or what others want them to see."

But Boris was no dissident. He would turn eighteen soon, draft age, and when I asked what he would do, he didn't need to think about it. "I will go to the army," he replied. "It's better than jail." I don't know what happened to Boris, but it seems unlikely that he would have stepped forward when a call went out in his unit for volunteers for dangerous missions. He was not unusual. There were kids like Boris throughout the Bosnian Serb Army, kids who would much rather watch MTV than risk their lives in a war that was destroying a way of life that had been quite agreeable to them.

There was a Wizard-of-Oz quality to the Serb military machine—look behind the curtain and you will not find the ten-foot tall monsters you expect. This state of affairs was illustrated, vividly, in the winter of 1992, when I visited the town of Rogatica, a choke point of the four-year Serb siege of Gorazde, where thousands were killed by the shells or the cold or the lack of food. Gorazde suffered a shortage of everything but ways to die. I was traveling with two British colleagues, and because we didn't have passes to be in the area, the commander at Rogatica greeted us by threatening to shoot us. We received the usual anti-NATO, anti-Muslim spiel, then were invited to his office, where the ashtray consisted of a spent artillery shell. One of us said something that enraged the commander and he proceeded to blow up again, grabbing my notebook and ripping pages from it.

After threatening, again, to kill us, he quieted down and apologized for his behavior. He returned my notebook. We talked some more and then accepted his invitation for a meal in his canteen. Over bowls of bean soup, he complained about his hard life on the frontline, telling me that his unit seemed to be forgotten by higher-ups, that he was bored, and that he hadn't had sex for ages. He asked when we had last had sex. An uncomfortable silence prevailed. When schmoozing with frontline soldiers, I prefer to offer appropriate answers rather than accurate ones, if the two happen to vary. But I did not know the appropriate answer in this case, and neither did my colleagues. Our interpreter volunteered that he had had sex with his girlfriend a few days earlier. This revelation cheered the commander. He liked being in the presence of someone who had carnal knowledge that was not months old.

I mention this incident only because the commander was a losing figure. Yes, he would not hesitate to order another round of shelling of Gorazde, but he seemed more interested in his own well-being and self-pity than anything else. Ho Chi Minh would have booted his fat ass out of the army. If Powell imagined Vietcong-like resistance and fortitude in the hills of Bosnia, I wish he could have been with me in Rogatica. Defeating these bullies would not have required massive intervention; in reality, the military equivalent of a nudge would have done the job, and eventually did.

Bosnia's government did not need foreign troops to fight its war; it had plenty of troops of its own, more than 100,000. It needed weapons. As the wars began in the former Yugoslavia, the United Nations imposed a weapons embargo on all sides in the disintegrating country, and this strategy played into Bosnian Serb hands, because they had ample stockpiles of armaments and a vibrant weapons industry in Serbia to resupply them. The newly formed Bosnian Army, however, had few weapons and no factories. It was surrounded by Serbia and Croatia (a part-time ally, part-time enemy) and resorted, in dire moments, to handmade mortars.

How could the UN refuse to protect the Bosnians *and* prohibit them from purchasing weapons to protect themselves? The rationale for arms embargoes is that if you starve a conflict of weapons, the fighting will stop or slow down, even if there is leakage due to black-market deals. In Bosnia, the rationale did not hold, because one side, which started the war, had plenty of weapons, and the other side, which had few weapons and did not want or expect a war, was being slaughtered. (About two hundred thousand people, mostly Muslims, were killed in the war, according to an estimate used by the United Nations High Commissioner for Refugees.) The embargo was immoral because it abetted genocide. It nonetheless suited the United States and its allies on the Security Council because they wished for the fighting to cease as soon as possible, and the embargo meant the Bosnians had to accept whatever terms the stronger Serbs demanded. The Bosnians needed to realize they could not win the war, and the best way to make them realize that was to make sure they could not acquire weapons that might enable them to win. It was the kind of realpolitik that brings great satisfaction to the Henry Kissingers of our world, and to the Colin Powells.

To better understand the unfortunate logic of the situation, imagine a lopsided boxing match in which the losing boxer has one hand tied behind his back and pleads with a spectator to free the tied hand. The spectator, who just wants the bloody spectacle to end, balks at the request and urges the boxer to take a fall.

The metaphor is a simplification but useful to keep in mind. Different experts provide different opinions on the effect of arming the Bosnians. My view, which is not a minority one, is that lifting the embargo—and, going a step further, providing the Bosnians with weapons—would have stopped the genocide and enabled the Bosnians to retake territory seized by Serbs in the first weeks of the war. After all, the Serbs were not great or even good fighters. When Croatia re-armed and, in 1995, retook a swath of territory that had been held by ethnic Serbs since 1991, the Serbs hardly bothered to fight. They ran. When NATO bombed the Bosnian Serbs in 1995, they caved in after two weeks. In the following years, when troops of the North Atlantic Treaty Organization made occasional arrests of Bosnian Serb war criminals, there were no revenge killings of NATO personnel. Notice a pattern?

It's important to remember, too, that the provision of weapons to Afghanistan's Northern Alliance, by Russia and the United States, played a key role—along with the U.S. bombing campaign—in giving Northern Alliance fighters the edge they needed to roll over the Taliban.

But what if the Bosnians committed atrocities with the weapons we supplied or allowed them to be supplied with? Would we have then become accomplices to their revenge killings? This was a frequently heard objection, and it had some validity. In 1995, when Croatia reconquered the Krajina region, the scene was not pretty; ethnic Serbs who had lived there for centuries were so terrified that they fled to Serbia, and many who stayed behind were brutalized or killed by vengeful

Croats. In 1999, when NATO's bombing campaign led to the withdrawal of Serb military forces from Kosovo, ethnic Albanians celebrated by "cleansing" Serb civilians who had not retreated; this retaliation was an embarrassment for the Western countries that had ended Serb barbarism, only to see it replaced by an Albanian variant.

Would the same pattern have occurred in Bosnia? I strongly doubt it. The Croatian troops who attacked in 1995 were fighting on behalf of a government that was every bit as nationalist and thuggish as the Serbian regime led by Slobodan Milosevic. The Kosovo Liberation Army, responsible for the killings of Serbs, was a generally disreputable assemblage of young men who wanted to purge every Serb from Kosovo; most Albanians in Kosovo shared their goal.

Bosnia was different. The Bosnian Army, despite the cruelties inflicted on civilians it was trying to protect, did not engage in systematic killing sprees when it managed to retake slivers of territory. Did atrocities occur? Yes. Were they widespread? No. The majority of Bosnia's Muslims did not wish to live in an ethnically pure state. To be sure, revenge killings would have occurred if their army had retaken Serb-held territory, but not, I believe, on a significant level. If we demand that an army be atrocity-free to merit international support, then no army including, our own, could ever meet that criterion. In Afghanistan, we have had no trouble looking the other way as Northern Alliance soldiers executed Taliban or Al Qaeda fighters.

Skeptics also argued that lifting the embargo would not have been enough. The United States, they said, would have needed to train the Bosnians to use the new weapons, and as everyone knows, military trainers are the first step on the slippery slope to full-scale intervention. This argument is no sturdier than a two-legged table. The warfare in Bosnia was primitive. The Bosnian Army needed simple materiel, such as anti-tank guns, mortars and artillery pieces, as well as ammunition. Little training or assembly would have been required by outsiders. The Bosnians were not in the market for smart bombs.

Pentagon and administration officials talked up a geopolitical doomsday in which lifting the embargo would spark a much broader conflict, because Milosevic might send the Yugoslav National Army into

Bosnia to defend Serbs, or perhaps the Russians would become involved, leading to a U.S.–Russia face-off in the Balkans. This scenario was paraded around like a strategic missing link, and it, too, was lacking in reality. As subsequent events showed in Croatia and Bosnia, Milosevic did not send in his troops to defend Serbs once they were attacked by stronger forces. And in 1999, when NATO bombed Serbia, the Russians stood aside, grumbling.

For the sake of argument, let us assume that maintaining the embargo was a wise policy. What other options were available, short of dispatching 250,000 troops? For three years, the Clinton administration and its European allies insisted that bombing could not end the war. David Owen, lead negotiator for the European Union, memorably accused pro-intervention editorialists of being "laptop bombardiers." But by the summer of 1995, Serb behavior in Bosnia became too odious for Western leaders to overlook any longer—the "safe haven" of Srebrenica had been stormed by Serb troops, who massacred thousands of prisoners and took UN peacekeepers hostage. Shortly after, a Serb mortar attack killed thirty-eight people in Sarajevo. A NATO bombing campaign was finally begun. It was a limited affair, with just thirty-five hundred sorties on Serb targets in Bosnia over eleven days; when compared to NATO's seventy-eight-day bombing of Serbia in 1999 with more than thirty-eight thousand sorties, the campaign in Bosnia is revealed as a mild slap. Even so, it worked, with no lives lost by the Western alliance. The Serbs swiftly agreed to a peace conference, held in Dayton, Ohio, that ended the war, although on terms that, it turned out, were unduly generous to the architects of the genocide.

To this day, many opponents of bombing insist they were right. The bombing worked in 1995, they say, because the Serbs were weaker, militarily, than they had been in previous years. This is true, but that only means the mild campaign in 1995 would have needed to be a bit stronger if it had taken place in earlier years. How much stronger? Impossible to say, of course, but the degradation of the Bosnian Serb Army was a slow-moving affair; the army that crumbled under NATO's bombs in 1995 wasn't that different from the army that existed in the first year or two of the war. Dragisa, the Serb with the big gun in the hills above Sarajevo, was not much of a warrior in 1992, nor was the commander in Rogatica.

Opponents of bombing also note that NATO's attack coincided with a summer offensive by Croatian and Bosnian troops that swept through northwestern Bosnia, threatening to overrun Banja Luka. Would the bombing have succeeded without that ground threat? The ground offensive certainly helped drive the Serbs to Dayton, but again, in its absence NATO had much more to throw at the Serbs from the air. In any event, once the Serbs became pinned down by NATO's warplanes, a ground offensive against them could have begun at any time during the war. From the first day, an aerial blitz by NATO would have tipped the conflict in favor of the Bosnian side, forcing the Serbs to retreat, militarily and diplomatically. The crucial role of the U.S. bombing in Afghanistan is a perfect illustration of the extent to which our Air Force can turn the tide of a foreign conflict.

The United States did not need to use its ground troops to stop the genocide. But what if it had? Our GIs would not have objected. Many foreign soldiers in Bosnia were dismayed because they had to stand aside as genocide unfolded before them. For all but the final stage of the war, the feeble UN peacekeeping force had strict orders to use its weapons only in self-defense; its mission was restricted to helping deliver relief supplies.

In the first winter of the four-year siege of Sarajevo, a cosmopolitan city that had hosted the Winter Olympics in 1984, I met Richard Roth, a sergeant in the 82nd Airborne and a farm boy from Maquoketa, Iowa. The Clinton administration opted, in the early years of the Bosnian war, to limit to a handful the number of U.S. soldiers in the United Nations Protection Force, and as far as I could tell, Roth was the only uniformed GI in Bosnia's capital, where he worked as a communications specialist at the residence of the UN commander. I sensed, as we talked in a reception room at the commander's villa, that Roth's bosses at the Pentagon would not have been satisfied with what he was saying.

"Everybody but the Serbs hopes the Americans will get involved," Roth said as we sipped tea from porcelain cups, which rattled on their saucers when a shell landed nearby. "I think the Serbs are the bad guys, but that's not the UN's position. I know we shouldn't go sticking our noses everywhere, but this is too close to our NATO allies to sit back and do nothing." Because there were no other American soldiers based in Sarajevo at the time, Sergeant Roth got a lot of attention when he walked around the city in his uniform, with an American flag on his sleeve. Everyone wanted to know, why doesn't America do something? I think he knew the sad answer but he shrugged it off, telling me, in the caustic way that grunts in Vietnam handled queries about the morass they knew they were in, "I'm not paid to think." Our cups rattled as another shell hit its target nearby.

Most men and women don't join the armed forces because the pay is good or the food delicious. They join for other reasons, including a dose of altruism. They believe that maybe they will have the opportunity to represent their country on a just mission that will save lives. They are not afraid to put their lives on the line. They are not Boy Scouts, although their timid leaders treated them as such in the Balkans.

Why are America's leaders reluctant to intervene except in the most obvious, national-security-threatening situations, as in the Gulf War? The Vietnam precedent plays a paramount role, of course. So, too, does the story of American intervention in Lebanon, where, in 1983, 241 U.S. soldiers who had been sent to Beirut as peacekeepers were killed in a suicide-bomb attack. More recently, the killing in 1993 of eighteen U.S. soldiers in Somalia pretty much eliminated any appetite Bill Clinton might have had for using the world's strongest military for anything beyond oil-protection duty.

The lessons of Vietnam should not be forgotten, nor should those of Lebanon and Somalia. But one of the lessons politicians and generals drew from those debacles—that the American public has no tolerance for sacrificing GIs overseas—is wrong. Those missions were a political mess, and the deaths they produced were close to pointless. Americans understood that. If a mission is honorable or if Americans believe it is honorable, they will support it. That was the case in the Gulf War, as it was when NATO finally bombed Serb targets in Bosnia in 1995, and four years later, when NATO bombed Serbia. And that was rousingly the case when the Bush administration started its war on the Taliban.

The 1948 Convention on the Prevention of Genocide requires signatories to punish genocide when it occurs. This convention puts a special burden on the United States, the world's "indispensable nation," as Madeleine Albright liked to say in her secretary of state days. Of course not every genocide can be stopped with a modest dose of military intervention, and it would be unfair to demand that the United States sacrifice as many lives as it takes to stop mass murder in country X or Y. There are limits to what the United States can do, and limits to what the United States should be expected to do.

What are those limits?

In the spring of 1994, as the genocide in Bosnia progressed like a plow digging into the earth, and as a new and worse genocide began in Rwanda, President Clinton's national security adviser, Anthony Lake, who had the most famous conscience in an administration famous for its famous consciences, explained that the U.S. government was not, unfortunately, in a position to stop the bloodbaths that were staining our television screens.

"When I wake up every morning and look at the headlines and the stories and the images on television of these conflicts, I want to work to end every conflict," he said. "I want to work to save every child out there. And I know the president does, and I know the American people do. But neither we nor the international community have the resources nor the mandate to do so. So we have to make distinctions. We have to ask the hard questions about where and when we can intervene. And the reality is that we cannot often solve other people's problems."

Lake's heart may have been in the right place, but his mind was not. The cowardice of other nations should not be an excuse for our own. As Lake was murderously slow in realizing, the U.S. government could have solved the problems in Bosnia and Rwanda at acceptable rather than extravagant costs, in political and military terms. Regarding Rwanda, just ask Romeo Dallaire.

In October 1993, Dallaire, a lieutenant general in the Canadian Army, was sent to Kigali, Rwanda, to command a lightly armed UN peacekeeping force of twenty-five hundred soldiers that was overseeing a fragile peace accord between the Hutu-dominated government and the rebel Tutsi army. General Dallaire sensed, early on, that Rwanda was slouching toward genocide. In fact, he had hard information from a senior official inside the Hutu Power movement that a mass extermination was being planned. The informant told Dallaire that lists of human targets were being drawn up, death squads were being trained and deployed, and provocations to start the killing were imminent. On January 11, 1994, three months before the genocide began, Dallaire sent a coded cable to his superior at the United Nations, Kofi Annan, who at the time was head of peacekeeping, and now is secretary-general.

The cable outlined the informant's story and requested permission, as a first step, to raid a Hutu arms cache. Dallaire also asked permission to provide protection to the informant. The response from Annan came quickly: The UN forces in Kigali were to do nothing more than oversee the disintegrating peace accord. Raiding arms caches and protecting informers was out of the question. "We wish to stress," Annan's cable concluded, "that the overriding consideration is the need to avoid entering into a course of action that might lead to the use of force and unanticipated repercussions."

It is understandable that Annan, or anyone, would hesitate to intervene *before* genocide occurs. Perhaps Dallaire was over-reacting, as commanders in the field might do. Perhaps the Hutus would pull back from the brink on their own accord, without the UN's firing a shot (which, who knows, could make matters worse, not better). It is difficult to sift the false alarms from the real ones. But the UN, like the Security Council members that decide its policies, has what seems to be a standing rule (or should we say a sitting rule?) to dither until blood begins to stain the carpets along the East River and at Foggy Bottom. Often the best and only chance to stop genocide is before the violence becomes widespread; we must be ready to act early and quickly, especially, as was the case in Rwanda, when the required acts are modest.

But Annan and the Security Council did worse than fail to act early and quickly. Once ten Belgian peacekeepers were massacred by Hutu extremists on the first day of the genocide, April 7, the Security Council decided to withdraw its force from the country, even though Dallaire urged the opposite course, insisting that with more troops and a mandate to use them in combat the violence could be stopped. The U.S. government played a key role in keeping the UN out of Rwanda's genocide. Dallaire has said, on many occasions, that he would have needed just three battalions to "break the embryo of genocide." In 1998, the Carnegie Commission assembled a blue-ribbon military panel to examine his claim. The panel consisted of more than a dozen senior military officials, including a half dozen U.S. generals.

"The hypothetical force described by General Dallaire—at least five thousand strong—could have made a significant difference in Rwanda," the report concluded. "A window of opportunity for employment of such a force extended roughly from about April 7 to April 21, 1994, when the political leaders of the violence were still susceptible to international influence. The rapid introduction of robust combat forces, authorized to seize at one time critical points throughout the country, would have changed the political calculations of the participants. The opportunity existed to prevent the killing—and to put the negotiations back on track."

It would be wrong, however, to condemn the U.S. government for failing to stop the genocide in Rwanda or the one in Bosnia. The situation was more shameful than that. The government failed *to attempt* to stop the genocides. It is only a slight exaggeration to say that President Clinton wished the killings would finish as quickly as possible, on any terms. For hardly the first time, the quick solution was preferred to the just solution, even though the just solution could be reached at an acceptable cost.

The blind spot at the Pentagon was exceptionally broad. In his occasionally candid memoir, *Waging Modern War*, published in 2001, General Wesley Clark, who commanded NATO forces during the bombing of Serbia in 1999, recalled that once he got involved in Bosnian issues in the summer of 1994, "I became increasingly concerned about our staff's lack of experience with the situation on the ground. No one had been there personally." The Pentagon brass received CIA reports and diplomatic cables, Clark wrote, and perused CNN and *The Washington Post*, but had not bothered to send anyone of importance to Bosnia to figure out, from a military perspective, what was happening there and what could be done.

In this way, the lesson of the genocides of the 1990s are not much different from the lesson of Vietnam: our political and military leaders can be so out of touch with on-the-ground reality—even if, as was the case in Vietnam, they have plenty of people on the ground—that they are 100 percent wrong in their analysis of what can be done. The delusions are visceral. In Vietnam, the White House wanted to defeat a communist insurrection and persuaded itself that this was possible to do, even though in reality it wasn't. In Bosnia, the White House and Pentagon feared that stopping genocide might become a quagmire involving massive intervention, and persuaded itself that this was the case.

It is not surprising that General Powell, long before he became Secretary of State Powell, threw around inflated force estimates in the early 1990s. He understood less about Bosnia, and what was needed to stop genocide there, than Sergeant Roth from Maquoketa, Iowa. Powell made the mistake of treating a genocidal policy as an unbeatable monster.

# 6

# A Drive to Globare

KIRA BRUNNER

In the summer of 2000, I met Scott Slaten, an American soldier who
had come to Pristina, Kosovo, two-and-a-half months earlier as part
of a NATO-led peace keeping force (KFOR) providing security for the
United Nations Mission in Kosovo (UNMIK). It was a little more than a
year since the end of the seventy-eight-day air war that NATO launched
on March 24, 1999, to stop Serbian ethnic cleansing. Slaten was sipping
coffee in one of the many outdoor cafés where shopkeepers make a
good living selling sodas and grilled cheese sandwiches to homesick
internationals. We talked in the shade of a Philip Morris umbrella. He
agreed to find a jeep and take me the following morning to the village
of Globare in central Kosovo. I wanted to find out how the process of
building a durable peace was working in a country in which ethnic
cleansing had taken such a toll. During the war, as many as ten thousand
Kosovo Albanians, who account for more than 80 percent of Kosovo's
two million inhabitants, were massacred. Eight hundred thousand more
fled to neighboring Macedonia.

How do victims and perpetrators live side by side in a country shattered by "ethnic cleansing"? How does such a country rebuild its civil
society and political structures? And what role should an intervening
power like NATO play in the rebuilding process, especially if there is
every reason to believe that new violence will begin if it pulls out?

Each day NATO troops become more entangled in the job of
rebuilding the country, which, as a result of UN Resolution 1244, is offi-

cially a UN, not a NATO, protectorate. Today Pristina, the capital city, is swarming with human rights workers, KFOR soldiers, and United Nations officials. In addition, a handful of entrepreneurs have arrived, their presence announced by the sudden appearance of American-style gas stations just outside Pristina.

The next morning, my translator, Virtyt Gacaferi, and I met Slaten by his Jeep, a large white SUV with KFOR stamped on the side. Gacaferi worked as a journalist for *Koha Ditore*, the preeminent Albanian newspaper, and the only paper that kept its presses running throughout the war. A wiry and quick-witted twenty-year-old, he had a sophisticated understanding of the region, in comparison with what I was soon to hear from Slaten, who was full of gung-ho ideals and easy answers to the complexities of war and intervention.

As we drove out of town, past checkpoints and NATO tanks, and entered the open farmland of central Kosovo, Gacaferi and Slaten began debating the country's future. Slaten was already fed up with what he described as the simple-minded, nineteenth-century nationalism of Yugoslavia's ethnic wars. He hated the way the ethnic hatreds that he encountered daily hampered the work of reconstruction. As an example, he pointed to the new Kosovo passenger train line that was under construction. "Both sides are against it," he said with undisguised sarcasm. "What if they started riding together? Oh my god, they might start living together, and what would happen then?"

Gacaferi, normally jovial and lighthearted, was offended. He responded patiently, not so much with a justification, but with a description of what daily life in Kosovo is like: "When an Albanian meets a Serb person for the first time, he thinks about 1912, then about World War I, then World War II, and then finally he thinks about the person standing in front of him." He was exaggerating only slightly. Even a train ride in Kosovo is never a simple matter. Every moment in the present carries with it the weight of repeated betrayals and grievances.

It is impossible to have any conversation about the political situation in Kosovo without getting a history lesson, but to understand the oppression that until recently shaped the daily lives of Kosovo Albanians, one doesn't have to go far back. In the late 1980s, the Serbian Parliament initiated a series of laws that steadily chipped away at Albanian rights in Kosovo. Starting in 1989, Belgrade passed measures that eroded the rights of Albanians in almost every sector of public and private life. The police force was purged. Serbs replaced Albanians. More than three thousand Albanian medical workers and journalists lost their jobs. Serbian managers took over radio stations, newspapers, and cultural institutions. And in a final blow, the government revamped the education system, replacing all Albanian language, geography, and history with a Serbian curriculum. As a result, few Albanians could remain in school. These legal mandates created an apartheid-like system, in which the Albanian majority—which had held public power until 1989—suddenly found itself subordinated to the Serb minority.

As far as the Serbs were concerned, their hold on Kosovo was historic, their ties to the land reaching back to 1389, when in a heroic struggle they were defeated by the Turks. Slobodan Milosevic, always the political mastermind, manipulated this sentiment for his own ends. At a 1988 rally in Belgrade, he told an enthusiastic audience, "Every nation has a love which eternally warms its heart. For Serbia it is Kosovo. That is why Kosovo will remain in Serbia." Although tensions were high in the late 1980s, Serbs and Albanians would not come to blows over Kosovo for another ten years. The nonviolent tactics of Ibrahim Rugova, the man who dominated what amounted to a Kosovo Albanian parallel government, helped prevent the outbreak of violence. And Serbia, preoccupied with its war in Croatia and Bosnia, could not afford to spread its resources too thin.

Everything changed in 1998 when the Kosovo Liberation Army (KLA) transformed itself from a hit-and-run military offshoot of the Peoples Movement for the Liberation of Kosovo (LPK) into a viable army, committed to secession and independence and willing to battle Serbia as well as engage in terrorist campaigns of its own against Serb citizens. By July, the KLA had one-third of the country under its control, but in late July, after over-extending itself in a campaign against the town of Orahovac, its soldiers were on the defensive. Belgrade—no longer mired in a war in Bosnia—now decided to fix its "Kosovo problem" once and for all and launched a counter-offensive. Soon its para-

militaries poured into Kosovo, overrunning the countryside, slaughtering civilians, burning villages, and forcing Albanians to flee on foot into
neighboring Macedonia.

As we drove through the countryside, we could still see destruction
everywhere. Entire villages had been reduced to tangled scrap heaps of
rubble. What was not destroyed had been carted away by scavengers.
During the war, Gacaferi continued working as a journalist and remembers the exhilaration he felt when the American-led bombing campaign
began in 1999. Like most Albanians, he saw the bombing campaign as the
only way to prevent a mass slaughter. The first day the bombs fell, he
stood on a rooftop in Pristina and cheered. "I never heard a single complaint against NATO, not once," he said. At this Slaten smiled approvingly.
"America," he said, "is not a geographical location. It's an idea in our
hearts and our heads that can be placed anywhere in the world. And the
Albanians like this idea," he declared.

But I was growing increasingly skeptical. I wondered what might lie
beneath the surface of such undaunted enthusiasm for all things American. In Pristina I had seen a portrait of Madeleine Albright taped to the
window of a cigarette kiosk. Now, as we passed through villages where
markets were once again bustling, I saw more KLA black eagles flying
than stars and stripes. The flags were a clear sign of the loyalty people
in the countryside still had to the KLA. Not surprisingly, the KLA cred-
ited its troops, not the Americans, with winning Kosovo's freedom from
Serbia. Although they had agreed to disarm under the U.S.-negotiated
terms, the daily retaliatory violence against Serbs still living in Kosovo
attested to the fact that the KLA had not completely disbanded and was
perhaps reluctant to grant NATO sole military power.

As we pulled into Globare, we attracted a great deal of attention. Children ran up to us, and three women walking up the road stopped to
wave. Slaten jumped out of the jeep, greeted the children, pulled lollipops out of his pockets, and tossed them to the kids as they laughed
and shouted, "America, America, thank you America." Slaten smiled
and posed for photos with his arms wrapped around a group of kids.
He clearly enjoyed acting the part of a World War Two liberation
hero.

When I caught up with the three women on the road, I asked them where they had been during the war. They and their children had fled to the nearby hills when the Serb paramilitary forces raided the village. As they spoke, my eyes drifted over their shoulders to the field behind them where a large, freshly dug grave of seventeen or so plots had been heavily strewn with flowers. The women followed my eyes, waved their hands toward the graves, shrugged their shoulders in resignation, and said, "Our men."

One of the women invited us into her house for coffee. Slaten was eager to accept her invitation. He was having fun. "I never get to do this, I never get to meet civilians. This is the best part." Slaten cut a sympathetic but slightly ludicrous figure. Trained for battle, he was now reduced to handing out lollipops and posing for photos. The U.S. air strikes, designed to avoid American casualties, had made it impossible for ground troops to play a significant role during the war. With the air war over, the main duty of the KFOR troops was to find a way to prevent retaliation by Albanians against the Serbs. NATO troops patrolled Serbian neighborhoods on foot. They guarded monasteries from vandalism, stationing tanks out front around the clock. Beyond keeping a lid on the daily violence, the troops helped coordinate the rebuilding of decaying power plants and obsolete sewer systems. Despite then-president Bill Clinton's declaration that U.S. troops would never become mired in nation-building, nation-building had, in fact, become a daily part of their duties.

For those who had lived through the war, it was clear why the wounds had not healed. As Slaten and I entered the woman's home, she described what she found when she returned from hiding. Her farm equipment was destroyed. Her house, although still standing, had been stripped of every piece of furniture. Even the plumbing was pulled out of the walls. In her living room, she pointed to the stucco wall on which Serb soldiers had engraved, with a knife, an image of a skull and crossbones, the Grim Reaper, and the words "Death Action," "Death Units," "Welcome to Hell." Whitewash barely covered the graffiti.

As we sat down to cups of strong Turkish coffee, a middle-aged man, clearly the head of the family, joined us. Excited by the presence of a KFOR soldier in his home, he began to seek reassurance from Slaten.

He wanted to know if NATO planned to remain in Kosovo. He was very nervous about the possibility of the international troops leaving or of some deal being struck with Belgrade that might allow the return of Serbian control. "If the old system came back, I would take my family away," he announced. By the "old system" he not only meant Serbian rule and political repression, but also the return of death squads, killing, looting, and destruction. "If they could kill a seventy-year-old man," he said, referring to his father, who had been beaten to death in a nearby field, "how can we trust them anymore?" He looked pleadingly at Slaten, sizing him up. Could he put his trust in this man or not? "We don't trust the Serbs, but do you? Does NATO? Does the United States? Were you truly fighting for the cause of the Albanian people and the KLA? Do you expect us to live with Serbs again? And, will you leave us here to die if we refuse?" Slaten struck both his hands firmly on the table. "That won't ever happen. We won't allow the old system ever to come back." He flashed the man an open smile. Then, catching my eye, he turned and winked.

This question, asked by a victim and answered by a representative of the intervening power, captures the complexities of the postwar dilemma that Kosovo presents. To men like Slaten, the answers were simple. He had a job to do, and he was in Kosovo to get it done. The Serbs who fled Kosovo during the American bombing left behind belongings and property. One day they will seek the return of their property. Then what? For Slaten, ethnic hatreds were just obstacles in the way of building a multi-ethnic state—the American ideal of democracy that can be "placed anywhere in the world."

Slaten is not alone in his hope of building an America in the Balkans. Even the turbo folk music pumping out of car radios and barrooms reveals the intertwining of Kosovo's own nationalism and an imported American patriotism. Aselina Ismaili, a popular turbo singer and Miss Kosovo 1997, wails to her mother on the radio of the beauties of Kosovo, from the patriotic battle in Drenica to the glory of the Albanian flag. "Mom, oh Mother, Drenica black and red, Mitrovica so beautiful and Pristina like our own little America."

Pristina is not America. It is a city struggling to co-exist with an occupying military power. And Kosovo is a country striving to rebuild its civil society and political structures. The actors in this theater of reconstruction are the no-nonsense NATO soldiers, the war-weary human rights workers who fly from one world catastrophe to another, and a generation of young Kosovo Albanians who, reared under Milosevic's rule, came of age during the war.

The story of this new generation of Albanians is a parable for the trials of Kosovo itself. As children they were torn from their classrooms by Serbian law, and as young adults they were tossed into the confusion of war. Today, they are struggling to find a place in the contemporary landscape of Kosovo. In the 1990s, laws passed by the Serb Parliament forced most Albanians to leave school. Although in the early nineties thirty-six thousand Albanian students finished primary school, the new law allowed only six thousand seats for non-Serbs in secondary school. In the university even stronger measures were taken; in 1993, the Albanian rector was fired and replaced by a Serb. The enormous difficulties that Albanian students faced in getting an education forced the establishment of a parallel education system. Teachers who had lost their jobs began to meet with students in private homes and garages. In 1998, the parallel system accommodated 266,413 primary school students, 58,700 secondary students, and 16,000 university students.

By 2001, the parallel schools, hospitals, and government created as a counter to the stifling laws of Milosevic's Serbia had collapsed. But the very fact that the parallel system existed attests to the ingenuity of a people who, during their darkest times, were able to exercise some control over their own political destiny. Today, they wish to rebuild those parallel structures, but this time with absolute control over them. Although the war was won, independence was not. Kosovo is still officially a part of Yugoslavia and is unable to create political institutions without Belgrade's approval.

Before the war, America rejected Kosovo's call for independence, fearing that it would lead to even greater turbulence in the Balkans. Now that this fear has dwindled, American foreign policy still objects to independence out of concern that it would look like a reward for the violent terrorist tactics undertaken by the KLA. For the moment,

Kosovo has been declared a UN protectorate, thus deferring the tricky problem of independence. Under the UN protectorate, NATO has taken over the job of creating virtual institutions, laws, and structures that may with time become real. But right now Kosovo exists in a limbo between self-determination and dependence on foreign aid and oversight.

Human rights organizations, the military, and a collection of non-governmental organizations (NGOs) now have a hand in every aspect of governing the country. They help administer the gas works, electric power, garbage collection, and food distribution, and they conduct the sticky negotiations involved in returning property to Serbian refugees. Although life is manageable, and economic subsistence is feasible for most Kosovars, it comes with a price. The Kosovars are dependent on foreign aid, limited in the practical initiatives they can take on their own. Milk, for example, is priced as low as fifty cents a carton, because an NGO is selling it below cost. The result is that it has become less profitable for an Albanian farmer to open a dairy than to negotiate import fees with the NGOs.

Young men like Gacaferi are prime examples of the entrepreneurial spirit that both takes advantage of and runs up against the new international forces in Kosovo. He profits from the influx of Western journalists, at times taking in as much as a hundred dollars a day as a translator. Yet he is skeptical of the instant success that Western attention and money bring. Reflecting on the hundreds of Westerners filling the streets of Pristina, he gripes, "Many of these guys who come under the pretext of humanitarianism are really just businessmen. They can make a hundred thousand dollars a year tax free. Retired U.S. police officers come to make money and see Europe. From here they can go to Turkey or Greece or Italy." True enough, but what also cannot be denied is that the intervening military force has brought stability to a region nearly destroyed by ethnic war. Gacaferi pauses and looks at an American officer sitting nearby and remembers that he prefers the new order to the old.

"Nobody likes police, but we can't live without them. Now we have, 'Please can you get out of the car.' Before we had, 'Get the fuck out of the car.'" It is a difference worth preserving. Yet, at times, the imposition of American rules and regulations on a Balkan culture seems so removed from reality that it can only be laughed at. New mandatory seat belt rules and radar speed checks result in a hundred dollar fine for any violator. The trouble is that the rules have no real weight in a country where the average monthly salary is less then fifty dollars.

There is a joke in Kosovo that goes, "Why can't an elephant go to primary school? He can't fit through the door. Why can't an elephant go to secondary school? He didn't go to primary school. Why can't an elephant go to university? Because he is working for an NGO." The joke points up how complex the end game in Kosovo has become with NATO, the UN, and NGOs in effect running the country. The role NATO has undertaken in the name of human rights is not only necessary, it is invaluable. NATO has been able to keep a lid on violent retaliation against Serbs still living in the region, and it has also provided a buffer between Kosovo Albanians and Belgrade. Without NATO's presence, Kosovo could easily slip back into war. There was proof of this vulnerability in the summer of 2001 when many KLA soldiers, frustrated by the constraints in Kosovo, crossed the mountains into Macedonia and threatened the capital city of Skopje.

Yet, leaving Kosovo indeterminately as a protectorate too easily allows NATO and the United States to slip into the role of an imperial-like occupier—a role that in the end undermines the values of humanitarian intervention. The power a protectorate gives NATO and the United States is open to abuse that can only be avoided if Kosovo and its people are helped to succeed in the much more complex task of achieving self-government.

# PART THREE
# Rwanda

# BEARING WITNESS

## Bernardine Niyirora

IT WAS AROUND THE 15TH OF APRIL 1994 that we started to spend
the night in sorghum fields and in the woods. People were being pursued during the day, killed or tortured. When I saw this, I put my little
brother on my back, for Mama was pregnant. The killers found me in
the forest and beat me on the feet. The girls with me were raped. It was
useless to hide. We knew we had to die.

So we returned to the place where we lived and found that our
houses had been burned. We took refuge in sorghum fields again and
spent the night there. In the middle of the night we climbed Mount
Kanyarira to try to reach Kabgayi. But it was impossible, for we ran into
a roadblock.

At daybreak we made it back to our old houses near Saruheshyi. It
was around the 25th. We were visited by a cripple who said, "Go give
yourselves up, for sooner or later you'll have to." He led us on the road
to Evode's house. Our clothes were taken. We were told to pray, for it
was our last day. After our prayer, they began to beat the old, for, they
said, the old ones knew the whole history of the Inkotanyi [Rwandan
Patriotic Front]. They took our grandfather, named Straton Ruhory-
ongo, and his sons, three in number, and beat them to death with nail-
studded clubs. They attacked everyone, even the little boys. I was
paralyzed where I sat. They took my little brother. I begged them, "This
one isn't a boy." They left him alone and took away everyone they had

chosen and went to kill them behind the house. They told us, "The women and girls can clear out."

So we took the Bukomero road and neared a group of school buildings, believing we could find lodging there. Instead, we found frightening young thieves who took away a girl among us. We continued on our journey and came to the asphalt road. There we received the order to go back.

So we turned in the direction of the commune to put ourselves in the hands of the authorities. We were led to the Women's Training Center, where we found many gravely wounded people. There we spent the night. The next day I noticed that policemen were carrying something that looked like a corpse. It was my little brother, seriously injured in the head but not yet dead. He was laid out in the vestibule. Unable to lift him, I dragged him along the ground. I saw that he was in agony and poured some water over his body and more in his mouth. A few moments later, I saw that Mama was dripping blood and water down her legs, which were very swollen. Her head was swelling up too, for she had received a blow from a club.

On the 29th of April buses came to take us on board. We were driven to the school of St. Joseph. By chance I found someone to help me carry my little baby brother. Arriving at the school, we realized that death was better than staying here. We spent the night under the sky, in the rain. The next day everyone was looking for someone to give him a piece of potato to eat. Food was prepared, but to get any you had to be strong for the fight. I approached a nun and showed her my trembling mother and my suffering little brother. She looked at them and took pity and brought them a cup of tea, even a bit of corn. She looked for a place to shelter them and left them in the henhouse. Mama, feeling that she was about to deliver, went to the maternity ward and gave birth. Then she came back to us. But she couldn't sit down, for she was unable to stretch out in any direction. Dysentery and hunger were exterminating us. We were dying like flies. In our compound, the henhouse was bombed but by a miracle no one was touched.

We continued this sad life until . . . the 2nd of June, around ten in the morning, when we heard bursts of gunfire. Then we saw the army of the RPF advancing among us. They opened the door, and those who could followed them. We left in the direction of Byimana.

# 7

# Road to a Genocide

BILL BERKELEY

Ethnic bigotry in Rwanda was born of history, amplified by an elaborate system of myths built up around that history, and broadly accepted by Hutu and Tutsi alike. It has often been remarked that Hutus and Tutsis—the latter make up just under 15 percent of Rwanda's population—meet none of the conditions normally associated with tribes. For centuries they have spoken the same language, lived on the same hillsides, and intermarried to such an extent that the physical characteristics stereotypically attributed to each—tall, thin, and lighter skinned for the Tutsi; short, stocky, and darker skinned for the Hutu—are often blurred. Specialists on the region commonly protest that the distinctions between the two groups are artificial. But sixty years of colonial rule followed by thirty-five years of Hutu domination (1959–1994) produced real distinctions: deep-seated stereotypes and even deeper reservoirs of envy, fear, and mistrust that were ripe for exploitation. The fact that leaders manipulated ethnic divisions for their own cynical ends does not change the fact that the divisions were there to be manipulated, in the hearts and minds of those below. Yes, Rwanda was a land of followers, but they were followers prepared to hate and fear.

Rwanda was a textbook example of the destructive legacies of "indirect rule." Before colonialism, it was a highly organized feudal kingdom. Tutsi chiefs were overlords, but ethnic distinctions were fluid and social mobility commonplace. First the Germans and then the Belgians introduced a system of rule from a distance, whereby the Tutsi chiefs controlled the Hutu majority and extracted its labor on behalf of the colonial power. Across the continent, indirect rule in the colonial era was a means by which minority groups and traditional chiefs were invested with power and privilege, educated, trained, and subcontracted to do the dirty work on behalf of the white man. Resentments grew accordingly, nowhere more so than in Rwanda and neighboring Burundi.

In Rwanda, the malignant consequences of indirect rule were magnified by an explicit racial ideology known as the "Hamitic Hypothesis." European racial theorists concocted the "scientific" notion that "white Africans" from the northeast had brought civilization to the rest of the primitive continent. The Tutsis of Rwanda were held up as just such a superior race: intellectually gifted, morally uplifted, born to rule. The Hutus, by contrast, were dumb beasts of burden, ill-suited to be anything more than soil-tilling subjects. Educational privileges for the Tutsis reinforced these stereotypes. A system of population registration—including ethnically based identity cards—cemented them.

Tutsis, not surprisingly, embraced these myths as justification for their privileged position. Generations of European and Rwandan Tutsi intellectuals elaborated on a pseudo-anthropology of Tutsi superiority and Hutu incompetence. Elitism evolved into racism, and a myth of historic Tutsi domination—and cunning—came to be broadly accepted by Hutus and Tutsis alike. Sixty years of humiliating subjugation gave rise among the Hutus to what the French scholar Gerard Prunier, author of an outstanding history of the genocide, *The Rwanda Crisis*, has called "an aggressively resentful inferiority complex," upon which their leaders were keen to build.

In the Hutu-led "social revolution" of 1959–1962, which drove out the Belgians and their Tutsi surrogates, upward of ten thousand Tutsis were murdered, and as many as three hundred thousand were driven into exile in neighboring countries. Thousands more were murdered and exiled in subsequent waves of repression. For the next three decades, Hutu politicians, no more democratic than their Tutsi predecessors, justified their rule by building on and reinforcing Hutu fears of Tutsi perfidy.

The slide toward genocide began in October 1990, after the Rwandan Patriotic Front (RPF), a rebel insurgency led by Tutsi exiles, invaded Rwanda from Uganda. Their aim was to pressure the Hutu government of President Juvenal Habyarimana to allow Rwanda's exiled Tutsis to return. Three years of fighting ended in stalemate, and President Habyarimana was forced to enter into a power-sharing agreement with the Tutsi rebels. But extremists within Habyarimana's embattled regime had already begun formulating a plan to subvert the agreement and destroy the rebels by exterminating their base of support—the internal Tutsi population.

A key component of the plan was a virulent propaganda campaign—crafted by prominent Hutu intellectuals such as Ferdinand Nahimana (now in custody at the UN International Criminal Tribunal for Rwanda in Arusha, Tanzania)—that tapped into and inflamed old Hutu fears and resentments. The plan worked. On April 6, 1994, Habyarimana's plane was shot down—most likely by his own hard-line "allies." Habyarimana's assassination was immediately blamed on the Tutsis. This was the pretext for the massacres to begin.

No one really knows what proportion of Rwanda's Hutus participated in the genocide. By some accounts as many people killed as were killed. The broad participation of tens of thousands of ordinary Hutus undoubtedly was a function of Rwanda's by-now notorious culture of obedience. I encountered a chilling illustration of this phenomenon in 1998, four years after the genocide, when I visited one of the provincial prisons. At that time some 130,000 accused *génocidaires* were held in such places across the country. In the eastern province of Kibungo, the main prison is a squat brick edifice built to house 1,000 detainees. On the day of my visit there were 3,196 inmates, virtually all of them genocide suspects, including 112 women and 132 minors. There were also twenty-five infants, growing up in confinement with their imprisoned mothers.

Conditions were typical of prisons across Rwanda, which is to say, unspeakable. An overpowering stench of weeks-old sweat, filth, and urine hit me as I pushed my way into the prison's densely packed dormitories. As my eyes adjusted to the dark, I became aware of hundreds of eyes peering out of the blackness from within inches of my face. There were no lights or toilet facilities. Prisoners used chamber pots to relieve themselves. The sleeping quarters were pitch dark except for the light from slim window slats. Ventilation was nil. There were no beds or mattresses. The prisoners slept shoulder to shoulder on flattened cardboard boxes arrayed on shelves akin to a chicken coop. Their clothes and other belongings hung like stalactites from the ceiling. The prison yard was packed to overflowing, covered with a coat of soot from smoke billowing out of the cooking tent at one end of the courtyard, where inmates stirred massive vats of beans and rice. Streams of fresh sewage dribbled around me. Lice, malaria, ringworm, typhoid, and dysentery were rampant.

In 1995, as many as nine prisoners per day were dying in Rwanda's prisons. Conditions were said to have improved by the time I arrived, but disease, dehydration, and suffocation remained common. It was hard not to think that—guilty or not—these people were enduring a fate worse than death.

My guide through Kibungo prison was the elected leader of the prisoners, a thirty-eight-year-old former businessman named Joas Kaburame, himself accused of genocide. He told me he was framed by a former lover who was jealous of his marriage to another woman. It could be true, I thought. Who knows? No trial was imminent, Kaburame said. The Rwandan government was estimating that at the current rate it would take four hundred years to try all those accused of participation or complicity in the genocide. I asked Kaburame what seemed to me an obvious question: Was there ever any violence in this awful place?

"There are no fights," he replied matter-of-factly, without a trace of irony. "It's forbidden to fight. They must obey the rules."

Here was the culture of obedience at the heart of Rwanda's darkness: three thousand accused mass murderers packed in horrendous conditions like snakes in a bottle—and no violence. They were forbidden to fight, and so they didn't. Perhaps this culture goes some way toward explaining the velocity of a mass slaughter that was orchestrated from on high but implemented by tens of thousands of ordinary civilians at the grass roots. Rwanda is a nation of followers, people who "must obey the rules," and do.

## Anarchy and Tyranny

In July 1994 the Rwandan Patriotic Front (RPF) finally routed the Hutu regime and ended the genocide that in a hundred days had taken some eight hundred thousand lives; two million Hutus fled the country, including many of the *génocidaires* and their leaders. In a familiar pattern, the latter re-armed, using UN refugee camps as a base, and they have been fighting ever since to return to power and finish what they started. The result is the present intractable situation. A minority-led regime is compelled by circumstances beyond its control to govern indefinitely as a military dictatorship, in which even the best intentioned leaders are trapped by a kind of Macbethian logic, compelled to shed blood merely to survive. Many advocates for justice in Rwanda, including supporters of the International Tribunal, believe that justice will lead to "healing" and "reconciliation" between Hutus and Tutsis. That is an unrealistic goal. There are too many other factors in play, like the ongoing civil war, that are hardening mistrust. The history is accumulating, and so is the bigotry.

Bigotry alone does not explain mass slaughter. Racial stereotypes, envy, resentment, scapegoating, fear—all helped to make Rwanda's genocide possible, not inevitable. In combination, they serve to explain why people followed, but they are not explanation enough. The bigotry was there to be manipulated and exploited by cynical and desperate leaders. The real question is, what sort of environment spawns such leaders in the first place and then rewards their tactics?

Rwanda is a textbook case of ethnic conflict produced by tyranny, a prime example of the links between tyranny and anarchy and between ethnicity and organized crime. There is a widespread belief in the post–cold war era that ethnic conflict is a byproduct of "failed states." Rwanda represented the opposite: a state that was all too successful in mobilizing its people along rigidly hierarchical lines from the top down, from the head of state and his ruling clique of co-conspirators down to the last village mayor. And it was this success that in 1994 made possible the slaughter of hundreds of thousands in barely three months, mostly with clubs and machetes.

Rwanda was a model of order. The country was divided into 12 prefectures led by *préfets*, 154 communes led by *bourgmestres*, 1,600 sectors led by *conseilleurs*, and tens of thousands of *cellules*—a top-down network of control rooted in the precolonial kingdom, codified by the colonizers, and preserved after independence. Once Hutus vanquished the Tutsi elite in the early 1960s, their leaders took over the pre-existing social structure and used it to exercise total control over the populace. This rigid hierarchy was not to be confused with the rule of law. The rule of the gun was paramount; enforcement was consistently arbitrary.

The psychologist Ervin Staub, in his valuable book *The Roots of Evil—The Origins of Genocide and Other Group Violence*, examined mass slaughters in this century, from the Turkish genocide of the Armenians to the Nazi Holocaust and Pol Pot's Cambodia. Staub found "certain characteristics of a culture and the structure of a society"—such as obedience and hierarchy—that enhance the potential for group violence. Rwanda is another case where culture and social structure worked together. But the social structure was more complex than is generally understood. We need to look more closely at Rwanda's slide into genocidal conflict.

In the years leading up to the genocide, Tutsis had been massacred across Rwanda with increasing frequency—and impunity. Four hundred were slaughtered in Kibilira in 1990, five hundred in Bigogwe in 1991, three hundred in Bugesera in 1992. No one was ever held accountable. The rest of the world paid no heed.

Many suppose that tyranny and anarchy are at opposite ends of a linear spectrum. But often they are side by side on what might better be described as a circle: the one is a product of the other, and vice versa. Anarchy is a vacuum that brings out the worst in socialized and acculturated men and women and selects the worst among them. The pursuit of power is a life-and-death struggle. Those who excel in this struggle distinguish themselves through nothing more exotic than boundless cunning and ruthlessness. The most successful of all become tyrants, and the anarchy in which they thrive is called tyranny.

Even the most rigidly institutionalized tyrannies—Rwanda was one, South Africa during apartheid another—rely above all on the radical absence of lawful accountability for the criminal abuse of power. These tyrannies harness the forces of anarchy to their own ends; the tyrants turn lawlessness and terror, murder and rape, arson and theft into instruments of rule. For them, anarchy is a way of governing.

Inflamed ethnic passions are not the cause of this Hobbesian war of all against all, but its consequence. In a lawless world, ethnicity is a badge of legitimacy and protection, even of justice. It is the bond by which people high and low adhere to a vigilante code. They may appear to be acting on mindless impulse; in fact, they are making rational calculations of their own self-interest or, more accurately, of their own survival. The depth of their pre-existing prejudices may explain the potency of the symbols that their leaders choose to exploit, but it is the logic of their lawless environment that transforms those prejudices into terror.

Ethnic conflict in postcolonial Africa is also a form of organized crime. The "culture" driving Africa's conflicts is akin to that of the Sicilian Mafia or of the Crips and Bloods in Los Angeles, with the same imperatives of blood and family that bind all such gangs together. Africa's warring factions are best understood not as tribes but as racketeering enterprises, their leaders calculating strategy after the time-honored logic of Don Vito Corleone.

It is the stakes in Africa that are different—multiplied exponentially in circumstances where the state itself is a gang and the law doesn't exist. It is as if men like Corleone seized control not just of "turf" on the margins of society, but of the state itself and all its organs: police and army, secret police, the courts, the central bank, the civil service, the press, television, and radio.

It is by now well established that Rwanda's catastrophe was "more than a simple tribal meltdown," as *Time* magazine put it. All too often, however, the calculated quality of Rwanda's genocide is cited to distinguish it from other, presumably more spontaneous African slaughters. In fact there is no such thing as a "simple tribal meltdown," not anywhere. There were elements in Rwanda that distinguished it from other African calamities, but calculation was not among them. All of Africa's present-day conflicts are orchestrated from on high. They are all products of calculated evil.

Rwanda's Hutu elite, which excelled in this lawless culture, established a clear example of the state as a racketeering enterprise. Juvenal

Habyarimana had governed Rwanda for twenty-three years after the model of his mentor, Mobutu Sese Seko of Zaire. Amply funded and armed by the French, who funneled huge quantities of weapons to Rwanda even during the killings of 1994, Habyarimana ran lucrative rackets in everything from development aid to marijuana smuggling. He and his in-laws operated the country's sole black-market foreign exchange bureau in tandem with the central bank. Habyarimana was also implicated in the poaching of mountain gorillas, selling the valuable skulls and feet of baby primates. Habyarimana's brother-in-law was the principal suspect in the murder of the American anthropologist Dian Fossey.

This was the criminal culture in which the Rwandan genocide was hatched. Like gangsters and despots through the ages, Habyarimana apparently was destroyed by the monster he created, and then the monster went on to ever greater destruction.

## Fear Above All

The genocide of 1994 had its predecessors. Rwanda's border with Burundi is not much further from downtown Kigali than Coney Island is by subway from mid-town Manhattan. In 1965, between five thousand and ten thousand Burundian Hutus were killed by a Tutsi-dominated army. That slaughter turned out to be a premonitory sign of the awesome carnage of 1972, when upward of a hundred thousand Burundian Hutus—some say two hundred thousand—were killed. In 1988, Burundi's army killed twenty thousand Hutus, and another three thousand in 1991. As many as fifty thousand Burundians—Hutus and Tutsis—were butchered after a failed Tutsi-led coup in 1993, and another hundred and fifty thousand have died in Burundi's continuing bloodshed since then. Some eight hundred thousand Tutsis and dissident Hutus were killed in the Rwandan genocide of 1994.

Tutsis killing Hutus, Hutus killing Tutsis—the common denominator in all this slaughter is the total absence of legal accountability for a single perpetrator at any stage over more than three decades. In the absence of individual accountability for a single general, tyrant, militia leader, or gangster, and with no commonly agreed-upon set of historical facts, Tutsis and Hutus alike have blamed the other for the killing that has taken such a toll of both. Each has been prepared to believe the worst about the other's intentions in times of chaos, making Tutsis and Hutus alike vulnerable to the machinations of the propagandists and eager to seek the protection that those wearing the badge of ethnicity claimed to afford.

Fear, not hatred, was the dominant theme of the Hutu propagandists in Rwanda, who relentlessly terrorized their listeners on two state-owned radio stations both before and throughout the genocide of 1994. These radio broadcasts fabricated tales of harrowing massacres attributed to Tutsi guerrillas and civilians. They warned Hutus that Tutsi-led rebels were bent on re-imposing feudalism, wiping out all the Hutus, and taking all their land. All too many Hutus, looking across that nearby border at what happened in Burundi, believed what they were told, and then did what they were told they had to do in order to survive.

In June 1994, I interviewed six admitted members of the Interahamwe militia who had been captured days earlier by the Tutsi-led rebels. We sat on benches in the filthy remains of an abandoned corner store in Kabuga, a rubble-strewn, rebel-held town on the outskirts of Kigali. Genocide was still unfolding in the South. The climactic siege of Kigali was underway. Hundreds of dazed survivors of the massacres, some of them wrapped in gauze bandages that barely concealed their ghastly machete wounds, lingered amid the wreckage of their lives in the looted and gutted ruins nearby.

These militiamen were illiterate peasants—husbands and fathers— with thickly callused hands. Most of them had spent their entire lives cultivating sorghum and sweet potatoes on the steep mountain slopes of Kibungo Prefecture in eastern Rwanda. Defeated, scared, disheveled, wearing grimy secondhand clothes and sneakers or rubber flip-flops, they spoke in dull monotones under the watchful eyes of their Tutsi captors. They appeared to be men of the herd; each one said he had never killed before this. Evidently calculating that it was pointless, and might be fatal, to deny their crimes, they spoke with surprising candor about joining up with the "Igitero"—a group of attackers, leaders and led as one.

"Many people contributed to killing one person," one of them told me. "Because they feared the blood of the victim ["a guilty conscience," my translator explained], each person was afraid to kill alone. We would kill in groups. Even that old man hiding in the sorghum plantation—when we discovered him, Leonard, the militia leader, ordered everybody to hit him. Even after he was dead, everybody was supposed to take part in the killing. I used a club."

Another said, "If someone was discovered, we would surround him with sticks and start beating him. Then the rest would come with sticks and machetes and finish him off."

I asked this man if he felt any remorse. "I felt guilty and I felt I was committing a crime," he replied. "I had never killed before, so I did not feel comfortable to kill, because I knew these people had committed no crime. But I had to save myself. I had only to do as I was told."

This was the line: they killed because they were forced to. Many were killed for refusing to kill, they said. But further questions yielded a more complicated picture. Fear, not hatred, may have driven them to kill, but it was fear not just of their leaders. It was also fear of those whom they sought to exterminate.

Emmanuel Kamuhanda, eighteen years old, wore a mangy, purple corduroy jacket, blue jeans, and plastic high-top sneakers. Sullen and withdrawn, he spoke very quietly, and did not look me in the eye. "I did not want to kill," he told me. "I was just compelled to kill by the leader of the militia." When I asked how many people he had killed, Emmanuel replied, "There were many. Perhaps those who had the lists know better. I can tell you in my village we killed fifteen people. After my village we went to other villages and killed many. To say there were hundreds would be an understatement. The top leaders of the militia, when they marched us to kill, they had a list of the victims. We were shown whom to kill on the list. If you resisted, they would threaten you. They said you must kill or you will be killed."

Yet when I asked Emmanuel *why* he was forced to kill, his reply suggested that he understood the reasons for killing, and that they made sense to him: he believed in what he was doing when he was doing it.

"The government always told us that the RPF was Tutsi, and if it wins the war all the Hutus will be killed," he said. "As of now I don't believe this is true. But at the time, because it was the government saying so, using the radio, and because I had not known the RPF before, I believed that the government was telling the truth."

His confederate added, "They were always telling people that if the RPF comes, it will return Rwanda to feudalism, that they would bring oppression."

A third put it this way: "I did not believe the Tutsis were coming to kill us and take our land, but when the government radio continued to broadcast that the RPF is coming to take our land, is coming to kill the Hutu—when this was repeated over and over, I began to feel some kind of fear."

## Responsibility

No one disputes that Rwanda's Hutu leadership must bear ultimate responsibility for the genocide. But what of the RPF? What measure of responsibility do Rwanda's rebels bear for provoking what, in the context of Central Africa, was surely a foreseeable mass slaughter?

General Paul Kagame, leader of the Tutsi-dominated rebel army that invaded Rwanda in 1990 and now the president of Rwanda, is keen to draw parallels between the Tutsis' experience of genocide and that of the Jews. He and his fellow Tutsi generals point to Israel's conduct in the Middle East as a model for their own behavior. Indeed there are legitimate parallels, and they help explain why policy makers in Washington in the years since the genocide have flinched at the thought of passing judgment on those who claim to be acting on behalf of Rwanda's Tutsis.

But the parallels between Central Europe and Central Africa are not exact, and they may obscure more than they illuminate. To begin with, the Jews of Europe were never armed. Nazi propaganda notwithstanding, there was no Jewish conspiracy to dominate Europe, nor was there ever. There had been no Jewish tyranny in Germany, as there were Tutsi feudal tyrannies in both Rwanda and neighboring Burundi. And there had been no Jewish-perpetrated genocides in, say, Austria, as there were Tutsi-perpetrated genocides against Hutus no fewer than three times in a generation in Burundi.

These differences by no means absolve Hutus who participated in the genocide, but they underscore the recklessness of Tutsi refugees like General Kagame who, in 1990, thought the solution to their exile was an ethnically based armed insurgency against an entrenched and brutal, Hutu-dominated regime in Kigali. No rational person could have looked at the history of repeated mass slaughters in Rwanda and Burundi since 1959 and doubted for a moment that at least one likely outcome of such an invasion would be massive violence against defenseless Tutsi civilians.

Kagame was not himself a defenseless victim. To suggest that he was would be to adopt the same logic that informed the genocide, namely that a Tutsi is a Tutsi is a Tutsi, whether armed or unarmed. Kagame and his RPF confederates were armed. The victims of the genocide were unarmed. Kagame can argue that armed rebellion was his only alternative under the circumstances; he surely did not intend his rebellion to provoke a genocide. He points out that Westerners, not least Americans, have often resorted to violence to achieve their ends. Fair enough. But Kagame, no less than the West, must bear a measure of responsibility for the unintended consequences of legitimate ends pursued through violent means.

Gerard Prunier tells the story of the RPF occupation of a town in Western Rwanda during the early stages of the war. An old Tutsi man remarked to one of the young guerrilla fighters who had come to "liberate" him: "You want power? You will get it. But here we will all die. Is it worth it to you?" Prunier goes on to say, "[I]t is improbable that in late 1990 when Paul Kagame was working day and night to turn the RPF from an alienated band of exiles into an efficient fighting machine, he ever stopped to ask himself what was really going to happen. And in a way it is quite normal. Action carries with it its own logic, and in such situations men who stop to think for too long are likely to end up dead."

In January 2000, I had an opportunity to pose the question about responsibility to Yoweri Museveni, the president of Uganda, who was Kagame's main ally in 1990 and after. Not least, in 1990 Museveni had backed the Rwandan Patriotic Front's armed invasion of Rwanda from Uganda, led by men who were among Museveni's closest military confederates.

I met Museveni in his suite at the Waldorf Astoria, where he was staying during a visit for what turned out to be fruitless meetings of the UN Security Council to try to end the war in Congo. I asked Museveni about the law of unintended consequences. He had waged an armed rebellion against Idi Amin, and then another against the successor regime of Milton Obote. Now he was backing an armed rebellion against Islamist tyranny in Sudan. He had backed Laurent Kabila's rebellion against Mobutu's tyranny in what was then Zaire. Now he was backing rebels fighting against Kabila's tyranny, in a war that, as of this writing, had claimed as many as two and a half million civilian lives. Had it not occurred to Museveni and his friends, I asked, that armed rebellions provoke massive reprisals against defenseless civilians? What was he thinking in 1990? Surely he was mindful that a Tutsi-led armed rebellion in Rwanda was likely to result in the mass murder of Tutsi civilians. That had been the pattern in both Rwanda and Burundi, not to mention Uganda itself.

"We did not conspire with the RPF in 1990," Museveni demurred. "But after they went, we did not want them to come back. We said stay there [in Rwanda]."

Did Museveni accept no responsibility for the bloodshed that followed? I asked. For that matter, did he accept no responsibility for the bloodshed unleashed in response to his own war against Obote? Does one who engages in violent rebellion—even justified armed rebellion against tyranny—bear no responsibility for the unintended consequences of his rebellion? When those consequences are foreseeable, as surely they were in Rwanda and Congo, as well as in Sudan, aren't the rebels responsible for protecting those who bear the brunt of the tyrant's repression?

Museveni was plainly contemptuous of this line of questioning.

"There is a thief who grabs a briefcase in the street," he said, eyes alight, staring me down. "When I try to restrain him, he starts shooting passersby. And then the journalist from New York says, 'Why did you try to restrain him? You are the one who provoked him.' Don't you think that's a bit … ?" He shook his head incredulously. "The authors of the genocide are to blame. We cannot have this blackmail."

Blackmail?

"Amin said on the radio, 'Museveni will be killed. His family will be killed.'" The president was recalling his first armed rebellion in Uganda, against Idi Amin. "That was blackmail—if you resist dictatorship, your family will be killed. The threats to my family should not doom resistance to dictatorship. I do my duty. If you want to kill innocent people, that's your own responsibility."

Museveni concluded with vehemence, "But I will not accept blackmail. Every dictator says, 'If you attack me, I will kill you.' Before 1986, a hundred thousand children were dying of six preventable diseases in Uganda. So people in a bad system are dying every day. That is the basis for deciding to resist a dictatorship. You are mistaken. The people who are killed in reaction to resistance are not as many as by dictatorship itself. There is a responsibility of regional actors to attack dictatorship."

Museveni had a point, of course. Even the best intentioned of Africa's leaders—and Paul Kagame is one of them—must choose between painful alternatives. Meek submission to tyranny would be unacceptable and nonviolent resistance almost certainly ineffectual. The latter could only be credible and effective—in the eyes of the tyrant as well as in those of his subjects—if there were many more regional actors prepared to support it, and if those actors were backed by the resources and prestige of outside powers.

That support and backing, however, were entirely missing in the Rwandan case, where both the UN and the Clinton administration declined to intervene even after the massacres began. And the next time?

# 8

# Echoes of Violence

DARRYL LI

S even years after the fact, the most enduring—and perhaps haunt-
ing—image of the Rwandan genocide is that of the nameless Hutu
peasant standing over a pit of putrid corpses, a machete in one hand and
a radio in the other. The manner of his gaze is unclear, but there is no
mistaking the tinny voice blaring from the tiny receiver as anything
other than the infamous Radio-Télévision Libre des Mille Collines
(RTLM), the station whose broadcasts were a background score to the
killings.

The semi-private "hate radio" station, linked to an elite circle of
Hutu hard-liners, was allegedly the brainchild of Ferdinand Nahimana,
a Sorbonne-trained historian currently on trial before a UN-run court in
Tanzania for incitement to genocide. During its brief existence as the
first licensed private broadcaster in the country, RTLM quickly sur-
passed the stilted, government-run Radio Rwanda in popularity with a
combination of virulence, humor, and style. "They talked off the cuff
about a subject they mastered: hatred," a former press liaison with the
rebel Rwandan Patriotic Front (RPF), which overthrew the genocidal
regime, told me.

For the notorious state-sponsored Interahamwe militia who were
the shock troops of the genocide, RTLM's broadcasts were orders, its
denunciations death warrants. In one well-known incident, an RTLM
reporter covering an attempt by UN peacekeepers to rescue a group of
refugees from the Hôtel Mille Collines in Kigali relayed the names of all

sixty-two evacuees on the air, including several prominent opponents of the regime. Soon thereafter, a group of Interahamwe stopped the UN convoy and singled out a number of those named on the radio for abuse; only intense diplomatic pressure saved them from being massacred. Tutsi civilians sheltered in a mosque in Kigali's Nyamirambo neighborhood in the first weeks of the genocide were not so lucky; after a cue from RTLM, militia and soldiers butchered some six hundred people inside, while the station gleefully reported the results.

In the summer of 2000, six years after it was knocked off the air in the wake of the collapse of the genocidal regime, reminders of RTLM could be found everywhere. The Kigali hostel in which I slept was owned by a nearby church, whose priest during the genocide, Wenceslas Munyeshyaka, allegedly carried a radio tuned to RTLM while singling out Tutsi members of his flock for elimination (Munyeshyaka later fled to France). Walking through the crowded streets, I often passed stalls where one could still buy cassettes featuring the extremist songs of Simon Bikindi (arrested by Dutch authorities in 2001 and sent to the UN tribunal), a staple of the RTLM diet. And in the city's central prison, I found many alleged *génocidaires*, most of them ordinary farmers, such as Frodouald Ndoliyobijya, who recalled RTLM's antics with a mischievous giggle one minute and in the next humbly told of how he murdered a Tutsi whom his father had tried to save.

RTLM's lingering omnipresence had to do with the fact that the Interahamwe were only a small part of a nationwide audience that tuned in for news, entertainment, and the latest instructions. The station spread hateful propaganda about the country's Tutsi minority, guided people to where the "enemy" hid, and goaded ordinary people into joining the killings—the most famous of its entreaties being the uncharacteristically blatant "The graves are only half full! Who will help us to fill them?" Hundreds of thousands of people heeded these calls by manning roadblocks, joining search patrols, looting, and steadily killing in their own locales.

"It's a lie if a farmer says he didn't like RTLM," said Bernard Rutaremara, who awaits trial in Kigali's central prison for participating in the killings. Bernard was probably right, but RTLM's near-universal popularity, like the infamous Rwandan "culture of obedience" it is often taken to represent, must be explained rather than taken for granted. Three months of conversations with detainees, survivors, and others made it clear that Rwandans actively debated and critiqued what they heard on competing radio stations—including Radio Rwanda and the RPF-controlled Radio Muhabura. Yet it was RTLM that somehow captured the national imagination. Understanding why this happened requires more than a look at what the radio station said. It requires knowing the ways in which its words were understood and the ways in which RTLM took advantage of the role of radio in everyday life in Rwanda.

Through radio, the genocide unfolded in thousands of locales, turning ordinary Rwandans into witnesses to the killings and bringing them into the massacres in ways at once both terrifying and mundane. As Mwamini Nyirandegeya, a woman of mixed ethnicity who survived the genocide as a servant to the militiaman who raped her, put it, *"RTLM animait dans l'ambiance du moment."* One also could say that the station's *animateurs* helped to shape that ambience as well.

The first time I saw Valérie Bemeriki, the infamous RTLM *animatrice*, was through the window of a reception area in Kigali's central prison. Short, limping, and slightly rotund, her pink prisoner's uniform reminiscent of an ill-fitting ballerina's tutu, Bemeriki hardly resembled the voice of genocide. I stood up when she entered the room. We shook hands and made small talk before I introduced myself.

Bemeriki acquired a reputation during the genocide for her impassioned, almost frenzied, announcing style. During our interviews, she dismissed RTLM transcripts as forgeries and swept aside uncomfortable questions, instead launching into long, rambling monologues about how massacres of unarmed Tutsi civilians were in fact battles between government troops and rebels. Furthermore, she said, she and her colleagues were not demagogues, but responsible journalists who always checked their facts and reported the truth, and if that resulted in their being falsely accused of genocide, so be it.

Despite the outrageousness of some of her claims, Bemeriki had a point. To the outsider's eye, RTLM's transcripts reveal few explicit instructions to murder. In the ideological universe of RTLM, one never spoke of killing, but only of "work" or "clearing the brush" (courtesy of "tools," rather than machetes or clubs, of course). The word "Tutsi" itself was used far less often than *inyenzi* (cockroaches) or *inkotanyi* (the self-given nickname of RPF fighters). This indirectness, which left nothing unsaid, is apparent even in the title of the Simon Bikindi hit "You Know What I'm Saying."

For these euphemisms to take on such meanings—to make roadblock duty, search patrols, and killing acceptable activities for people to take part in—RTLM appropriated three ideas that had shaped postcolonial Rwanda's understanding of itself: History, Democracy, and Development. The narrative of History provided a raison d'être for the postcolonial regime through comparisons with the merciless exploitation of Hutu farmers by Tutsi collaborators during the era of Belgian rule. Democracy, meaning little more than the crude arithmetic of ethnic majoritarianism, scapegoated Tutsi to mask the dominance of a narrow clique of northern Hutu under a shared bond of ethnicity. And the elusive goal of Development, promising a vague future of prosperity, justified *umuganda*, a weekly ritual of communal labor forced on nearly every peasant in the country. For decades before the genocide, these ideas were the foundation of an authoritarian, single-party state that micromanaged the population and in which Tutsi were marginalized but almost never attacked.

The genocide turned these concepts upside down, weaving a coherent ideological tapestry that made euphemisms such as "work" into powerful metaphors for making sense of one's actions, no matter how terrible the implications of those actions may have been. RTLM invoked History, Democracy, and Development to mobilize people rather than to render them docile, using these familiar ideas to mask unthinkable ends.

RTLM regularly compared the genocide to the 1959 revolution that overthrew Tutsi hegemony, collapsing past into present to raise the terrifying specter of a return to the ancien régime. In what was an almost constant refrain, Kantano Habimana, RTLM's star *animateur*, warned listeners: "Masses, be vigilant. . . . What you fought for in '59 is being taken away," implying that the gains of the revolution, the postcolonial state, and progress itself were hanging in the balance.

When speaking of democracy to justify the killings, the station urged Hutu to put aside differences and close ranks against the common Tutsi threat. RTLM fetishized the language of majorities and minorities, styling itself as the voice of the *rubanda nyamwinshi* ("numerous people"). The station argued that the numerical superiority of the Hutu meant both that their cause was just and their victory inevitable. By extension, only the Tutsi could be blamed for their fate—"Will those people truly continue to commit suicide against the majority?" Habimana once asked with rhetorical incredulity.

In its announcements, advice, and encouragements, RTLM cast participation in the genocide in the mold of *umuganda*, likening extermination to controlling soil erosion or preventing forest fires, efforts in which everyone had to pitch in. "Hello, good day, have you started to work yet?" RTLM asked its listeners every morning. Indeed, many of the tasks of the genocide eerily resembled *umuganda*, with farmers turning up for their shifts under the same supervisors with the same tools (mostly machetes and hoes), as if it were just another day of clearing fields or planting trees.

Yet the code of the genocide, like all totalitarian languages, sometimes could not help contradicting itself at times. One Rwandan told interviewers that RTLM "called for all the Tutsi to be exterminated. Bemeriki would say, for example, 'Kill! Kill! Go to Nyamirambo! I have just been there, and there aren't any bodies in the streets yet. *It's still tidy. You have to start cleaning!*" On another occasion, as news spread that France was sending troops to Rwanda to bring humanitarian aid and cover the withdrawal of the collapsing genocidal regime, Bemeriki told Hutu to welcome the troops warmly. After months of mixing anti-Tutsi invective with superficial assurances that not all Tutsi were bad, it was only sensible for her to make it absolutely clear that these white men were different from the hated Belgians. "If you are told to do something, you are not told to do the opposite," Bemeriki insisted. "If we are saying that we should welcome the French, that does not mean that we should throw stones at them."

A few months before the genocide, Claver Kizungu, a Tutsi farmer living east of Kigali, happened upon a spectacle in the local market. The editor-in-chief of RTLM, Gaspard Gahigi, had arrived with a mobile studio and was broadcasting live in front of a crowd of several hundred locals. "He said that the Tutsi were bad and that they killed many people when they were in power, and that you had to know they are the enemy and get them," Kizungu recalled. During the monologue, a neighbor—Vedaste Nteziryayo—looked over in Kizungu's direction and menaced him with a slashing motion across the throat. The same Vedaste Nteziryayo went on to kill many people during the genocide, although another of his Tutsi neighbors insisted that he was a good man who had saved lives as well.

Whether in person or on the air, RTLM's *animateurs* helped listeners experience the genocide as a series of small performances upon which the edifice of larger ideologies could be built. They adroitly navigated and manipulated the hierarchies and bonds within audiences, trying to turn the very act of listening into a form of participation in the genocide.

Sometimes, RTLM played with its listeners as much as it played to them, using already widespread mistrust and fear to build unity. During one interview at a roadblock, a man boasted of having helped to kill five *inyenzi*. Habimana encouraged him to "keep it up" and then advised listeners, "When testing if people like a radio station, you must ask the following question: who are the *animateurs* of the radio whom you know? Who are the RTLM *animateurs* you know? . . . If you do not know them that means that you do not like this radio." The pressure to listen—and to be seen listening—to the station was immense. "Some people were against RTLM, but didn't have the strength to say so in public," recalled Jamad Nkundintware, a Hutu mason. Venant Musirikare, an elderly Tutsi, was so terrified by the hardening attitudes of his neighbors that he bought a recording of Bikindi's songs to convince them of his loyalty. His fears were not unfounded; another time, Habimana announced that all Tutsi who were not against the regime should man the roadblocks alongside Hutu, only to tell people the next day, "Look around, the enemy is among you."

Although few of the station's listeners had access to a telephone, RTLM found ways of actively involving audiences. *Animateurs* relayed personal messages from listeners, while soldiers and militia spontaneously brought suspected RPF collaborators to the station's studios to be interrogated on the air. Similarly, RTLM's announcements provided practical advice that went into planning day-to-day activities. One Hutu farmer I spoke to recalled several of his neighbors proclaiming, "Kantano [Habimana] said there are no RPF troops here, so we can continue our work."

In a sense, ordinary Rwandans, too, performed RTLM's broadcasts. Almost every personal message, public service announcement, and piece of gossip transmitted found its way by word of mouth beyond those who actually heard them, making each radio a potential spawning ground for new performances. According to one of his former neighbors, a murderer of some notoriety named Hakiri used to spend mornings sitting on the corrugated metal roof of his shop outside Kigali with a radio to his ear, listening to RTLM. His mood darkened during the broadcasts, and he would climb down and gather people to tell them what he had heard of the latest Tutsi atrocities. Across the country, thousands of listeners were relaying, embellishing, and even misrepresenting RTLM's broadcasts. In *We Wish To Inform You That Tomorrow We Will Be Killed With Our Families*, Philip Gourevitch writes of a prominent Hutu extremist who, taking pity on some Tutsi children at a roadblock, admonishes the militiaman harassing them, "Don't you listen to the radio? The French said if we don't stop killing children they'll stop arming and helping us."

In seeking to turn listeners toward a common goal, RTLM treated them as thinking subjects rather than obedient drones. But it was for this very reason that, like all totalitarian systems, it could be nothing but imperfect. For just as thousands of Rwandans like Vedaste Nteziryayo chose to kill some Tutsi and to save others, they could also invoke RTLM for their own ends—even, at times, to resist the genocide.

More so than Radio Rwanda or the RPF's Radio Muhabura, RTLM's *animateurs* developed personas in which listeners invested authority and trust. Kantano Habimana captivated audiences with his electrifying announcing style, narrating the results of massacres as if they were victories on the football pitch (he is rumored to have died in a refugee camp in Congo after the genocide). The raucous, hard-drinking Noël (Noheli) Hitimana was much beloved from his years at Radio Rwanda.

RTLM even had its token white man, a Belgian named Georges Ruggiu. Though he was far from the most popular of RTLM's *animateurs*, his uniqueness made him memorable, if only as an object of curiosity.

Ruggiu's case is also interesting because he is the only non-Rwandan to have been indicted by the UN tribunal (he pleaded guilty to incitement to genocide in June 2000) and was the only *animateur* without journalism or broadcasting experience. In fact, there appeared to be no reason to hire him other than the fact that he was white. Samson Karungura, who killed ten people during the genocide, remembered speculating that Ruggiu's being on RTLM meant either that he couldn't find a job in his own country or that the station had the strength of foreign support. "Moderates said if there is a white man working [for RTLM], they would be able to destroy any opposition," recalled Protegène Shyaka, a Tutsi shopkeeper.

Some of Ruggiu's monologues seemed to do little other than leverage his Europeanness for credibility. During one evening program broadcast several weeks before the genocide, Ruggiu read passages from Machiavelli's *The Prince* on the air, expounding on the necessity of disingenuousness in politics, while classical European music droned on in the background. "Here then is Nicholas [sic] Machiavelli, who speaks through my voice," Ruggiu announced, as if taking on the role of a spirit medium. Centuries of "civilization" hung in the air like overripe fruit, dangling just out of the reach of the Rwandans listening in rural hilltop homes.

Rwandans obviously resent whites as much as they respect them. So rather than making him into a latter-day Kurtz, Ruggiu's race was at best a gimmick. Furthermore, only a fraction of the population knew enough French to fully understand him. But just as radio broadcasts do not travel in the ether, listeners do not exist in a vacuum. According to several people I interviewed, educated French speakers, themselves often local organizers of the genocide, regularly translated and explained Ruggiu's broadcasts for others. The result was a sort of mutual reinforcement, enhancing the credibility of these elites while at the same time extending the reach and authority of Ruggiu's words.

Ironically, the only people who seemed curiously unaware of the significance of Ruggiu's whiteness were those whose duty it was to exact justice upon him. The UN judges who sentenced Ruggiu to twelve years in prison cited his European background and consequent unfamiliarity with Rwanda as mitigating factors in determining his punishment, but never mentioned that his being European was key to his involvement with RTLM in the first place.

We were crouched in the shadow of the mud-brick house, wary of the hot sun and of the listening children peeking through the cracks in the fence. James Nshogozabahizi, a Hutu farmer, described daily life during the genocide on the hill where he lived, east of Kigali. The "work" of manning roadblocks or searching houses began in the morning, when some locals would report to the authorities. It would continue until 5 P.M. or so, and then people would gather in the local bar to drink, chat, and listen to RTLM before retiring to bed and waking up the next morning. Several dozen kilometers away I met Tito Rutaremara, a Tutsi, who recalled that during breaks in the work day, locals would gather in groups as large as a hundred to listen to RTLM, closely following the information relayed to plan the next day's activities. I asked if this happened every day. "Of course," he replied. "It was work. It was to know what to do."

Much of the killing in Rwanda in 1994 was marked not by the fury of combat or paroxysms of mob violence, but by a well-ordered sanity that mirrored the rhythms of ordinary collective life. After all, what is striking about the genocide is not simply that the priest, the schoolteacher, and the radio *animateur* spoke with one voice of the necessity to "work," but rather that they did so during the weekly sermon, the daily lesson, and the hourly bulletin.

Radio's subtle presence was a key entry point of the state into the lives of its citizens. For the people I spoke to who owned radios, listening was often the first thing they did in the morning and the last thing they did at night. For others, catching the latest news was often a major reason for visiting neighbors or swinging by the local bar. In a country with few newspapers or televisions, the medium's portability and many uses enable it to cross boundaries of public and private life and to punctuate daily schedules. Of RTLM's *animateurs*, none had a more intuitive grasp of this than Noheli Hitimana.

After a decade on the air at Radio Rwanda, Hitimana was a part of the lives of millions of Rwandans. During the early morning shift, widely listened to by farmers rising to tend their fields, he was known for calling out to the farthest mountains in the country, issuing greetings to various regions, and saluting individuals with whom he had shared a drink the night before. "He showed that Radio Rwanda was interested in its listeners," explained confessed *génocidaire* Elie Ndabamenye, adding that a greeting from Hitimana was something like a small honor, a moment of celebrity and recognition for hard work.

Hitimana carried on in a similar vein at RTLM. His monologues featured litanies of places where local residents were warned to remain vigilant or urged to hunt down *inyenzi*. Similarly, Hitimana converted his habit of saluting individuals into a means of denouncing them. According to a report by the press freedom NGO Article 19, one of those threatened was opposition journalist Joseph Mudatsikira. "Let me say Hello, child of my mother," Hitimana said, adopting a tone of playful familiarity. "Let me salute you, as you are the same as Noheli [that is, also a journalist] ... If you die just as everyone else has been speaking about you, it is not like dying like a sheep, without having been spoken of. When we have spoken about you, you have effectively been spoken of." Mudatsikira was killed several days later. Hitimana's broadcasts on RTLM exploited a decade's worth of familiarity in order to insinuate the genocide into everyday life, to make its presence felt even in small homes in rural areas at dawn—including the many in which Tutsi were being hidden. For the Hutu who risked their lives to shelter others, however, the intimacy of Hitimana's broadcasts made them more than death threats. It made them betrayals, signals to listeners that underneath all that defined their world, even routines followed in the privacy of the home, lay the possibility of treachery, of being attacked by a Tutsi neighbor or accused of treason by a Hutu friend. Providing an example of what to emulate and a warning of what to avoid, Hitimana showed that it was better to denounce than to be denounced and that even personal ties could be subordinated to the imperatives of the genocide.

"You Americans cry a lot when someone dies," Jean d'Amour, my interpreter, told me with surprise one day as we waited for lunch. "I see it on television." When we first met, he mentioned that his parents had been killed in the genocide; we never spoke of it again. Months later, I looked for an account of the conversation in my journal, but found that it had not even merited a mention. Another time, an acquaintance of mine, called Richard, told me that after the genocide, he ran into the man who had killed his parents, a family friend named Emmanuel, and did not know what to do. Or rather, he wanted to do so many things at the same time that he did nothing. "If you need anything, any help, just let me know," Emmanuel told him sincerely. Richard nodded and went about his life.

After some time in Rwanda, especially the weeks spent working at the Kigali prison, I became habituated to these stories. While handing me a packet of life-saving malaria pills, a doctor once said that he lost ten relatives in the killings; I acknowledged the statement with a nod as I left his office, thinking not of his loss but only of my burning fever. I would not object to being called insensitive (or anything worse), but, as Jean d'Amour asked rhetorically, "How can one cry so much for one person when so many have died?"

Rwandans are not an incredibly stoic people who have simply shrugged off death, nor have they achieved some elusive stage of "closure" and "moved on." Rather, the genocide lives on in the grief, pain, and anger that has saturated everything to the extent that one's loss seems to have been reduced to only a single piece of an imponderably vast suffering. It seems that Rwandans have been able to continue with life only by accepting the inescapability of death, while mutual suspicion and tension gnaw at the edges of nights and days.

The genocide's continued hold on everyday life seven years later is a reminder of the fact that it involved the direct efforts of hundreds of thousands of ordinary people on a day-to-day basis, shattering the ties of neighborliness, friendship, and love. It is often said that in times of war or conflict, there is a point where people cease to be shocked or disgusted by the wanton taking of human life and thus find it easier to kill as well. Yet despite this fact and despite the desperate poverty, immense state coercion, and other rationales that can be summoned, something about the Rwandan genocide remains inexplicable. I don't mean its cruelty, which was unspeakable but not unprecedented, nor even its sheer enormity. What is uniquely unimaginable about the Rwandan genocide was that rather than the violence becoming normal, normality itself was somehow co-opted in the service of violence.

Like the killings, RTLM, too, was omnipresent, routinized, and intimate. By articulating a coherent language of massacre, bringing listeners together as witnesses and performers, and infiltrating everyday routines, RTLM may even have been the key to transforming the Rwandan genocide from a state-led campaign into a mass-participatory nationwide project. Without RTLM there might have been, during the late evenings in bars after a shift at the roadblock, or in the midst of a nighttime walk home past a banana grove, machete in hand, at least some stillness, a bit of silence, a moment to think alone.

# 9

# Justice on a Hill

George Packer

O n a ridge in southern Rwanda, a few miles from the Burundi border, lies the town of Butare. The National University is there, and
for many years both the town and the province of the same name
enjoyed a reputation for tolerance. In 1994, the proportion of Tutsis in
Butare was far greater than anywhere else in Rwanda—there were
140,000 throughout the province—and in town Tutsis made up a full
quarter of the population. The rate of intermarriage between Hutu and
Tutsi was higher here than elsewhere, so high that Hutus in the north
of Rwanda sometimes said that there were no real Hutus in Butare. In
early April of 1994, when the rest of Rwanda was consumed with mass
murder, Butare held out. Only after April 19, when the president of the
interim government and other leading Hutu Power figures came to
Butare and told its Hutu citizens to quit shirking their national duty, did
the killings begin in earnest there. But once the genocide reached
Butare, it accelerated at a frenzied pace, and by the end of April tens of
thousands of Tutsis were dead. When the genocide was over, 75 percent
of the province's Tutsis, more than a hundred thousand people, had
been eliminated.

Laurien Ntezimana, a Hutu theologian who distinguished himself in
Butare in 1994 by working to feed and save Tutsis, told me, "Butare is
the most dangerous place in Rwanda." In fact, the province seems relatively peaceful today. What Ntezimana meant was that its history of
interconnection, together with the scale of its slaughter, have left a pool

of bitterness that is deep and toxic even by Rwandan standards. Eight years after the genocide, there is a great deal of talk about justice and reconciliation in Rwanda. I went to Butare because it seemed as tough a place as one could find to test the meaning of these words.

The road that winds south and west to Butare from Kigali, Rwanda's capital in the center of the country, passes through a stunning landscape. Behind every green hill there's another hill, with eucalyptus groves and banana trees and terraced fields of sweet potato and manioc and corn. The cottages nestled in the hills have terra-cotta tile roofs and little mullioned windows. Everything is on a miniature scale, hidden away, intensely settled, too much human imagination concentrated in too small a space ("the human head has many ideas," a genocide suspect in Kigali Central prison said). As I drove, the hills and the cottages looked like the landscape of a fairy tale on which there had been laid a curse.

In the northern part of the province, the paved road passes through the ancient royal capital of Nyanza, seat of the regional court of appeals. On my way to Butare I made a stop at the court, a two-story colonial building on a hilltop, because I wanted to talk to the prosecutor-general about *gacaca*. The word (pronounced ga-CHA-cha) literally refers to the flattened grass where, in Rwandan tradition, elders sit under a tree and render judgments on property disputes and cattle theft. Rwanda is now adapting this old and local form of trial to seek justice for the clearest case of genocide since the Holocaust.

Rwanda's prisons and lock-ups house close to 112,000 genocide suspects and another five thousand convicts. The number is so great, and the condition of Rwanda's judiciary so poor, that it's often said it would take at least a century to try all the cases. The Rwandan Patriotic Front (RPF), which has had a monopoly on political power in Rwanda since it ended the genocide in 1994 by defeating the Hutu Power regime, has always claimed that the country's devastation, its continued lack of resources, and the enormity of the crime explain the excruciatingly slow turning of the wheels of justice. There is evidence, though, that manipulation by the RPF has delayed some trials, altered others, led to false arrests, and kept thousands of prisoners from even reading their files and knowing the charges against them. At the same time, untold numbers of *génocidaires* remain at large, both inside Rwanda and outside.

Faced with criticism abroad and a strain on resources and social relations at home, the RPF has launched a daring experiment in participatory justice based on the tradition of *gacaca*. Beginning this year, all but the most serious genocide cases will be tried outside the court system, by tribunals of elected judges in the communities where the crimes took place, with the local population in attendance as audience and potential witnesses for the prosecution or the defense.

The prosecutor-general of the Nyanza appeals court is responsible for preparing *gacaca* in his jurisdiction by arraigning prisoners whose files are empty—some of them have been locked up seven years without a court appearance—before the local populations. Jean Marie Mbarushimana, a large, self-assured man with a Gallic blue, double-breasted suit jacket and thick sideburns, is himself a survivor of the genocide. After four years in Canada he came home, as he said, "healed," to participate in the monumental task of bringing justice. He seemed undaunted as he smoked a cigarette by a large window that opened onto an airy second-floor porch where a pair of birds fluttered and swooped. He had no doubt about *gacaca*'s ultimate success. The genocide had been a collective effort, a national mobilization requiring everyone's involvement. *Gacaca* would untie the knot in the same way.

"The government wanted to incriminate the whole population," he said, "to cover up the genocide. So that it was almost impossible to be neutral, stay at home, remain outside it. You had to show you were for it. Because the orders came down—the orders—to be at the roadblock, to join the night patrols, and you had to take your stick and show you were part of it."

He was describing what it was like to be a Hutu in Rwanda in the spring of 1994. This effort involved a high degree of imagination and restraint on his part, but it is an effort that seems essential for *gacaca* to succeed. The point of taking the cases out of the courtroom and onto the hills is to create a setting where the fullest possible truth can be told. "Synergy" is how Laurien Ntezimana described it: "The two parties in conflict work together to bring light to the matter. They work together even when they contradict each other. *Gacaca* works in the heart of a family, on a hill, among people who have an interest in living together."

Genocide is an absolute. It doesn't admit of moral degrees. But more than anywhere else, in Rwanda, where tens or hundreds of thousands of ordinary people from one group joined in the attempted elimination of another group, genocide was made up of countless individual choices, deeds, omissions, evasions, rationalizations, compromises. What were they? At this distance we think about the Rwandan genocide as a singular horror, a truth reducible to two unbelievable figures: one hundred days, eight hundred thousand deaths. But for every Rwandan involved— and there was hardly a Rwandan who was not, in one way or another— the genocide meant the particulars of his or her own experience. Jean Marie Mbarushimana told me that he wanted to make a film about the genocide to show Rwandans how it happened everywhere in the country. I said that most foreigners understood it *only* as a whole; what we had more trouble understanding, and perhaps did not want to understand, was how it happened in this or that corner of Rwanda.

I was not interested in ideologues or sadists, though Rwanda has produced its share of both. They seem exhaustively examined and at the same time fundamentally unknowable. I wanted to find the ambiguous cases; I wanted to talk to Hutus whose conduct during the genocide would force you or me to ask what we might have done in their place.

The prosecutor-general put out his cigarette. On the way to his door I asked if there was a case in the Butare prison that I might find especially interesting in light of our conversation. He thought about it. "There's a prisoner named Camille Nzabonimana. He used to sell solar-heating panels. He saved a lot of Tutsis, but he's accused of leading killers. Look into his case."

There is a long history in Rwanda of mass action under state compulsion. During the time of the *mwami*, the precolonial Tutsi king, it took the form of regular communal work called *umuganda*. The Belgian colonizers exploited *umuganda* to conscript forced laborers in road-building and other public works, a practice continued after independence, especially by Juvenal Habyarimana, the Hutu dictator whose plane was brought down over Kigali on April 6, 1994 by a missile fired by attackers who remain unknown to this day. The genocide that followed his death—for which his death provided an excuse—was another variation on the theme of collective enterprise, an apocalyptic *umuganda*, the responsibility of everyone.

In a sense, *gacaca* follows in this Rwandan tradition of mass mobilization. The preamble to the *gacaca* law, passed on January 21, 2001 and disseminated in the name of President Paul Kagame, gives a strong whiff of command justice, declaring that the "duty to testify is a moral obligation, nobody having the right to get out of it for whatever reason it may be." The genocide was organized to incriminate everyone it didn't eliminate. *Gacaca* will make everyone who survived the genocide a defendant, a witness, or a judge. So *gacaca* presents a paradox, or rather, many paradoxes. It falls back on Rwandan traditions to resolve their terrible legacy—and yet nothing is more traditional in Rwanda than the idea that survival means figuring out what the authorities want. It depends on grassroots participation mandated by the state. It makes the assignment of individual responsibility for the genocide a collective business. It is premised on there being a community whose existence is open to serious doubt.

In October 2001, 90 percent of the population turned out in their local areas to choose the *gacaca* judges, known as "people of integrity." I arrived several weeks later, so I had to rely on Rwandans' accounts of how, for example, one man whose name was put forward by neighbors was rejected when someone else pointed out that he drank too much, or how a Tutsi recused himself because he admitted to harboring anti-Hutu bias. Across the country, 260,000 people of integrity were selected by their neighbors to make up the *gacaca* tribunals at all administrative levels. To me, this extremely public exercise in character analysis spoke of a degree of consensus and sheer nosiness that few American neighborhoods could achieve. But Rwandans seemed to accept the process as natural, and most people pronounced the elections a success.

Each tribunal has nineteen judges. Those at the cell level—a jurisdiction of about four hundred people—will collect accounts of crimes of genocide committed in their area, divide the suspects into four categories of severity (those in the first category, organizers and zealots of the genocide, as well as rapists, will not receive the benefit of *gacaca*), and go on to judge the Category 4 offenses, those against property. At the next level up, that of the sector, tribunals will hear Category 3 cases, involving crimes that resulted in injury. The district-level *gacaca* courts will hear Category 2 cases, involving killing but not leadership of killers (by some estimates, three-quarters of those in jail fall into this group). From each level an appeal can be made higher up, with provincial tribunals as the final courts of appeal.

The *gacaca* law allows for substantial reductions in sentences if the accused confesses. A Category 2 defendant, facing twenty-five years to life, can have his sentence reduced to twelve to twenty-five years if he confesses at trial; and if the confession comes before *gacaca* begins, the sentence drops down to seven to twelve years, which means that some killers who were arrested just after the genocide will be freed based on time already served. Others will benefit from doing community work in place of half or more of their remaining term.

Prospects like these have made *gacaca* a hard sell among genocide survivors. "A widow who sees the guy that killed her husband return to his own house and sleep with his wife?" speculated a woman who happened to be Hutu. "For her to think that they're making love right now, while I'm here alone? I imagine it could lead to killings, maybe by machete, maybe by poison." Some Rwandans assume that *gacaca* will liberate tens of thousands of killers; far likelier is a prisoner exchange, with some going free, others newly arrested after denunciations during *gacaca*, and the majority staying where they are to finish their sentences in prisons that will remain intolerably crowded. A proposed law of compensation payments has made *gacaca* more acceptable among survivors—but the law hasn't been enacted, and there's no money for it anyway. In the end, most of the survivors I talked to supported *gacaca* for their own well-being. As long as trials are delayed, they won't see justice.

Prisoners and their families have their own suspicions. In Gisovu, a remote prison high in the fogbound tea plantations of western Rwanda above Lake Kivu, one prisoner said he'd heard that all *gacaca* judges would be Tutsi. There was a rumor that all those who confessed would be trucked to Gitarama prison in the center of the country and killed.

The confessed—most of them low-level participants—were receiving threats from influential prisoners and asked to be segregated. Others were warned not to confess because the coming Hutu war of liberation would release them soon. Thus far, the rate of confessions in the prisons is very low—in Butare, less than 10 percent—though the authorities believe that once *gacaca* begins and some prisoners go free after trial, the number will rise dramatically. Most of the prisoners at Gisovu, with little solid information and an ingrained suspicion of the Tutsi-dominated state, regarded *gacaca* as an opportunity that probably concealed a trick.

There is something in *gacaca* for everyone to dislike. Human rights groups point out the obvious procedural deficiencies: no defense counsel; prosecution, judge, and jury one and the same; low standards of evidence; ample room for manipulation and corruption. Psychologists warn of the potential for "retraumatization" as stories of killing and rape and torture are told in the most public possible forum. Somehow Rwanda's five thousand policemen are going to have to keep order at more than a hundred thousand trials where in many cases Tutsi survivors and Hutu defendants will look at each other for the first time since the spring of 1994. And yet I found literally no one, Rwandan or foreign, who was willing to oppose *gacaca*. No one had a better idea. Everyone seemed to understand that it is the only possible way out of the trap set by genocide.

In Rwanda, authority has always flowed from top to bottom. With *gacaca*, those in power are courting the possibility that the direction could be reversed, with unpredictable consequences. This is what makes the traditional idea revolutionary. "There are many things wrapped up in that one thing *gacaca*," said Peter Uvin, a scholar at Tufts University's Fletcher School who wrote a report on the subject for the Belgian government. "Politically, it's a brilliant piece of work. It offers something to all the groups—prisoners, survivors—it offers them all hope, and a reason to participate. It's brilliant." He pointed out that *gacaca* calls into question the idea of the RPF as an authoritarian government in a culture of obedience and fear. "Once they start, who knows when they'll stop talking? Hutus judging Hutus—it doesn't square with a govern-

ment that needs to control everything. Intelligent thinking, a major
political risk, and they take it. Is it really because they think it's going to
amount to nothing? Are they that cynical? I don't know. Make up your
mind and let me know."

Before the genocide, Seth-Robert Nzeyimana was a community development worker in the Methodist church—first in Kibuye, by Lake Kivu,
where he was born, and then in a neighborhood of Kigali, where he was
transferred in 1993. Léopold Rurangwa dealt with the mail and personnel files in the office of the mayor of one of Greater Kigali's districts.
Each man was, in the words of Seth-Robert, "a good functionary," and
as I listened to their stories on a bench outside Kigali Central prison, it
didn't seem to make much difference that one was religious and the
other civil.

At ten in the morning on April 8, a day and a half after the president's plane had gone down, Seth-Robert's neighbor came to his door.
"He said they were killing Tutsis since Tutsis were complicit in the
death of the president. He said I should join my neighbors on the road
to Rebero. Everyone was obliged to go. When I went, I saw people taking Tutsis out of their houses and killing them with machetes, in plain
view."

It started as the work of ten "fanatics of the president," local members of the *interahamwe*, the Hutu Power militia. But soon they had
recruited a large crowd, including Seth-Robert, who left his house with
a bread knife and an unsharpened spear.

"You couldn't say: Wait, I'll think about it and get back to you in a
week. Even if you know killing is wrong—and everyone knows it—you
couldn't let on that you were opposed. I had to look like the others. I
told myself that my hand, my own hand, mustn't kill, mustn't shed
blood."

I asked what he would have done if he had been ordered to kill.

"Maybe I would have—I couldn't know. Maybe I could have
wounded someone. It's possible I'd have done it, I was so afraid of dying
and my family dying. I'd only been married a year and there was still
only tenderness in my heart."

Seth-Robert's involvement in the genocide, he said, amounted to joining groups of killers in his neighborhood between April 8 and April 12, when he and his family fled Kigali. He had never before seen someone die, but now he watched forty or fifty Tutsis being killed every day, and it struck him how many of them did not resist. "They just sat there calmly. They didn't try to flee—that's what I didn't really understand. Few cried, even the women. It was a courage that impressed me."

At night he returned home and tried to sleep a few hours. I asked if he discussed what was happening with his wife. He shook his head.

"We were frozen. We were cold. It was as if life had stopped. I said to myself: It's as if Rwanda is dying. Life had stopped. No ideas came to mind. It was as if we'd become prisoners in the country that now existed. I'd become like a piece of wood, if I can say."

Seth-Robert, who is forty-one, was wearing brown loafers and gray socks below his pink prison shorts. He told his story in a soft, calm voice, the voice of a good functionary of the church, with a long, mournful face, and at the hardest questions he smiled in a gentle sort of pain and paused a moment with his head tilted at a reflective angle before answering. Several times during the two hours of our conversation he excused himself, stood up, and turned his back. The first time he did this I thought he was weeping, until he pulled a handkerchief from his pocket and carefully but loudly blew his nose.

Léopold, thirty-five, the mayor's assistant, had a high furrowed brow, pursed lips, and a blue-capped pen in his prison shirt pocket. By his own account, he had joined a mob that killed a man suspected of spying for the RPF. Léopold said that he delivered blows with the flat of his machete, intending only to extract information. "But unfortunately, my colleagues hit him without control, and he died. I went to inform the mayor, and then went home. The mayor said there was nothing to do, he had to be buried."

As Seth-Robert and Léopold described it, their overriding emotion in those days was fear. I heard this again and again from prisoners. The more Tutsis were killed, the more Hutus became afraid: of those doing the killing, those ordering it, and those—the soldiers of the RPF who were advancing throughout Rwanda—who might avenge it. They knew that not all their Tutsi neighbors could be RPF infiltrators, yet as the genocide proceeded apace and the propaganda machinery played on and the bodies piled up, they began to believe it. "Between Hutu and Tutsi there was this suspicion," Léopold said. "If a Hutu met a Tutsi, he thought he'd be killed. And vice-versa." Vice-versa was how it always seemed to turn out, yet in Seth-Robert's and Léopold's telling, they had been swept up in a fearsome catastrophe no less than their Tutsi neighbors. It was something that happened to them, not something they did.

Seth-Robert sounded happy only once during the conversation—when he recounted how, after he'd made it across Rwanda's killing fields back to Kibuye, he managed to save the Methodist mission's hospital equipment and musical instruments from looters. His satisfaction at this exceeded any pleasure he seemed to feel at the rescue of Tutsis by other Hutus that he sometimes mentioned—for he himself rescued no one, though a Tutsi hid in his yard without his knowledge. "Even if someone came to ask me to hide him, it would be useless, they'd come search the house and find him. I'd advise him to pass through the bush and either try to join the RPF or else leave the country."

When it was time for them to go back inside the walls, I asked Seth-Robert if he felt any guilt. There had been none in his telling; there wasn't really even sorrow. I was troubled by their absence, for he and Léopold seemed like decent men.

Seth-Robert smiled and nodded slightly, as if he'd been preparing for this question. Suddenly I felt like a confessor priest.

"After much reflection, I've told myself this: apropos of what happened, I felt myself guilty of cowardice. That's what I can tell you. I was cowardly in those first days of the massacres, and that's why I decided to plead guilty." I asked what he meant. "Cowardly because I didn't make a decision right away, before the situation got more serious. I could, for example, the day after the plane went down, I could have fled with my family without bringing any belongings. The love of material things made me wait. There, that's cowardice."

We said good-bye before I could bring myself to ask whether the love of material things was worse than the death of Tutsis.

In Rwanda I spoke with many prisoners who have confessed. They felt, or allowed themselves to feel, different degrees of remorse. But it always had to be drawn out of them with persistent prompting, and it always stopped well short of horror. A thirty-two-year-old technical school instructor named Bertin Bagaragaza sat with me in the dim little library of Butare prison, clutching a ruler, his right eye drooped shut. In June 1994, as the RPF advanced on Butare, Bertin had attended a meeting at which the mayor, a zealous administrator of the genocide in his district, discussed how to parcel out the goods left behind by the Tutsis who had been exterminated.

"My sin was this," said Bertin, holding the ruler upright like a scepter. "At the meeting I said this: As long as there are still Tutsis in families, and there are Hutus who hide them, we can't easily fight the war. So we have to hunt them, and we have to punish those who hide them. So that's my sin. That's the first sin I committed. The words I said could have had an influence on the hunt in the hills." He had also looted a washbasin, five packets of Omo detergent, and some bicycle parts.

I asked whether the Tutsis in the hills weren't hiding to save their lives.

"Normally, they hid to save their lives," he agreed. "But with the war that was in the country, I was afraid that the presence of the Tutsis in the country, with the army of the *Inkotanyi* [an old battlefield term applied to the RPF] could hurt us afterward." He paused. "That's what I feared." He looked at me with his left eye. "Me, that's what I thought."

How did he become convinced that he had been wrong?

"What convinced me—inside myself, I thought—an idea came to me. A simple peasant doesn't prepare hatred for another, or participate with the military. He doesn't mix in what doesn't concern him. I keep returning to the situation that was there before the war. If we look back at how we lived together before the war, there was no reason to hunt them. And then the idea of confession came to me—with reflection. Of what happened in life—that I'd done badly. That I'd behaved badly. I felt guilty."

After listening to Bertin, I left the Butare prison and went into town to meet Laurien Ntezimana, the lay religious leader who fed and protected Tutsis during the genocide. We sat at a table outside the Hotel

Ibis, where *interahamwe* leaders had installed themselves when the genocide started here. I told Ntezimana that the confessed prisoners did not
seem to grasp what had been done in 1994. They believed that the genocide was a spontaneous expression of popular anger upon the death of
the president, rather than the meticulously planned and brilliantly
administered conspiracy that it had been. They seemed to regard their
own fear and peril as equal to the Tutsis'. In most cases, confession
seemed more a matter of sentence reduction than tormented conscience. They had pleaded guilty to genocide, but they didn't tremble at
the word.

"The person hasn't realized what he's done," Ntezimana said, and
his eyes and teeth flashed with a ferocity that seemed incongruous for a
white-haired theologian, but made sense in light of his record. Good-
ness alone might not have been enough. "That's the work of religious
confessors, and they aren't doing it. This is where it's necessary to go
past religion into spirituality. Priests cut short the process, saying
directly, You're damned, you're pardoned. You have to make the person
understand who he was at the time and ask him if he's still that person,
and whether he wants to follow another path."

I thought of the words on a sign outside the Catholic church of Nya-
mata, south of Kigali, in which ten thousand people were slaughtered,
and which has become one of Rwanda's many genocide memorials: "If
you knew who I was and who you were, you would not have killed me."

One hears various theories about why so many Rwandans didn't know
who they were: A culture of obedience; the historical inequality
between Tutsi and Hutu that was fatally manipulated by the Belgians;
the violence and impunity of Hutu rule; land pressure in Africa's most
densely populated country; the origin myths, the dehumanizing propaganda—Tutsis were called *inyenzi*, cockroaches; the logic of kill or be
killed. Simon Gasabirege, a social psychologist at the National University in Butare, believes that Rwandans suffer from a weak and disorgan-
ized *personalité de base*. Christianity replaced traditional values but never
penetrated far or took root; its message was told but not lived,
Gasabirege contends. "The personality that everyone shares, the infrastructure of the community that holds it together, more or less strong,

more or less weak—when you have a situation like this where you had such disorganization, then you have terrible damage. With these gaps in identity, violence comes out very strong. So for the survivors, it seems as if their neighbors changed overnight. Before, they were fine."

Indeed, survivors often spoke in such terms. The wife of an episcopal bishop in Butare said, "At the moment of the genocide there was a brusque change, people became animals and killed, but before there was no wickedness." A Tutsi woman in a rural area west of Kigali, who seemed to be the only survivor in her village, said, "Before the war, we were fine. If someone needed water or firewood, we shared. And we're that way again. But man can change in a moment." A teenage boy who was twelve during the genocide said, "I only knew I was a Tutsi because they killed my parents." And Hutus insisted even more vehemently on the friendly relations they'd always enjoyed with their Tutsi neighbors.

"Ah ah ah—that's false, that's false, that's *false*," said Jean de Dieu Mucyo, Rwanda's minister of justice. If you had a longer memory and looked below the surface, he said, mobilization for genocide began in 1959. It was carried on at home, at school, in public life. Rwandans, who seemed to become different people overnight on April 6, 1994, had been prepared to kill for years.

Mucyo is so youthful and his smile so shy that when I was shown into his office at the ministry, where he was working on a Saturday morning (the RPF is nothing if not purposeful), I glanced beyond him for an instant to find the minister. He comes from Butare; I'd heard that thirty-two members of his family were killed during the genocide. A sergeant in the Rwandan Patriotic Army (RPA) during the war, he rose quickly to the highest level of the regime, where he presides over the genocide trials and is the most public RPF voice on *gacaca*. It's a fairly hard-line voice, though with me Mucyo spoke so softly that at times he was barely audible, and he sat quite still, as if—this, too, was a recurring quality of those in authority—the effort of self-restraint was very nearly immobilizing.

I raised the question of ambiguous cases—a prisoner, for example, who had protected some Tutsis and killed others, perhaps even killed in order to be able to protect—and how *gacaca* would deal with them. Mucyo brushed it aside. "Ask him why are there people who protected and didn't kill?" I pressed a bit: in effect, the *gacaca* law only covers crimes committed in the name of Hutu Power. Members of the RPA are thought to have killed thousands of civilians during and after the war, but these crimes won't go to *gacaca*, which at the very least raises questions about the government's own willingness to be held accountable.

The topic is an explosive one in Kigali, but Mucyo kept his cool. "We've explained many times that these cases should go to court." It was true: Kagame and others in the RPF have often argued that the genocide was a crime of the state, while the RPA killings were individual excesses. I told Mucyo that I accepted this distinction, but for a Hutu widow on a hill it might not matter; that she might look at a Tutsi widow at *gacaca* and feel there was a double standard of justice; that, for *gacaca* to work, the Hutu widow would need to be able at least to speak of her own loss. Why else should she agree to participate?

"If it's to speak, there are always meetings on the hills where she can speak. *Gacaca* is for justice." Mucyo said softly, "You had to be here in '94 to know. Trucks and trucks carrying corpses. *Interahamwe* shouting. You had to be here in '94."

For the justice minister, *gacaca* will separate the genocide's guilty from the innocent, and the nuances in these categories don't matter. For him, the truth is a simple thing; the only question is whether the people have the courage to speak it.

How one sees *gacaca* depends in part on how one sees the genocide. The *gacaca* law states that the genocide was "publicly committed before the very eyes of the population, which thus must recount the facts, disclose the truth and participate." Broadly speaking this is true—but both genocide and *gacaca* are composed of thousands of separate pieces that have to be assembled into a whole, like the film the Nyanza appeals court prosecutor wants to make to show Rwandans the extent of what happened. "No one was present at the genocide," said Thomas Kamilindi, a radio journalist who was nearly executed twice. "Everyone knows only his corner of it." The deeper you look into the details of one corner, the more nuances begin to disturb the law's clarity. "There is no such thing as one truth," said a Westerner involved in preparing for *gacaca*. "It's even more the case with genocide and especially this genocide, where the persons who committed the genocide are members of the same population as the victims of the genocide. Lots of people didn't want to see lots of things. Perhaps you would have done as I would have done, which is to spend as much time as possible in my fucking house. The survivors saw it at night or when their protectors were marching them from one place to another. Others participated, but at different levels. Can you imagine the kind of shumble rumble fucked-up panicky situation you would be living in this country, and then six or seven years later pile up testimonies about what happened?"

Then there is the larger truth of circumstances and motives—those cases where the facts are clear and the witnesses prepared to give accounts, but the actions of the guilty demand a deeper understanding. A Hutu girl protects a neighboring Tutsi family, and only the father of the family is killed. After the genocide, the family adopts her. Several years go by, and finally she can't stand it any more and confesses to them that she betrayed the father to his killers. She goes on living with the family, but nothing can be the same again. Joseph Kanyabashi, the mayor of Butare, spends the first days of the genocide guaranteeing safety to Tutsis displaced from other areas. At several meetings in mid-April, he urges collective resistance against attacks. Then the Hutu Power authorities descend on Butare on April 19 to demand cooperation, and Kanyabashi, who has a Tutsi wife and has been criticized for his friendships with Tutsis, stands before the assembly and pledges his support to the regime. Yet later that afternoon, he reportedly tells a crowded meeting at a sector office not to give in to the killings, although he cannot say how this can be done. Then he stops resisting. When his sister-in-law asks him to rescue her and her children from a besieged church, he sends word that he can do nothing. Soon he is ordering the destruction of Tutsi houses and issuing firearms to civilian "self-defense" groups; but when young thugs use them for plunder and indiscriminate killing he tries to toughen the regulations. In June, as the RPF moves toward Butare, Kanyabashi manages to save some of the last surviving Tutsis before fleeing to Zaire. He is later arrested in Belgium and this spring will go on trial at the international tribunal in Arusha, Tanzania.

Kanyabashi was neither the best nor the worst of the men in his position. He wanted to keep the genocide from reaching his district, but he was too cowardly or too attached to his job or too used to following authority to put up resistance when it did. Then he began his slide down the slippery slope. Alison des Forges, a leading American expert on Rwanda who will testify against Kanyabashi at Arusha, repeated to me what she was told by a Tutsi: "The only people who should be allowed to judge are we the survivors, because we're the ones who know the kind of pressure they were under." Des Forges challenged the notion of a terminally compliant population. "The capacity to reach down to every individual doesn't mean there is blind obedience on the part of every individual. People look for ways to evade the state. During the genocide, reactions varied. People had ways of avoiding the order—it was the same with road building." A Hutu student in Butare told me that it was possible to avoid participating—he jumped out a back window every time *interahamwe* knocked on his door—but it took courage, and it helped if, like him, you weren't well-known in town.

The possibilities of evasion put an added burden of guilt on those who wouldn't make use of them. But if, as Laurien Ntezimana said, *gacaca* only works "with people who have an interest in living together," then it will have to present the full context of each prisoner's response to the madness swirling around him.

Camille Nzabonimana received me inside the walls of Butare prison as if I had come to interview him in his living room. We sat opposite each other at a table outside the prison director's office, Camille with his hands folded together, a wedding ring on one finger, smiling in polite expectation, as if to put me at ease. At forty-eight, he was balding, with a small beard and a mole under his left eye. Only the brown discoloring of his upper teeth suggested that he had spent the past seven years in prison.

In a rich smooth voice, Camille told me the story of his life. He studied physics at Patrice Lumumba University in Moscow in the seventies, and in 1983 he received training in alternative energy in Florida. He married and had three children with the daughter of a man who had held a rare political place as a Tutsi member of the Hutu political party that assumed power at independence. His father-in-law's example convinced him to stay out of politics, and he never joined any party. Instead, in 1987 he left his research job at the National University and opened a shop selling solar panels, mostly for the rural villas of wealthy Rwandans. It was so profitable that in 1993 he started to build a hotel near Butare, which remains unfinished.

When the killings started in Kigali, his wife's relatives fled to Butare, which was still calm, and Camille hid them in his house behind the shop. On April 20, at 4 P.M., they heard the noise of a large plane—a C–130— and assumed it was the Presidential Guards. In fact, the plane had come from Nairobi to evacuate European nuns and United Nations observers; the Presidential Guards had already arrived by bus the same day. "And the killings started. We can never know how. I was in the middle of town— I heard gunshots. I knew it was bad, and from the twenty-second to the twenty-fifth we stayed inside—my brother-in-law, his whole family, five people, and my family. A Tutsi neighbor who lost his family ran to us and said, 'They killed my parents.' I said, 'OK, you can stay with us.'"

"So casually?" I asked.

"I didn't know the scale of the killings. With the earlier troubles, you could hide a Tutsi without being killed yourself. I didn't know the scale."

He had shown courage, but he wanted to be honest about the extent of it: if he had known more, he might have shown less. But now he had a problem, for there were seven Tutsis hidden in his house, including his wife (by the rules of Rwandan identity politics, his children were Hutus like him). At 9 A.M. on the twenty-second, while Camille was still in his pajamas, *interahamwe* wearing the red and yellow headbands of Hutu Power beat on his door. They were young and violent, and they entered by force, demanding to see identity cards. "I had a very quick reaction, knowing my wife had a Tutsi card. Her older sister was there with her husband, who had imagined this problem long in advance and changed their cards to Hutu. So he and my wife's sister now had Hutu cards, though they were Tutsi. I told my wife, 'Hide your card, say you've lost it,' and she threw it under the bed."

But one of the militiamen insisted that his wife, Jeanne Chantal, was a Tutsi. Thinking ever faster for her life, Camille said, "No, it's not possible," and he gave two reasons: her sister's card said "Hutu," and her father had been a big man with the Hutu party of independence. "It was a more or less consistent argument." Finally he offered to go for a replacement card with two militiamen to the mayor. This was Joseph Kanyabashi, who three days earlier had publicly committed himself to the genocidal regime. "But he knew me well and respected me a lot."

On the way, Camille and the militiamen became separated in the confusion of the town. Camille continued alone to the mayor's house, but Kanyabashi was out. "I couldn't go home, they'd demand the card. I got a friend in town to call a lieutenant, a friend of mine, and I explained very rapidly. I didn't say whether or not my wife was a Tutsi, just that they were going to kill her. The lieutenant went with another soldier and dispersed the group at my house, saying, 'What are you doing? There are no Tutsis here.' The *interahamwe* had knives and machetes, but the soldiers had guns and threatened to shoot them."

Camille eventually reached the mayor by phone, and within three days Kanyabashi, now fully involved in rounding up Tutsis, issued a Hutu identity card for Jeanne Chantal. "That was the first episode, for my wife."

"Around the twenty-seventh of April I had a notion to go see my mother-in-law in her village. Part of the house was destroyed and no one was there. I asked the neighbors what happened." A neighbor said my mother-in-law had been killed the day before, a brother-in-law the day I arrived. And they told us that the daughters had gone to hide in the sorghum field—it was the season when it grew high." Two nights later, taking advantage of a heavy rain that had cleared the militias from the roadblocks that were now up all over Butare, Camille drove with the lieutenant friend in a military vehicle and found ten people hiding in the field—"boys, girls, some from Kigali, distant relatives, even Tutsis from the area who had no relation to us." It took three days, but eventually they all joined the people he was already hiding in his house. By this time Camille had more than fifteen Tutsis with him.

"There were more threats. I didn't know how long the killings would last. I remained in a psychosis of fear, the whole time until July." Camille alone ventured out to the market for rice and potatoes; he even opened his shop a few times. Twice the *interahamwe* came back to his house, and both times the lieutenant's vehicle was parked outside. "They concluded that I was always guarded, so they didn't come back. A great bit of luck. So I was saved this way."

Two months after the RPF takeover, soldiers came to his house one night and brought him in for questioning. "They took me directly to this prison. And I remain here until today."

I had forgotten where Camille's story was leading. He sat before me in prison pink, still smiling but with a trace of irony. A bakery owner in Butare had accused him of joining killers in a church massacre in which the man's son had died. "You see how in business people are jealous." Over the years new accusations were made by other people whom the bakery owner put up to it, Camille said, while old ones were withdrawn, though he couldn't be sure of the details, for he wasn't permitted to see his own file. "It's a deduction from the questions they asked me that I know what's in the file. 'Your vehicle participated in massacres.' 'Which vehicle do you mean? The luxury SUV or the Mitsubishi?' In the file it said the Mitsubishi. I said, 'OK, the Mitsubishi wasn't in the country, it was in Burundi, I rented it to Doctors Without Borders.' Then they said it was the SUV that was with the *interahamwe*. If it wasn't one vehicle it was the other."

Letters written by the Tutsis he'd saved had no effect. Jeanne Chantal, who had lost many family members in the genocide, fell into a deep depression and left Rwanda with the children for France. Camille's case didn't move.

"And you did nothing?" I asked.

"Frankly, I'm guilty of nothing."

When Camille said this, he scrunched up his forehead and frowned, shaking his head. There was something mechanical about the expression, and for the first time I had a doubt about him.

I left him and went back into town to find his accusers.

Margueritte Mukabazanira, a secretary at the school superintendent's office, was at home when I came by. She appeared to be in her fifties, with wire-rim glasses, an African print dress and matching head wrap, and a muted air. When I mentioned Camille, she exchanged a smile with the two teenage girls in the living room with her. "I can't talk about it. For personal reasons." Nonetheless, she invited me to stay for lunch.

We ate beef and potatoes while the television blared a French program about seahorses. On the wall was a photograph of Fred Rwigyema, the first leader of the RPF, and a wedding picture of Margueritte and her husband. I tried to find a subject other than Camille, hoping we would return to him.

"Did you cook the lunch yourself?"

"No, there's a maid. But I know how to cook."

"Of course," I said, gesturing to the two girls, "you're the mother of children."

"No," she said quickly, "they killed them all. And my husband."

I put down my fork. "How many did you have?"

"Five. It's too long a story, I can't tell it. This is why it traumatizes me when people come here asking questions. No one ever comes to ask how we live, only to ask questions about these *interahamwe*."

I fell silent and stopped eating, but she insisted that I continue. She wondered how I liked the country. I offered that the landscape was lovely.

"Yes, it's a nice country except that they kill so many people here. It's very nice except for that."

Margueritte's face and voice remained dull. A Rwandan psychiatrist once told me that a long-term disorder not found in the *Diagnostic Statistical Manual* had appeared among genocide survivors. He called it "traumatic grief." "To grieve for one person is easy," the psychiatrist said. "When it's ten or twenty and you don't have any social support, then it's horrible."

The two girls were also survivors, from Gikongoro. They visited once a month because they too had lost everyone and they had taken Margueritte as their mother.

Lunch was over. "You want to free Camille?" she asked.

"I want to know what he did. I heard he saved a lot of people."

"Of course, they all say that," she scoffed. "At *gacaca* I'll tell everything. But now, even if I know a lot of things, I won't say."

Nonetheless, she was willing to help me find the bakery owner. His name was Martin Uwariraye, and we tracked him down at his surviving

Portrait, with the heads carefully defaced, found in the ransacked house of a Muslim family living in a Sarajevo suburb. The portrait was found by the young girl in the photo who, after a four-year absence, returned home in the winter of 1996, following the Dayton peace accord of November 1995. Before leaving, Serb forces looted the family's furniture and appliances and removed the window panes from their house. *Credit: Ron Haviv/VII*

Muslim prisoners of war kept in a cowshed at a Serbian-run concentration camp in Manjaca, Bosnia, during the summer of 1992. *Credit: Ron Haviv/VII*

A Muslim woman, a survivor of the 1995 Srebrenica massacre, screams in frustration at a UN soldier in a refugee camp set up in the town of Tuzla. Weak UN forces did nothing to prevent the slaughter by Serbs of 7,000 Muslims, the largest massacre in Europe in fifty years, in what was supposed to be a safe enclave. *Credit: Ron Haviv/VII*

Serbian Tiger leader Zeljko Raznatovic, aka Arkan, poses with his paramilitary unit and a baby tiger he liberated from a Croatian zoo in the fall of 1991. Arkan's Tigers were responsible for a large part of the ethnic cleansing that occurred at the beginning of the war in Bosnia. *Credit: Ron Haviv/VII*

Instruments of genocide: machetes left at the border of Zaire and Rwanda by retreating Hutu militia in 1994. *Credit: Antonin Kratochvil/VII*

The corpses of eight hundred Tutsi killed in a 1994 Hutu-led massacre in Kibuye, Rwanda. The dead were left on the floor of the town's Catholic church for family members to discover. *Credit: Antonin Kratochvil/VII*

The death of Bernardino Guterres, seen running in his plastic flip-flops while the Indonesian police chase him. Guterres has a pin on his cap with a picture of East Timorese leader Xanana Gusmão. These are the first recorded photographs of Indonesian police killing an East Timorese. They were taken in August 1999, four days before East Timor voted to be independent from Indonesia. *Credit: John Stanmeyer/VII*

Bodies of Croatian citizens lie unburied outside a hospital in Vukovar in the fall of 1991. The Serb shelling was so intense during the final days of the siege that it was impossible to bury the dead. *Credit: Ron Haviv/VII*

children's school. Martin was a heavy-set man who laughed nervously when I mentioned Camille. He seemed not to speak French, and Margueritte addressed him at length in Kinyarwanda. His answer was brief.

"He knows nothing," she said.

Martin gave me his hand and a smile; he was trying to leave. I held onto his hand.

"Is Camille guilty, Monsieur Martin? Is he guilty?"

Margueritte answered for him. "Is there a Hutu who isn't guilty?"

"You can understand how a woman in her position, who's alone, who lost all her children, how she might think that all Hutus killed," Innocent Kayitare told me that night, in the small office next to the bar he owned. Margueritte had given me his name as a possible witness against Camille, but Innocent had spent the whole genocide in a friend's ceiling—where he lost seventy pounds, while his protector went out every day to kill—and he had witnessed nothing. On the wall above his desk was a picture of his murdered five-year-old son. Innocent had the slightly incredulous manner of a man who was still trying to get his bearings, a man who's had his peace permanently disturbed and doesn't want to be caught off guard again. He was not hopeful about *gacaca* bringing Hutu-Tutsi reconciliation in Butare. "Those people drinking in my bar—there are Hutus and Tutsis drinking together. They won't say it, but if the government told the Tutsis that they were free to kill the Hutus, they'd do it." He added, "Living together doesn't mean we have to love Hutus. It means we don't threaten each other. But we don't have to love each other." As for Camille, Innocent was certain of his guilt. "He lived very close to the roadblock."

It was true: Camille's old shop, and the house behind it, stood almost directly across from where the most notorious roadblock in Butare had been set up. On the other side of the main street there was a plot of overgrown grass that in 1994 had been the house of the local organizers of the genocide—the minister of gender and social affairs and her son, an extremely violent militia leader, both now on trial at Arusha. On my last day in Butare, I stood a hundred feet up the main road from Camille's shop and saw for the first time how close to the killers he and those hidden with him had been. My companion, a young human rights worker, was describing how a group of prominent survivors in Butare, including Martin Uwariraye, used their connections with the local prosecutor and the justice minister to keep wealthy Hutus like Camille in prison. The prisoners' goods were sold off and the profits contributed to a survivors' fund that supported women like Margueritte Mukabazanira.

"Do you think Camille is innocent?" I asked.

My companion stared down the road, as if he was seeing April 1994 again. "He must have had some relations with the roadblock," he said, avoiding the terms innocence and guilt. Camille had to have paid the militia, or given beer, or loaned his vehicle. Otherwise, they would never have allowed someone as well known as he to hide so many people so close to the roadblock and the house of leading *génocidaires*.

Much later, back in New York, I learned that Camille's name appears on a list of contributors to the war effort against the RPF, in his case more than five hundred dollars—though many were forced to give. There was more: at a town meeting on the night of April 26, he was named a leader of a security patrol in his neighborhood. Looking through my notes from our interview, I realized that his narrative jumped from the twenty-fifth to the twenty-seventh. Placing a leading businessman on a patrol would have given the administration of genocide in Camille's corner of it more legitimacy. But the minutes of the same meeting show that the need to "cut the brush" around town was also discussed, to deny the cockroaches their hiding places. The next day Camille had his notion to drive out and look for his wife's family in the sorghum fields.

Is he a *génocidaire*? Perhaps it will all come out when he, and the Tutsis he saved, and Margueritte Mukabazanira and Martin Uwariraye, and others, face one another at *gacaca*.

It troubled me to think too much about the dilemmas of Hutus like Camille. After all, there was nothing ambiguous about the mass graves at Gisozi, a hillside overlooking the main ridge across which Kigali spreads out. A new memorial is being built on a site where bones collected around the city were buried in 2000. Gisozi will be Rwanda's Yad Vashem. My guide was Evode Kazasomako, a psychologist who now holds office in the municipal government and oversees the project. He took me through concrete and tile rooms where display cases will contain bones, machetes, and other relics of the killings, and then upstairs where a library will inform visitors about what happened in 1994. When I asked how the history of the genocide would be presented, he seemed not to have given it much thought. There was a genocide, everyone knew it, and the memorial would tell the story. But he was quite sure that, if it were up to him, the words "Hutu" and "Tutsi" would not appear anywhere in these rooms.

"We want to erase that, we want to put it in the past," Kazasomako said as we walked out into the sunlight. "Those words, that thinking, it's what the colonizers brought us. Before, we were well together."

We descended a flight of stairs down the hill to an iron-roofed shelter. Inside, a great mound of clothes lay heaped on the ground, stiff with dried blood and sewage, awaiting display. Scattered among the clothes were unsorted bones and personal effects: a rosary, a wallet, a green national identity card. I picked it up. The picture inside showed an unsmiling young man with a thin mustache. The first line read "Ethnicity: Hutu, Tutsi, Twa, Naturalized." The booklet was too badly damaged to make out the entry.

"We want this to be talked about as something in the past, as history," Kazasomako said. "We want Rwandans who are young now not to know what the words mean when they grow up." He added, "And it's political. The government doesn't want it."

There is now a law in Rwanda that makes ethnic sectarianism a criminal offense. There is also an unwritten law that keeps people from talking about Hutu and Tutsi in polite company. Mucyo, the justice minister, told me, "I want us all to say, 'I'm Rwandan,'" which is also the RPF's line. But unfortunately it is not the way most people think. The old categories remain in place, more firmly than ever, in the way people construct their own and others' identities. "If you ban these terms," said a Hutu woman named Geneviève Mukandekezi, "they take a different form that's even more exclusive." Rwandans ask each other, *Ni uwacu?*— Is he one of us?

Given all the damage the terms have done, the taboo against "Hutu" and "Tutsi" is an understandable effort to break out of the vicious cycle of Rwandan history. But it's also an extension of that history, another silence imposed from above, and I didn't see how it could be squared with the other purpose of *gacaca* besides justice, which is reconciliation. It seemed to me that no one will be reconciled if Rwandans can't speak openly about the crimes of the past and the suspicions of the present— certainly not through *gacaca*, which insists that Rwandans address one another in the most public setting about the most difficult things. "One is in the same circle: authority doesn't accept criticism of its faults," said Thomas Kamilindi, the radio journalist. "When you criticize, they repress. That's why *gacaca*—what chance does it have with all that? There will be another chapter not yet written."

But the chapter being written now has no precedent in history, any-where, and no one in Rwanda knows how *gacaca* will turn out. "That's why the government regards it jealously," said Laurien Ntezimana, who was imprisoned in Butare this past January after his small organization's newsletter printed a word meaning "rebirth of energy" that was also used by a banned political party. "They don't want us to throw ourselves into it—while we don't want the government to be involved. It's too important to put in their hands."

On one of my last days in Rwanda, I had an early view of what *gacaca* might be like. Under an enormous tree in a village an hour west of Kigali, a thousand people gathered from all over the sector. Fifteen pris-oners arrived in the back of a pick-up truck clapping and singing: "Save me, because I have a human body! Save us, because there's war!" These were prisoners without files; the purpose of this "pre-*gacaca*" presenta-tion was to gather evidence for the trials to come.

"What happened in 1994 everyone knows," a prosecutor from Jean Marie Mbarushimana's office told the crowd. "A lot of people died. They didn't kill themselves—others did it. They're in prison, but a lot of them are innocent. Those who died in '94 loved their lives, they were Rwandans, they had a right to their life. The prisoners also have a right to their life, though they're in prison. We bring these people here so you the population can say what you know."

One by one, the prosecutor called each prisoner forward and asked if anyone knew anything about him. The population, which was overwhelmingly Hutu and largely female, said little. Whether they mistrusted the authorities or were reluctant to testify against Hutus, here was Rwanda's culture of conformity and fear in plain view. At first only a few solitary Tutsis came forward to give testimony: a man in a khaki fishing hat; a young woman clutching an umbrella.

She said, "People who met us told us this was the one who killed my family," and she pointed in the prisoner's face, while he bowed his head. "He had dogs and he was pursuing Tutsis."

Rwandans are taught to measure their humanity by the extent of their self-control. Although the young woman was standing close enough to strike the prisoner, she did not lose her composure. The last time she had seen him, in 1994, she was as hunted as a rabbit, and he possessed the power of life and death. Her extended finger had to express all the fury and grief of the years since then.

As the afternoon wore on, there were cases where Hutus and Tutsis argued about the guilt of a prisoner; and there were even cases where Tutsis spoke on behalf of prisoners, two of whom were released.

"They're going to kill us," a survivor muttered as he walked away after making an accusation. "Really, they're going to kill us."

"Rwandans are wicked," a prisoner standing behind me said. "They keep quiet even when they know me."

So it went. The Tutsi survivors seemed utterly isolated. The Hutu population seemed uninterested in guilt. The standard of evidence was extremely low—hearsay, one person's word against another's. Justice and reconciliation after genocide? How was it possible? Here were only fifteen prisoners—I was exhausted contemplating the task ahead. And yet, unmistakably, it was beginning. The population headed home under late-afternoon rain clouds. The two prisoners who had been set free received the embraces of family and friends. The others were loaded into the truck and driven singing back to prison, where they will await *gacaca* with Camille Nzabonimana and a hundred thousand others.

# PART FOUR
# East Timor

# BEARING WITNESS

## Filomena Suares

ALL AROUND TOWN HOUSES WERE BURNING. We heard gunfire all the time. On the 5th of September 1999 the police came to us and said that if we wanted to stay alive, we had to come to the police station. We went. It was packed with people, hundreds were there. We just wanted to stay alive. We stayed there for three days. Then we left and went to a nearby town to stay with my husband's relatives. Soon, though, the militia came there too.

On the 13th of September, the militia came to the house and said my husband needed to go to the house of the Liurai, a village leader. We thought he would be safe there. It was dark and I didn't want him to go by himself, so I went with him. When we arrived, there were so many people. My husband's brother was there too. They told me they only wanted men, not women. They said I had to leave. I said I wouldn't go, that I wouldn't leave him. One man threatened to stab me. I had to go, but I was so afraid for him.

I waited all night, awake. Each hour I kept telling myself he'd come home. He must be on his way now. At four in the morning, I was shaking, I could not stand waiting anymore. I went back to the house, back to where the militia were, where I had last seen my husband. I asked them where he was. They said they couldn't tell me. They said, "Now it's war." I kept asking, and they told me that if I didn't leave, I'd be killed too. I knew he was dead. I knew they had killed him. I came back again in the morning and they confessed. They said all of the men were dead. They were proud.

On September 20, we were forced to go to West Timor. They told us if we didn't leave we'd be killed. I stayed in the camp there till the end of October. When I came back the people investigating the killings told me what had happened that night. After they killed my husband, they put his body in a rice sack. They did the same with all the men. Then they took their bodies to a house, threw them inside, and burned it down.

# 10

# "If You Leave Us Here,
# We Will Die"

GEOFFREY ROBINSON

On the afternoon of September 13, 1999, I joined one of the last United Nations patrols to venture out into Dili, the capital of East Timor. Clad in flak jackets, but unarmed, we toured the city in three vehicles. In what had been a bustling city of a hundred thousand, there were now almost no local people in sight—only scavenging black pigs, a handful of Indonesian soldiers, and militiamen wearing red and white bandanas, loading up trucks with loot, heading for the border with West Timor. Just two weeks after the historic UN-supervised vote in which some 80 percent of the population had opted for independence from Indonesia, the city was a hollow, smoking shell.

Within hours of the end of voting on August 30, pro-Indonesian militia groups and members of the Indonesian armed forces (TNI) began a rampage of violence so sustained and so ugly that it surprised even seasoned observers who had predicted a backlash. Over the next few weeks, most towns and villages in the territory were burned to the ground. Supporters of independence were beaten and raped, while others were killed. By the middle of September, 70 percent of all the buildings in the territory had been burned or destroyed, an estimated four hundred thousand people—more than half the population—had been forced to flee their homes, and at least one thousand had been killed.

Helpless in the face of the mounting violence, the United Nations Mission in East Timor (UNAMET), which had vowed to remain regardless of the outcome, evacuated all of its district offices. In Dili, armed militia gangs laid siege to the UN compound. Inside were some five hundred UN staff and more than fifteen hundred local people who had sought refuge there. Those of us inside worried that the militia might come over the wall at any time, unimpeded by the Indonesian army soldiers who were ostensibly protecting us. But many of us were also worried about being party to a humanitarian disaster. Haunted by memories of UN inaction or flight in Rwanda and Srebrenica, we wondered what the legacy of our mission might be.

There was quiet rejoicing in the compound when we learned that the Indonesian government had agreed to allow an international military force to "assist" the TNI in ending the violence. And there was relief when all of the refugees in the compound were safely airlifted to Australia on September 14, and something close to glee when an armed international force was deployed less than a week later. But the fact remained that the violence had been widely predicted, and the UN had failed to prevent it. The questions were troubling, and impossible to avoid. Why had the UN decided to proceed with the vote in spite of widespread predictions of violence? Why had peacekeeping forces not been deployed before the vote to prevent the violence?

In one sense the answers lie simply in the self-serving policies of the United States and other Western governments, which were reluctant to offend the government of Indonesia, and so resisted calls for armed intervention both before and after the vote, and sought quickly to restore ties after the violence had subsided. This weak posture had its roots in a long tradition of international acquiescence in Indonesia's occupation of East Timor and in its appalling human rights record; and it helps to explain why later on the idea of an international tribunal for East Timor was so quickly abandoned. Yet, this simple view cannot easily explain why these very powers decided to intervene militarily in mid-September 1999. The fact is that without that intervention we might be speaking today of tens of thousands killed rather than one thousand.

Some observers have blamed the tragedy instead on the incompetence of the UN. There is some truth in that assessment. As the reports on UN failings in Rwanda and Srebrencia, as well as a recent report on UN peace operations, make clear, there is room for improvement in the UN's handling of humanitarian and political crises. But the portrait of UN incompetence does not really capture the political and moral complexity of the situation in East Timor. As anyone who has worked within it can attest, the UN is not a monolithic organization. Even at its highest reaches its capacity for independent action is always constrained by the views and interests of the most powerful members of the Security Council. Moreover, while it is true that the UN as a whole failed to prevent the widely predicted violence in East Timor, and chose to move ahead in spite of dire warnings, some within the UN acted in ways that saved lives.

More to the point, it is not at all obvious that it would have been preferable to cancel the referendum. To do so might have prevented the post-ballot violence, but it would also have deprived East Timorese of a chance to determine their own future and to escape finally from a brutal twenty-four-year occupation in which nearly one third of the population had already died. Whatever its failings, it is worth recalling that the UN helped to achieve something in August 1999 that had long been considered impossible—a legitimate act of self-determination for the people of East Timor.

For roughly three centuries, the territory now known as East Timor was a colony of Portugal. As the rest of the colonized world fought for and won independence after the Second World War, East Timor remained largely unaffected, and lived more or less harmoniously with its enormous neighbor, the Republic of Indonesia. That arrangement began to unravel rather dramatically in 1974 when, in the aftermath of its own revolution, Portugal set about to relinquish control of its colonies. Portuguese disengagement stimulated the growth of political parties in East Timor, including a social democratic party called Fretilin, which declared independence on November 28, 1975.

That declaration was the final straw for Indonesia's President Suharto, an army general who had come to power in a military coup in 1965. In the months after that coup, Suharto had helped to organize the killing of between five hundred thousand and a million members of the

Indonesian Communist Party and the imprisonment of about a million others. Ostensibly acting against the threat of communist insurrection and political instability on its border, in early December 1975 Indonesia launched a combined land, sea, and air invasion of East Timor. The annexation was formalized in July 1976, but resistance continued, and the human toll mounted.

Using U.S.-supplied OV-Bronco warplanes, Indonesian forces conducted large-scale aerial bombardment of the countryside. Populations thought to be supporting the resistance were resettled in an Indonesian version of the strategic hamlets strategy used by U.S. forces in Vietnam. The bombing and forced relocations led to widespread famine and disease. By 1980 church and human rights sources estimated that two hundred thousand of a pre-invasion population of less than seven hundred thousand had already died. Although the scale of the killing declined somewhat over the next two decades, Indonesian forces continued to be responsible for human rights violations on a staggering scale.

Indonesia's claim to sovereignty over East Timor was never recognized by the UN. Indeed, the UN Security Council and General Assembly passed a series of resolutions deploring the Indonesian invasion and recognizing the inalienable right of the people of East Timor to self-determination. In keeping with those resolutions, the UN continued to regard Portugal as the formal administering power in the territory. The problem was that for more than two decades no concrete action was taken to give effect to these resolutions. No state with any real power in the UN had the inclination to challenge so important a political and economic player as Indonesia—the fifth (later fourth) most populous country in the world, a bastion of anticommunism in Asia, and an economic prize—for the sake of a half-island the size of New Jersey. On the contrary, those best placed to help, such as the United States, declined to do so.

The December 1975 invasion, for example, was launched just one day after a meeting in the Indonesian capital, Jakarta, between President Suharto, U.S. President Ford, and Secretary of State Kissinger. For more than 25 years the detailed transcript of that meeting and other key documents were either kept secret or were so heavily censored before being declassified that it was difficult to know with any certainty what was said.

During the same period, Kissinger steadfastly denied suggestions that he and Ford had given the "green light" to the invasion; indeed, he insisted that East Timor was not even discussed at the meeting with Suharto.

Happily for historians, but not for Dr. Kissinger, some of the documents in question have now been released in uncensored form. They reveal that East Timor was indeed discussed with Suharto and that the United States did give its approval to the invasion. The transcript of the December 1975 meeting, for example, reveals that President Ford assured Suharto that the United States would "understand" if Indonesia deemed it "necessary to take rapid or drastic action" in East Timor. Kissinger was even more emphatic. "Whatever you do," he said, "we will try to handle in the best way possible." The two men asked only that any Indonesian action be delayed until they had returned to Washington so that, in Kissinger's words, they could "influence the reaction" and lessen "the chance of people talking in an unauthorized way." The document also reveals that Kissinger went out of his way to provide Suharto with a pretext for the invasion. Conscious of the illegality of using U.S.-supplied weapons to attack another country, Kissinger told Suharto that an invasion could be construed as an act of "self-defense." Suharto and his aids must have taken heart from the meeting.

The supportive posture of the U.S. government and its allies became even more clear in the months and years after the invasion. According to the U.S. State Department's own estimates, roughly 90 percent of the military equipment used in the 1975 invasion was supplied by the United States. And in the years after the invasion, successive U.S. administrations—both Democratic and Republican—funneled hundreds of millions of dollars of economic and military aid to the Indonesian regime and protected it from any serious political challenge to its illegal occupation of East Timor.

America was not alone in lending its support to Indonesia. Anxious not to alienate an important neighbor, and eager to capitalize on the economic opportunities that cooperation would ensure, Australia chose not to interfere with the 1975 invasion, and later became the first and only major power to give de jure recognition to Indonesia's claim over East Timor. In 1989, Australia reaped its reward, signing the Timor Gap Treaty with Indonesia for the joint exploitation of the oil and mineral wealth lying off East Timor's south coast. It is now known that Australia was privy to Indonesian plans to invade in 1975 and had details of the atrocities that Indonesian forces committed throughout. For most of the ensuing twenty-four years, however, a succession of Australian governments sought to downplay reports of gross human rights violations in the territory and provided substantial military training to Indonesian forces. Gareth Evans, the foreign minister from 1988 through 1996, has now admitted that much of Australia's military training "helped only to produce more professional human rights abusers."

With this sort of backing, and with support from many other countries as well, it is hardly surprising that for more than twenty years Indonesia refused to contemplate any challenge to its claimed sovereignty in East Timor. Nevertheless, events on the ground in East Timor and shifts in the international arena began gradually to weaken Indonesia's position through the 1990s.

The watershed event was the Santa Cruz massacre of November 12, 1991, in which as many as 270 people were gunned down or beaten to death by Indonesian soldiers. Video footage of the massacre was broadcast worldwide, prompting outrage and stimulating the formation of East Timor support groups throughout the world. A further critical development came in 1996, when two East Timorese, the international spokesman for the resistance, José Ramos Horta, and the Bishop of Dili, Monsignor Carlos Filipe Ximenes Belo, were awarded the Nobel Peace Prize. The Nobel Prize raised hopes for independence to unprecedented levels and further increased the leverage of East Timor support groups and nongovernmental organizations (NGOs). Yet in spite of the widespread sympathy for the victims of human rights abuse and the international legitimacy bestowed by the Nobel Prize, the prospects for East Timorese independence looked bleak. Indonesian authorities were adamant that East Timor would remain a part of Indonesia.

The beginning of the end of this impasse came in May 1998 when Suharto was forced to step down after more than thirty years in power. When he named his vice president, B. J. Habibie, as his successor, few expected change. But in January 1999, in an astonishing break with past government policy, Habibie announced that the people of East Timor would be given a chance to express their views on the political future of the territory. Clarifying the policy, the foreign minister, Ali Alatas, said that East Timorese would be asked whether they accepted or rejected a UN plan to grant the territory "special autonomy" within Indonesia. If they rejected it, he said, Indonesia would withdraw and East Timor would be on its own. This remarkable shift in the government's position seems to have been set in motion by international pressures, specifically by a December 1998 letter from Australian Prime Minister John Howard to Habibie urging the government to adopt a more flexible approach on East Timor. However, the boldness of Habibie's move surprised even those who had been urging a policy adjustment.

Clearly much had changed, but much had stayed the same. For one thing, the U.S. government remained extremely reluctant to offend the Indonesian authorities, as I discovered at a working dinner on Indonesia policy with Madeleine Albright in February 1999. There, to my amazement, I learned that State Department officials were still searching for alternatives to a direct popular ballot in East Timor. When I asked why the administration was reluctant to support a referendum, one official explained that it was because Indonesia's foreign minister Ali Alatas was opposed to the idea.

Also unchanged was the overwhelming power of the Indonesian Army in East Timor and the implacable opposition of most of its officers to independence. Army leaders reportedly put up little resistance to Habibie's proposal in cabinet, but that did not mean they supported it. Indeed, by the time the decision was announced, the army had already set in motion plans to ensure that the vote would favor integration, or would never happen at all. As East Timorese took advantage of Suharto's fall to demonstrate openly in favor of independence, reports began to trickle out about the mobilization of militia groups dedicated to maintaining the tie with Indonesia. And with Habibie's announcement in January 1999, the trickle became a flood.

It was soon evident that these militia groups were involved in a major campaign of terror and intimidation against supporters of independence. It was also clear that they were mobilized, trained, and supplied by Indonesian authorities, and that the violence was coordinated, or at least condoned, at a very high level. In February and March 1999, dozens of people were reported killed—some in very gruesome ways—

and tens of thousands were forced to flee, after which their houses were burned. Many of those who fled sought refuge in nearby churches or in the private homes of prominent citizens. It was against these people, and in these places of refuge, that some of the most egregious acts of militia violence were committed in April of 1999. The violence included a mass killing at a church in the town of Liquica and another at the home of a pro-independence leader in Dili.

Despite these ominous developments, when Portugal and Indonesia met under UN auspices in March and April, they agreed to the idea of a direct ballot, paving the way for a set of accords known as the May 5 Agreements. The main agreement, between Indonesia and Portugal, stipulated that East Timorese would be asked to accept or reject the special autonomy package. The rejection of that package, the agreement made clear, would set East Timor on the path toward independence.

If that part of the May 5 Agreements appeared too good to be true, there was another element that from the outset was fatally flawed—the agreement that placed sole responsibility for maintaining law and order in the hands of Indonesian security forces. The UN itself, including its civilian police (CivPols) and military liaison officers (MLOs), would be unarmed. Even a brief glimpse at the history of the Indonesian armed forces and their behavior in East Timor would have indicated what a dangerous approach this was.

Some of those privy to the UN-sponsored negotiations of early 1999 have suggested that the agreement on security was a necessary compromise; that insistence on an international armed force was simply not politically "realistic" in light of Indonesia's opposition to the idea. Like most arguments about realism in politics, this is a dubious one. So many previously "impossible" things happened in 1999 that one simply cannot say with confidence whether, if vigorously advocated, the idea of international forces might have been accepted. It seems clear that the argument for such a force was abandoned without being seriously tried. In a press conference in New York announcing the agreement, Ali Alatas told reporters that "throughout our discussions, UN peacekeeping forces have not been an issue that has been raised." Once again, old habits and assumptions ruled. As a Jakarta-based diplomat later admitted, "everybody conceded too much" in the course of those negotiations.

The dangers in the agreement on security were not lost on outside observers, nor even on those who helped to negotiate it. UN secretary-general Kofi Annan was so concerned about potential trouble that in a separate memorandum, dated May 4, 1999, he set out several criteria by which he would judge whether the security situation was acceptable. These included an immediate ban on rallies by armed groups, and the prompt arrest and prosecution of those inciting or threatening violence. He also made it clear that he would stop the referendum process should he find that these criteria were not being met.

With that fragile guarantee, in late May 1999 UNAMET began to deploy its personnel in East Timor with the seemingly impossible task of conducting a referendum some time in August. Almost immediately the question arose about whether it was wise to proceed with the vote—and that remained a preoccupation throughout the summer.

One of the responsibilities of the political affairs office in which I worked was to provide advice on that question to Ian Martin, the head of mission in East Timor. It was only one of many units offering advice, and events would prove that its influence was limited. But we took our responsibility seriously, and it cannot be said that the decision to proceed was taken lightly. Nor was it a foregone conclusion, as some critics have implied. In a series of internal assessments written in June and July, for example, the political affairs office argued that none of the security criteria spelled out in the secretary-general's memorandum of May 4 had been met and that the referendum should therefore *not* go ahead. In mid-July the head of mission expressed the same view, on behalf of UNAMET, in a number of memoranda to headquarters. In the end, however, that position did not prevail. Although there were two brief postponements, the process went ahead without significant interruption.

The decision to proceed stemmed partly from the fluidity of the situation on the ground and indications that the violence might yet be brought under control. Martin and others believed that sustained political pressure might convince the Indonesian authorities to rein in the militias and allow the ballot to proceed with only minor disruptions. Although some within the political affairs office remained skeptical on this score, most UNAMET staff came to believe that it would be best to proceed. And it must be said that the arguments in favor of proceeding had merit. Perhaps most important, they coincided with the views of the main resistance leader, Xanana Gusmão, and many other East Timorese who thought the vote should proceed without delay. They pointed out that any delay would only benefit the side responsible for the violence, the side that did not wish to see a free expression of popular will. This is where some critics, frankly, get it wrong, or tell only part of the story. The fact is that it is far from clear that it would have been preferable, morally or politically, to postpone the process.

Those critics are correct, however, in thinking that the decision to move ahead was strongly influenced by political pressures emanating from the UN in New York and from the capitals of major powers. As one official of the UN Secretariat told me, there were simply no advocates of a delay at headquarters. At the political level, the UN position was constrained primarily by the five permanent members of the Security Council—the United States, the United Kingdom, France, Russia, and China. It was also influenced by a group of five states specially convened in New York for this purpose, the United States, the United Kingdom, Australia, New Zealand, and Japan, together known as the Core Group. As far as I could tell from Dili, the Permanent Five and the Core Group were anxious to move ahead with the referendum, despite warnings of danger, and reluctant to do anything that might unduly upset the Indonesian government and military.

The decision to proceed, like the earlier decision to leave security in Indonesian hands, was also influenced by the personal representative of the UN secretary-general for East Timor, Ambassador Jamsheed Marker of Pakistan. A diplomat of the old school, Marker was a firm believer in the value of cordial face-to-face discussion. In keeping with that philosophy, and because of his friendship with Indonesian foreign minister Ali Alatas, he was more inclined than others in the UN to accept assurances of good faith offered by Indonesian officials. For some time, Marker had the ear of the secretary-general, and of his chef de cabinet, Iqbal Riza, a fact that inevitably led to a softening of the positions that UNAMET advocated from the field. From our perspective in political affairs, Marker had a tendency to understate the seriousness of the security situation and to let the Indonesians off the hook far too easily. Insofar as this approach was expressed in public, it also gave a skewed impression of what UNAMET actually knew and thought about security and political conditions.

As it became clear that the vote would proceed in spite of the dangers, some UNAMET staff, not to mention East Timorese, took the view that an armed international peacekeeping force ought to be deployed *before* the vote. As one East Timorese health worker commented to a foreign journalist, "If there is trouble, the UN will send in peacekeepers, right? Because there will be trouble."

Although UNAMET was never formally asked for advice on this issue, as early as July some of us began informally to convey this view to UN officials in New York and to any visitors who would listen. Among those who did listen, and who reached similar conclusions, was a joint parliamentary-NGO delegation from Canada. At the end of its visit, on August 12, the delegation's spokesman said, "Unless Indonesia is going to live up to its obligation, we believe it is critical for a peacekeeping force to be sent to the territory immediately." A U.S. congressional delegation made an equally emphatic statement in late August.

However obvious the need for peacekeepers seemed to those who had been in East Timor, the idea never got off the ground. The reason was simple: in the course of negotiations in April 1999, and throughout the summer, it was either ignored or actively opposed by elements within the UN Secretariat and by key powers in the Security Council, most notably the United States. This is not to say that these powers remained silent in the face of the mounting violence. There was plenty of criticism, and even some veiled threats, for example, at a donors meeting for Indonesia in Paris in July, and again as voting day approached in late August. But peacekeepers were never mentioned. Instead, the concerned states stuck steadfastly, one might even say pigheadedly, to the position that security was the responsibility of the Indonesian authorities.

When UN staff or outside observers asked about or urged the possible deployment of peacekeeping forces, the answer was more or less the same: it would be impossible to deploy peacekeepers without Indonesian approval, or by invoking Chapter VII of the UN Charter. Because it was assumed that neither of these things would happen, we were told it was "unrealistic" to expect peacekeepers. We were also told, as early as July, that it would take too long, three months at least, to mobilize such a force, so there was no point in discussing a pre-ballot deployment. The more practical and cost-effective approach, a series of policy and planning memoranda from New York explained, was to insist that the Indonesian authorities live up to their obligations for maintaining peace and security.

Significantly, when the Security Council finally lent unanimous support to the Australian-led Multi-National Force (MNF) in mid-September 1999, its resolution invoked Chapter VII of the UN Charter and gave the MNF authority to use all necessary means to restore security. Moreover, notwithstanding the earlier claim that a force would take at least three months to deploy, the MNF was on the ground within a week of the Security Council resolution. This was possible, it turned out, because Australia had begun to mobilize troops as early as March 1999 for this very purpose and by late June had a contingent of six thousand troops ready to go. The United States had also drawn up contingency plans and would certainly have been in a position to deploy troops had the command been given. In other words, all that had been said about the impossibility of deploying peacekeepers was untrue. What had prevented it from happening earlier was not political reality, nor even logistical difficulties, but an acute lack of political courage, imagination, and leadership.

Some measure of the lack of support for the peacekeeping option may be found in various post-ballot planning documents developed within the UN Secretariat starting in mid-July 1999. None of the plans I saw discussed the matter of peacekeepers at all. Instead they repeated the mantra that, regardless of the outcome, in the post-ballot period the Indonesian authorities would continue to be responsible for maintaining security. It was as though by mere repetition this pipe dream would come true. Within the UN Secretariat, the argument against a pre-ballot deployment of armed peacekeepers was put most stridently by the Department of Peace Keeping Operations (DPKO); and its objections effectively overrode any support for such a deployment that existed in other departments. The DPKO position coincided with the views of powerful states within the UN Security Council, particularly the United States.

U.S. opposition stemmed in part from concerns that the United States would have to foot a large part of the bill. It was also the legacy of the death of U. S. peacekeepers in Somalia in 1993, and the presidential directive that followed from it (PDD 25), which imposed strict conditions on U.S. support for any UN peacekeeping mission. The strongest opposition to the peacekeeping option in the United States appears to have come from the Pentagon, though the White House also resisted at least until some time in the second week of September. Nor was there much serious support for the idea in Congress until very late in the game. Although the State Department gave the idea more support, it scrupulously avoided mentioning peacekeepers in its public statements. At the UN, U.S. Ambassador Richard Holbrooke, who would later criticize Congress for slashing peacekeeping budgets, gave no hint of support for peacekeepers in East Timor until well after the referendum.

Whoever the architects of the policy were, opposition to peacekeepers prevailed in the United States and the UN until September 10—almost two weeks after the militias and the TNI began their campaign of violence. So it was that the UN found itself utterly unable to do anything as the violence descended on East Timor.

When the polls opened at 6:30 A.M. on August 30, 1999, most voters were already in line. Defying threats by armed militias, many had walked for hours in their Sunday best for the chance to vote. When the figures were tallied at the end of the day, UN officials announced that an extraordinary 98.6 percent of registered voters had cast their ballots. The decision to proceed in spite of predictions of violence appeared to have been vindicated. Almost immediately, however, the wisdom of that decision was thrown into question. Within hours of the end of voting, pro-Indonesian militia groups and members of the TNI began an unprecedented campaign of violence.

The first known victim was a local UN staff member, João Lopes Gomes. A fifty-year-old school teacher and father, Gomes was stabbed in the back and killed as he helped to load ballot boxes into a vehicle near Atsabe village in Ermera, just after the polls had closed. The news came to UN headquarters in Dili in a garbled radio message. The next day, I joined a small investigation team that flew to the scene of the attack by helicopter. Although our work was cut short by the escalating violence, we were able to establish that Gomes's assailants had been local militiamen, sporting red and white bandanas and armed with swords, home-made guns, and knives. We also learned that, at the time of the attack, they had been accompanied by TNI soldiers and the local military commander.

Within a few days, all UN officials had been drawn back to the headquarters in Dili, and the compound was effectively under siege. UN staff who ventured outside saw militias burning and looting while TNI soldiers and police looked on. On the morning of September 6, we learned that militias had attacked refugees who had sought shelter in the cathedral in the town of Suai, killing dozens. The same morning we heard that militias had attacked Bishop Belo's residence and the office of the International Committee of the Red Cross (ICRC), where many had sought refuge. The militias were said to have killed scores of refugees on the spot, while herding hundreds of others onto trucks and buses. Again Indonesian Army and police forces had done nothing. As the situation deteriorated, some two thousand East Timorese, the vast majority of them women and small children, sought refuge in the compound. They brought news of further abominations—including rape by militiamen and TNI soldiers. Huddled inside the compound, we slept on scraps of cardboard and grew accustomed to the constant clatter of automatic and homemade weapons fire outside. While we sat immobilized inside, the country burned.

Thanks largely to a handful of journalists who had stayed on, news of the dramatic escalation of violence began to make its way out of East Timor, where it prompted furious reactions from religious leaders, legislators, and citizen groups. In Lisbon, huge crowds lined the streets to greet Bishop Belo. In Australia, Canada, and much of Europe, angry demonstrators demanded swift international intervention. The news of the attacks on the bishop's house and the ICRC reached New York early on Monday, September 6. At a meeting of the Core Group later that day, the Australian ambassador argued for the first time that an international force must be deployed without delay. That evening Kofi Annan spoke by telephone to the president of Portugal, to the Australian prime minister, and finally, after 10 P.M., to President Habibie. He called on the president to bring the situation under control within the next forty-eight hours or to allow the international community to do so. Later that evening, Habibie declared martial law in the territory with effect from September 7. Far from improving, however, the security situation worsened.

With each day, the situation inside the compound grew more critical. Although many of the refugees had brought some food with them, certain basic necessities—rations, drinking water, fuel—began to run low, and the logistical problems of housing two thousand people started to become serious. Without any doubt, however, the darkest day in the compound was September 8. That evening, a decision was taken to evacuate all remaining UN international staff, effectively leaving some fifteen hundred refugees to their fate. The recommendation to evacuate was made by the head of mission, Ian Martin. The decision provoked a storm of protest within the compound and brought to a head fundamental questions about the UN's priorities and responsibilities.

Four of us from political affairs and humanitarian affairs were given the task of conveying the news to the community leaders in the compound. Surrounded by people like the courageous Sister Esmeralda and others whom we had come to know in the preceding months, we could scarcely find the strength to speak. Instead we wept, because we were sure that when we left all those inside would be killed. Worse still, we were asking fifteen hundred people to decide in a matter of just a few hours, whether to stay and await that fate or to flee through the night into the hands of the militia and TNI soldiers.

Sister Esmeralda waited patiently for us to finish. And when we had, she spoke. "Whatever else may happen," she said, "this referendum has removed any doubt that East Timorese wish to be free. For conducting it, we will always be grateful to UNAMET." Wiping tears from her eyes, she went on: "We knew there would be violence after the vote and we hoped that you would stay. And yet, we are not surprised that you plan to leave us now. We are used to being abandoned in our times of greatest need." Finally, saying that she and the others had no more time for talk, she excused herself and left. Overcome with shame, we delegated one of our group to approach Ian Martin and convey our view that the decision to evacuate was wrong. Martin did not disagree, but explained that the heads of security, CivPol, and MLO had all strongly advised evacuation. The heads of those units, he said, had given the impression that the majority of their staff were demoralized and anxious to leave.

Meanwhile, a sense of outrage began to grip other UN staff and the handful of journalists and observers who had taken refuge in the compound. Those feelings fueled a rebellion of sorts. A group of journalists demanded to speak to Martin, threatening to denounce the evacuation decision publicly. Outside I was confronted by a journalist from the *Sunday Times* who demanded that I make an exception to get an East Timorese friend and his family on to the UN evacuation flight and likewise threatened media exposure if I should fail to do so. As it happened, the man in question, Antonio Belo, was also an old friend of mine, whose safety I would have done almost anything to secure. I told Antonio and the journalist this, although I was deeply pessimistic at the time that Antonio or anybody else would be able to leave.

Notwithstanding the earlier claims by security, CivPol, and MLO chiefs that most of their staff were anxious to evacuate, by about 9:00 P.M. there was a strong sentiment that international UN staff should not leave before the fifteen hundred refugees had been taken to safety. More precisely, a quick straw poll conducted at Martin's request had revealed that at least eighty of the hundred or so international staff still in the compound were prepared to stay on even if the evacuation went ahead. Surprised, but I believe also heartened, by this show of resolve, Martin conveyed the news to UN officials in New York by telephone. At the same time, he informed them that General Wiranto, TNI commander, had urged UNAMET to stay and said that the TNI officers on the ground had concurred.

By the end of the evening the decision to evacuate UN staff had been postponed by twenty-four hours. As the news spread through the compound, there was quiet jubilation. In retrospect, it may seem odd that a one-day reprieve would be the cause for rejoicing. But the reality was that, against the backdrop of the original plan for a total evacuation that very night, twenty-four hours seemed an eternity. More important, there was a sense that a critical turning point had been reached. Indeed, although more than four hundred local and international UN staff did evacuate as planned some twenty-four hours later, a skeleton UN staff stayed in the compound until the safety of the refugees could be secured.

As the days passed, we waited anxiously for news of the international intervention that we assumed was now inevitable. We were encouraged to hear that France had dispatched a navy vessel to the area; that Canada's prime minister had said the international community would have to step in if the violence continued; that the secretary-general of the North Atlantic Treaty Organization (NATO) had called for urgent international intervention; that Japan's prime minister had said that the world "cannot just stand by"; and that Australia's defense minister had said its forces could be ready to move within days.

But it was deeply distressing to read in the press that Ambassador Marker, a member of our own team, had "refused to lend credence to reports of [Indonesian] military support for the militia" when for months we had carefully documented and argued precisely that case. And we learned with disbelief that the most important state of all, the United States, was still equivocating. When asked why the United States had not taken the lead in resolving the mess in East Timor, National Security Advisor Sandy Berger reportedly said that his daughter's university dorm room was also a mess but that didn't mean the U.S. government should clean it up for her. The sheer stupidity of this comment aside, it made it clear that the United States was still insisting that responsibility for restoring order rested with the Indonesian armed forces. Passed by word of mouth through the compound, this news was greeted with groans of disbelief. Everyone understood that it was precisely those forces that were orchestrating the violence. It was preposterous to insist that they now be entrusted to stop it.

Then, just as fear had begun to turn to despair, the picture began to brighten. From my perspective in Dili, the critical turning point was the visit of the UN Security Council delegation on September 11. After a series of meetings with Indonesian military authorities, the delegation came to the UNAMET compound. Crammed two or three deep in Ian Martin's office, the delegates were briefed on the crisis. The message was unambiguous: Indonesian assurances were meaningless, and swift international intervention was essential.

The most powerful message, however, did not come from UNAMET officials, but from East Timorese refugees, during a tour of the compound guided by Sister Esmeralda. Out of nowhere, a young woman rushed up to the head of the delegation, Martin Andjabe of Namibia. Seizing his hand, she said, "Please do not leave us here. We are so afraid." Andjabe first answered somewhat stiffly, saying that the UN would do everything possible to ensure their safety. Having heard this line before, the woman interrupted and, still holding his hands, said, "No, you don't understand. If you leave us here, we will die. You must promise." At that moment, Andjabe's countenance changed. Looking straight into the woman's eyes, and then wrapping his arms around her, he said, "We will not leave you. I give you my word."

Outside the UN compound, beyond Dili, in the capital cities of powerful nations, on the streets and on front pages, over telephone lines to the offices of Indonesia's president and armed forces commander, the pressure had begun to build—indeed, the critical decision may already have been made. That was a story I would learn many weeks later. But, as far as I was concerned at the time, the tide of our fortune had turned with those words: "We will not leave you. I give you my word."

Although we did not realize it until later, an equally critical turning point had come twelve hours earlier on September 10, when Kofi Annan issued an unusually strong public statement about the crisis. "The time has clearly come," he said "for Indonesia to seek the help of the international community in fulfilling its responsibility to bring order and security to the people of East Timor." He urged Indonesia to accept this help, and warned that "if it refuses to do so, it cannot escape responsibility for what could amount, according to reports reaching us, to crimes against humanity." The allusion to crimes against humanity buoyed our spirits considerably because it indicated a new level of commitment on the part of the UN.

Just as important, the statement indicated that the secretary-general was prepared to bring to bear the full weight of his office in finding a solution. By this point, Annan was personally involved in every detail of the crisis; in the words of one UN official, in those weeks he became "the desk officer for East Timor." His statement of September 10 reflected his strong personal views on the matter and in particular his belief that claims of national sovereignty must not be allowed to stand in the way of effective international action in defense of human rights. On September 9, the night before the statement, Annan had spoken to U.S. President Bill Clinton and Australian Prime Minister John Howard by telephone, asking what they were prepared to do. Later that night, he called Xanana Gusmão and told him that he was determined that the UN would not leave East Timor.

Perhaps by coincidence, although probably not, September 10 was also the day that the United States finally changed its tune on the question of peacekeepers. The day before, Clinton had issued an executive order severing ties with the Indonesian military, though not yet ending arms sales. Now, on his way to a meeting of the Asia-Pacific Economic Cooperation group in Auckland, New Zealand, Clinton said that Indonesia must accept an international force. The same day, the International Monetary Fund, citing the problems in East Timor, decided to suspend talks with Indonesia on its economic recovery program. That decision meant, in effect, that the IMF would not disburse some $460 million in mid-September as planned. At about the same time, the World Bank announced that it had frozen $300 million that had been scheduled for disbursement the following week. Shortly thereafter, the president of the Paris Club of creditors announced that the group had decided to delay any decision on credit for Indonesia until the next year because of the situation in East Timor.

The next day, September 11, the British foreign secretary announced the suspension of all arms exports to Indonesia; a move later followed by the European Union. In New York, there was an unusual open debate in the UN Security Council, in the course of which some fifty states spoke, most of them arguing in favor of urgent international intervention. In Auckland Clinton announced the suspension of U.S. military sales to Indonesia and reiterated U.S. support for the idea of an international force. Indonesia, he said, "must implement the results of the balloting, and they must allow an international force to help restore security. We are ready to support an effort led by Australia to mobilize a multinational force to help bring security to East Timor under UN auspices." That afternoon, the Security Council delegation met President Habibie in Jakarta, and discussed the deployment of international forces and the evacuation of the refugees.

After that meeting the Indonesian cabinet convened to discuss the same issues. Habibie emerged from the cabinet meeting in the evening and made the announcement that effectively brought an end to the crisis. Gathered anxiously around a radio in the UN compound with East Timorese friends, we listened as he declared that Indonesia would welcome the assistance of the international community in restoring peace in East Timor. The final obstacle had been removed. Two days later, all remaining UN staff and refugees were safely evacuated from Dili to Darwin by giant Hercules C-130 aircraft, and the next day the UN Security Council passed Resolution 1264, lending its full support to a swift deployment of a multinational military force. Within a week those forces began to land in East Timor.

What brought this dramatic change in the posture of the international community, and, in particular, what finally changed the policy of the United States? What was it that made international military intervention a possibility in mid-September when so recently it had been said to be impossible?

Part of the answer lies in the shocking television images and other media coverage of the events of early September. One senior Western diplomat involved in the East Timor issue told me that his country's policy "was not driven by realpolitik but by reactions to images on the television." These images, together with the realization that the violence was being abetted by the Indonesian military, generated widespread outrage among ordinary citizens and provided the basis for mobilizing protests and demands for international action. On September 7, the UN's Department of Public Information notified Kofi Annan that they had already received sixty thousand messages calling for urgent action to assist East Timor. The outpouring of concern was so great that the department had to set up a separate computer server to handle all the messages.

The impact of media reporting was accentuated by the presence of international UN staff and a handful of foreign journalists and observers in Dili as the violence descended. Terrible as it may seem, without the possibility that foreigners would die, key governments might never have felt compelled to act. The preoccupation with the safety of foreigners was evident even in the statements of officials known for their sympathy toward the East Timorese. In pressing for UN intervention in early September, for example, New Zealand's foreign minister said, "What one hopes comes out of the Security Council of course is that you can somehow cordon off those UN-related people over there and give some kind of protection for them." Political leaders were also moved by some of the decisions and actions taken by UNAMET staff in Dili. The refusal of many UN staff to evacuate from Dili on September 8 forced key UN member states to act to avoid sharing responsibility for a political and humanitarian fiasco.

Still, it is unlikely that media images and reporting would have translated into a change in policy had there not already been a sophisticated worldwide network of legislators, religious leaders, and grassroots organizations in place long before the crisis. When I asked a Canadian diplomat what it was that had finally convinced his government that it must support intervention, his answer was unequivocal—it was the NGOs. Canada was not alone in this regard, though the precise composition of the NGO network varied from place to place. In the United States, much of the work was done by private advocacy groups that had been working through the Catholic church and Congress since the 1970s. Elsewhere, NGOs such as Amnesty International had built up an unusually rich portrait of the human rights problem in East Timor and had established channels of access not only to the media but to government decision makers and officials at the United Nations. This essential groundwork meant that when the crisis came, the lobbying effort did not have to start at square one.

Historical memory also played a key part. From the outset, the 1994 genocide in Rwanda and the 1995 massacre in Srebrenica were on the minds of UN officials in Dili and in New York, and they played a role in the deliberations of various states. The parallels were difficult to ignore, especially for those with some direct involvement in the earlier debacles. That group included Madeleine Albright, who was ambassador to the UN when the United States blocked the Security Council from sending peacekeepers to Rwanda during the genocide; Kofi Annan, who had been head of the UN's department of peacekeeping operations at the time of the genocide in Rwanda; and his chef de cabinet, Iqbal Riza, who had served under Annan at that time.

Memories of Rwanda and Srebrenica probably influenced members of the Security Council, too, particularly those who had stood in the way of effective intervention. Whether or not that was the case, Security Council action, and in particular its visit to East Timor, was critical in forging a consensus on concerted international action. Through their personal experience of the violence and the mendacity of Indonesian officials, the delegation was transformed into a powerful advocate for intervention. Likewise, the personal commitment of the secretary-general, and his decisive diplomacy at the height of the crisis, were critical in bringing about a change in the political balance.

Faced with this combination of forces, even the most reluctant of the major powers, as well as such institutions as the Pentagon, found it virtually impossible not to act. It is sobering to think that without such pressures they would in all likelihood have done nothing at all.

As one of those trapped inside the UN compound in September 1999, I was deeply relieved to hear that military forces were coming. And the fact is that the troops that arrived in late September did an admirable job in bringing an end to the violence and easing the militias and the TNI out of the territory by the end of October. In that sense, the military intervention was an enormous success. Only a few months later, however, it was clear that the international community had failed to resolve, or even adequately address, a number of other serious problems. Paramount among these was the question of justice.

Egregious human rights violations lay at the heart of the need for international intervention in September 1999 and led initially to calls for international investigations and even an international tribunal along the lines of those established for Rwanda and the former Yugoslavia. UN experts duly visited East Timor in November and December 1999 and proposed that further international investigations should be conducted with a view to bringing those responsible promptly to justice. Unfortunately, these investigations and the idea of an international tribunal very quickly lost the support, if they ever had it, of the United States, Australia, the European Union, and other key governments, which began to push instead for an Indonesian judicial process that everyone knew would ultimately fail.

The main reason for equivocation by the United States and its allies on the matter of human rights investigations and trials in East Timor was a desire to restore good relations with Indonesia as quickly as possible, in particular with its armed forces. The United States, the EU, Australia, and other governments were never keen on breaking ties with the Indonesian army, and they did their best to restore those ties as quickly as possible after the mayhem in 1999. One way of reassuring the TNI of their friendship was to ensure that it would never have to face any serious accounting for the crimes it committed.

Conveniently, a special investigation team of the Indonesian National Human Rights Commission was quickly established to look into the violence. Its report, released in January 2000, called for the indictment of thirty-two people, including the then–TNI commander, General Wiranto. While greeted by some outsiders as a refreshing sign of change in Indonesia, there was deep concern among the East Timorese and human rights experts that the Indonesian report would simply be used as a foil by the military to deflect demands for an international inquiry and tribunal.

By early 2000, it was clear that this was exactly what was happening, as the United States and other major powers began to soften demands for an international inquiry and to suggest that an Indonesian judicial process might suffice. In February 2000, and perhaps earlier, the Pentagon began quietly to restore military education and training (IMET) programs that had been cut in mid-September, and the European Union formally ended the arms embargo that it had imposed about the same time. In July 2001 the Bush administration announced its intention to seek a full resumption of military sales and ties to Indonesia. These moves sent a clear message to the TNI that it was being eased off the hook, long before any serious measures had been taken to resolve the matter of justice.

Pentagon officials have sought to justify the resumption of military ties on the grounds that they are the best way to guarantee respect for human rights and civilian rule in Indonesia. But this argument overlooks the fact that thirty years of close cooperation with the TNI did nothing to prevent the widely anticipated violence in East Timor in 1999. Nor did such cooperation stop the violence once it had begun. Indeed, it was only after the United States and other governments cut their military ties and arms sales to Indonesia that the worst violence and killing were brought to an end.

The folly of the velvet glove approach has been brought home by a number of alarming developments since 1999. In September 2000, Indonesian security forces stood by and watched as militiamen killed three staff members of the UN High Commissioner for Refugees at their office in West Timor, and then burned their bodies beyond recognition. The victims were among the humanitarian workers assisting the East Timorese who had fled their homes in 1999, and the perpetrators were the very militiamen who had forced them to flee. The murders were met by a storm of international condemnation—from the United States, the World Bank, and the UN Security Council, which condemned "this outrageous and contemptible act." But the basic policy did not change, and the matter was left in the hands of Indonesian authorities. Several months later, the prosecutor in the case announced that the six alleged perpetrators would only be charged with assault—a decision described by a diplomat as a "despicable whitewash"—and in May 2001 they received sentences of between ten and twenty months.

Meanwhile, Indonesian authorities continued to drag their feet in a most disgraceful way. In a largely successful attempt to deflect international attention, the government announced plans to establish ad hoc human rights tribunals to try those responsible for the 1999 violence. But as legal and human rights experts noted, there were fatal problems with the mandate and makeup of these courts. Most glaringly, a presidential decision (No. 96/2001) limited their jurisdiction to violations that had occurred in April and September of 1999 and in only three of East Timor's thirteen districts. The decision effectively guaranteed that the majority of crimes committed in East Timor would never be investigated or tried. When the trials finally got under way in early 2002, they confirmed the worst fears of lawyers and human rights observers. Key suspects, including General Wiranto, were not among the defendants, and the proceedings seemed designed to ensure that those who were tried would either be exonerated or would receive only token sentences.

This depressing scenario is not likely to be rectified any time soon. Particularly in the aftermath of the attacks of September 11, 2001, the arguments in favor of maintaining ties with abusive regimes will only become stronger, and the prospects for remedying crimes against humanity committed by those regimes will grow ever more remote. The costs of such expediency will also be high for Americans and for the credibility of the U.S. government's war against terrorism. For the story of East Timor illustrates that there is a sound basis for the skepticism with which U.S. policy is viewed in much of the world and good reason to doubt the sincerity of America's professed opposition to the use of violence against civilians.

# 11

# The Shark Cage

RICHARD LLOYD PARRY

Early every Sunday morning, Bishop Carlos Filipe Ximenes Belo, the winner of the 1996 Nobel Peace Prize, held Mass in the garden of his residence in the East Timorese capital, Dili. The day before the referendum on independence from Indonesia, when East Timor changed forever, I went there hoping to hear him preach. The dawn service was always an occasion of soft dignity, with prayers and singing beneath the flowering trees. On this Sunday, August 30, 1999, more people than usual were in the garden, although Belo had gone to a service on the south coast. A priest read out a message on the bishop's behalf: "Brothers and sisters, many people here in this time are very afraid. Do not be afraid. Be brave, and choose the future of East Timor. This is the generation that will create history, and one day people all over the world will speak of us, of the warrior people and the brave-hearted."

All afternoon, cars drove out of Dili as diplomats, electoral observers, activists and journalists dispersed across East Timor for voting day. A group of us squeezed into a Jeep and drove toward Maliana, a three-and-a-half hour journey to the west, close to the Indonesian border. In every village along the way there were guard posts manned by members of the pro-Indonesian militia. In the previous six months, with the undisguised support of the Indonesian Army and police, the militia had driven people out of their villages, burned their homes, and killed activists of the independence movement in an effort to intimidate the population and sabotage the referendum. The closer we got to Maliana, the more alarming the picture became. Half an hour out we saw a mixed group of machete-wielding militia and rifle-carrying soldiers; a few miles further on was another militia group, carrying its own M–16s.

Since the referendum had been announced, Maliana had been the site of intense and violent militia activity. Stone-throwing militiamen had attacked the local office of UNAMET, the United Nations Mission in East Timor, and the mood among its staff was quite different from that of their colleagues in the capital. In Dili they were wary of journalists, but here they felt isolated and neglected, and their isolation made them eager to talk.

They talked about the Besi Merah Putih, the local militia whose name meant "Red and White Iron." They spoke of the local military commander, who made no effort to disguise his relationship with the militias and his contempt for the UN. Several independence supporters had been murdered by the militia, and there were constant threats against UN staff. Three nights earlier, the house where the UN's military liaison officers lived was under fire for three hours. Four thousand people, one-third of Maliana's population, had deserted the town.

The Australian who ran UNAMET's Maliana office thought that his bosses in Dili did not take his concerns seriously. The violence, he believed, was not random and opportunistic but part of a carefully laid plan that would climax in a militia attack on the UN and on known independence supporters. It would take place in the next few days, after the referendum. Automatic rifles would be distributed among the militia. The electricity supply would be cut to the entire town.

"And then?" I said.

"Then they can do whatever they like," he said. "The students have been attacked three times already, and they'll be the first to go. Then they'll probably go for the priests, and then they'll try it on here, but with something a bit stronger than rocks. So they'll be out there with their guns, and we'll be in here unarmed, trying to get out."

It had been eight months since my last visit, and I only had to look around to see that something drastic had happened to East Timor. At Dili airport, there was an air of bustle and urgency among the luggage handlers and the taxi drivers. Even after dark, there were young men and children on streets that formerly had been silent and deserted. But the biggest and most obvious sign of change was on the roads. Power-steering their way around every corner, parked in front of every official building, were the emblem of the United Nations in the third world: white Toyota Land Cruisers. Radio aerials curved from their potent hoods. Along the cliff roads and above the sea, in the markets, they glided through the rabble of bicycles and station wagons, like diesel-powered swans among ducklings. A white UN helicopter, stenciled with the blue symbol, buzzed to and fro. Children waved and cheered as it passed overhead. "UNAMET!" they shouted. "Hooray for UNAMET!"

It had all happened so quickly.

Indonesia invaded the Portuguese colony of East Timor in 1975, and during that time, by the most commonly quoted estimate, two hundred thousand people had died from the effects of war, disease, and famine. In 1997, on my first visit, Dili was a town of fear and spies, still living in the shadow of the most notorious of East Timor's massacres six years earlier, when hundreds of young mourners had been murdered by Indonesian soldiers in Santa Cruz cemetery. Then in May 1998, President Suharto, the Indonesian dictator, was forced from power by protests in Jakarta. Suddenly, the East Timorese had more freedom than at any time since the invasion.

Large-scale demonstrations were held and warily tolerated by the military. The clandestine groups opposing Indonesian rule had publicly set up shop in an office in the center of town. Even the East Timorese guerrillas, Falintil, were spending more and more time in the town, sneaking down from the jungle for meetings, rest, and conjugal visits.

In New York, the governments of Indonesia and the former colonial ruler, Portugal, continued to hold desultory meetings on East Timor, as they had done fruitlessly for years. The most recent talk was of an "autonomy package" that would give the province control over certain of its internal affairs. But everyone was taken by surprise when Suharto's protégé and successor, B. J. Habibie, suddenly announced that if its people rejected autonomy, East Timor could have its independence.

By the beginning of May 1999, after further talking in New York, Portugal and Indonesia reached an agreement: the UN would supervise something called a "popular consultation." It would involve a period of political campaigning, a choice between two options (autonomy or its rejection), and a popular vote. It sounded like a referendum, but Indonesian national pride was at stake, and so, officially at least, it could never be referred to as such.

There was jubilation among ordinary East Timorese and dismay on the part of Indonesian officials, army officers, and the powerful minority of East Timorese civil servants and regional chiefs who supported integration. Around the country, pro-Indonesian, anti-independence paramilitary groups, known as the militias, sprang up. In April they threw hand grenades into a church where fifteen hundred refugees had sought shelter, and shot and macheted dozens of them as they fled. The Aitarak, or "Thorn" militia, attacked the house of an independence leader in Dili and killed thirty more people. Reports of organized violent intimidation came from all over the country, but mostly from the west of the territory, close to the border with Indonesia. One element was common to all of them—the involvement of the Indonesian police and army, both as passive observers and active participants.

There were stories that Indonesian government officials—barred, under the UN agreement, from any part in the referendum—were already running pro-autonomy campaigns in the mountain villages. There were rumors that the militias were planning a "sweeping" operation in which thousands of them would descend on Dili to kill and drive out their opponents. In the larger towns, the supporters of independence mustered huge crowds in peaceful rallies; the pro-autonomy demonstrations inevitably ended in street fights, knifings, and deaths. The militia told their victims that this was what they could expect for supporting independence, and that if they were stupid enough to vote against autonomy, worse would come. And amid all this in May 1999 the United Nations landed in Dili, and the UN Mission in East Timor, UNAMET, was born.

UNAMET's Dili headquarters were on the campus of Dili's former teachers' training college, a place known to everyone as "the compound." It consisted of a walled rectangle a few hundred yards long, wedged up at the rear against a steep hill. The offices were plain, white-washed structures, many of them former classrooms, shaded by big green trees, and every vacant space was occupied by a Toyota Land Cruiser. I still dream about the compound; few places live so vividly in my memory. But on my first visit it made little impression.

The press office was responsible both for relations with the media, and for the public information campaign that UNAMET would soon launch on its own account. In charge was a dry, British-educated Canadian named David Wimhurst. On weekdays, he gave a briefing in the room next to his office, although in the early days of UNAMET there was often nothing to say. On such mornings, the game was to ask questions anyway, in the knowledge that sooner or later he would make the inevitable mistake.

"UNAMET just doesn't have the authority," Wimhurst would say tetchily after another question about why the UN wasn't doing more to thwart the militias. "The Indonesian police are entirely responsible for security matters up to, during, and after the referendum."

"Er, you just said 'referendum,' David," someone would point out.

"Popular consultation," Wimhurst would say quickly. "You're quite right. It's not a referendum, it's a popular consultation. And the Indonesian police are responsible for its security."

This was the problem. The UN knew what it was doing when it came to elections. In the weeks leading up to the vote, it would create an electoral register and conduct a public information campaign by radio, television, newspaper, pamphlet, and public information tours throughout the territory. It would distribute ballot boxes, ballot papers, and electoral lists, supervise the voting, transport the ballots back to Dili, and count them. For all these tasks, it had adequate numbers of experienced personnel. But it had only 270 civilian policemen—or "CivPols"—and just fifty military liaison officers—or MLOs. They were a picturesque force. Each wore his national uniform while on duty: the police sergeants from Japan and the army men from Uruguay. The chief of the MLOs, a Bangladeshi brigadier, strode about in dark glasses brandishing a little cane that quivered as he walked. His swagger stick was the heaviest weapon that UNAMET had at its disposal, for these were not "peacekeepers." Under the terms of the agreement signed in New York, responsibility for all aspects of security lay with the Indonesian police. And far from being the solution, the Indonesian police, along with the Indonesian Army, were the root cause of the misery that followed.

The police made no more than a token effort to disguise their enthusiasm for the militia cause. During the massacre in the church two months earlier, survivors reported seeing Indonesian infantry and members of the police mobile brigades, or Brimob, looking on. The gesture that many people regarded as the most flagrant insult to the UN had come the week before when the police had appointed a new head of the Dili branch of a local body of volunteer constables. The man they chose was Eurico Guterres, the "commander" of the Aitarak militia.

Should anyone have been surprised? The Indonesians in East Timor were notorious as thugs, torturers, and sadists. This was the way it had been for twenty-four years. Anyone could have predicted that they would fight to hold on to the place, using every vicious tactic they knew. How could the UN have hoped for a peaceful referendum under such conditions? Why had it not insisted on armed peacekeepers with the power to arrest, investigate, and, if necessary, to shoot those who used terror to get their way?

Afterward, when it was too late, the question was put repeatedly, and various answers were proposed. One suggestion was that the UN had been distracted. The period of most intense negotiations coincided with the crisis and then with the air war in Kosovo, when the concentration of the organization had been focused elsewhere. Another response was that the UN had caved in, capitulating to the Indonesians on this as it had so often done since 1975. But the most convincing answer was that the UN had little choice.

President Habibie's decision to allow the referendum was a historic opportunity. If he were forced out or replaced (as he would be, by the end of 1999) that opportunity might be lost forever. "The UN could have said no, and the whole thing would have been called off," one of the UNAMET staff said to me, "and for the next twenty-three years, we'd have had chunks ripped out of our sides for the great opportunity that we'd thrown up. But we didn't, and we're here. The system's not perfect, in fact it's terrible, and God knows what's going to happen before this is over. But it will get done, and whatever happens, the world will see it."

A bit later, he said, "We're asking for one last act of bravery from the people of East Timor."

After it was all over, when there was much bitter talk about UNAMET and its responsibilities, I sometimes recounted that conversation to Timorese who had lived through the violence. Some of them had lost as much as one can lose. But not one of them said that it was a mistake, or that it would have been better if UNAMET had never come to East Timor in the first place.

On the day of the referendum, I dressed before dawn and walked with my East Timorese guide toward Maliana's polling center, a grubby sports hall that faced onto the town green. He gasped as we turned the corner. It was a remarkable and thrilling sight.

There was more than half an hour to go until the polls opened, but already the green was filling with thousands of people. They streamed in from all directions, in groups large and small, carrying bundles of food, infants, and even rolls of bedding. The older men and women wore batik headdresses, the younger ones wore cleanly pressed jeans and rubber sandals. They pressed close against the wide, barn-like doors of the hall. But there was no shoving and shouting, no obvious excitement, not even much smiling. Many of the expressions were earnest, even anxious. They were there for a reason: to vote and then to get back home as quickly as possible. On the outer fringes of the crowd, people squatted on the grass and unwrapped small breakfast parcels of rice and vegetables. A group of militiamen, apparently unarmed, stood beneath a large sandalwood tree. An invisible force field surrounded them: despite the surging volume of the crowd, no one approached within ten yards.

Eventually, the crowd parted enough for us to squeeze narrowly into the hall. Inside, final preparations were being made before the doors were opened. The polling station staff were sealing up the ballot boxes after showing their empty insides to the observers. A line of tables had been set up, bearing pens, pencils, a box for the registration forms, and a plastic bottle of ink for marking the fingers of those who had voted. Outside, the UN staff organized the crowd into a rough queue. At exactly 6.30 A.M., the first voters were allowed in.

First inside was Guillherme Dos Santos, the regent of Bobonaro, a notorious sponsor of the Besi Merah Putih, plump and sleek in shiny batik. "Of course, we're not supposed to give preferential treatment to anyone," said the UN volunteer at my side. "It's a compromise, but look how happy he is." The next to be admitted were the very elderly and the infirm.

Among them was a middle-aged man supported on two broken sticks. His legs were bent permanently beneath him by accident or disease, and it took him five minutes to cross the room, collect his ballot, and shuffle into the booth in front of me. I should have looked away, but I watched, and saw him painfully mark his cross in the lower of the two boxes, the one rejecting continuing association with Indonesia. He folded the paper, and began the painful walk to the ballot box. It was the second vote of the day; across the country, hundreds of thousands remained to be cast. But at that moment I stopped wondering about the result. If such a man was able to ignore terror and infirmity to make his choice, there was little doubt what the rest of his brave people would choose.

Whatever other mistakes UNAMET made, as an electoral exercise the referendum was an astonishing success. By lunchtime, across East Timor, four out of five of those who had registered had cast their votes. The final turnout was 98.6 percent. In the whole country, only 6,000 people had failed to vote out of an electorate of 438,000. Had any free election anywhere in the world ever secured such a remarkable turnout? Nobody I asked could think of one.

That night, the UNAMET helicopter flew around the polling centers, collecting the ballots and bringing them back to Dili. In Ermera, two votes were lost when a ballot box split open as militiamen fired blunderbusses and threw stones at the staff who were loading it onto the helicopter. In Atsabe, a Timorese who was working for the UN was stabbed through the lung and died two hours later. His name was João Lopez Gomez. He was the first UN worker to die. But overall the day had gone more smoothly than anyone had dared hope.

The predicted attack on Maliana did not come that night. There were no reports of significant intimidation. Ambassador Jamsheed Marker, the grandiloquent Pakistani who was Kofi Annan's special envoy on East Timor, spent the day flying from town to town, and the experience stirred his poetic soul. "I returned with vivid impressions of the awesome majesty which is manifest in the power of the people," he told a press conference in the Mahkota Hotel, late in the evening when the observers and journalists had returned to Dili.

"Many who went to the polling stations today did so under conditions of considerable hardship. They defied poverty, distance, climate, terrain, and, in some cases, dark intimidation in order to exercise their God-given right to vote in freedom. . . . Whatever the outcome, the eagle of liberty has spread its proud wings over the people of East Timor and nothing, by God's grace, will ever take it away."

Marker was not slow to identify the agency responsible for this heartening outcome: the Indonesian police. Their conduct, he said, had been "of the highest order." The leadership of their commanding officer, Colonel Timbul Silaien, had been "superb."

The result was announced in the ballroom of the Mahkota Hotel at 9 A.M. on Saturday, September 4. The announcement was not due for another three days, but the count had gone quickly. It must have seemed a good idea to get the news out as soon as possible, and to catch unprepared the plotters and the conspirators. But later people cursed UNAMET for this decision. Ordinary Timorese, too, were making their plans—plans to leave the towns and head for the hills or the countryside, to send into hiding children and friends in the independence movement or, at the very least, to gather supplies in preparation for days or weeks of danger and isolation. By Saturday, none of these plans had been completed. Much later, a Timorese friend said to me: "People died, I think, because they announced the result early."

The ballroom was packed. Ian Martin, the special representative of the UN secretary-general, walked in quickly and read out the results. He was a thin, bespectacled man with a patient, bureaucratic manner which tended to enfeeble his angrier and more forceful statements. When the announcement came, it was almost anticlimactic. Strict instructions had gone around the UN staff not to show any visible reaction to the result, and among the journalists this had also been agreed. "In fulfillment of the task entrusted to me," said Ian Martin. "I hereby announce that the result of the vote is 94,388 or 21.5 percent in favor and 344,580 or 78.5 percent against the proposed special autonomy."

Four out of five East Timorese had voted for independence.

Martin read out a statement on behalf of the secretary-general, Kofi Annan, but even before he finished, people were walking out of the room. A murmuring crowd was gathering in the hotel's dingy lobby. People smiled thinly at one another, and congratulated the few East Timorese who were standing around. My driver, a man named John, was there, and as I walked toward him he ran forward and embraced me, pressing his face into my shirt.

"John, John," I said. "Independence! *Independencia*. East Timor is free."

He let me go and shook my hand gravely. Tears were on his cheeks. He looked terrified.

On the steps of the hotel, people were standing around uncertainly. There were no cheering crowds, no jubilation. Apart from a single vendor, the street was empty. Whatever else happened, it seemed important to buy a lot of cigarettes. As I was paying the vendor and stuffing the packets into my bag, a pair of Aitarak men drove slowly by on motorbikes, eyeing the front of the hotel.

From the Mahkota to the Hotel Turismo, where most journalists were staying, was ten minutes on foot, but this morning nobody wanted to walk. John's jeep quickly filled up with people who needed rides. At the quayside was a large barge, and in front of it a crowd of people waiting to sail to Indonesian West Timor, burdened with infants, mattresses, refrigerators, motorbikes, and even pieces of furniture. Small groups of women and children were converging on Bishop Belo's garden, where hundreds more were already camping out beneath the trees.

Inside the Turismo we went to our short-wave radios and computers to check the headlines. It was strange: here we were, witnesses to this remarkable news, and yet for the moment what we had seen with our own eyes was less important than the rest of the world's reaction to it. People called out the headlines as they came up. From his house arrest in Jakarta, the Falintil commander Xanana Gusmao said, "This day will be eternally remembered as the day of national liberation." José Ramos-Horta, who had shared the Nobel Peace Prize with Belo, had words for the defeated supporters of autonomy: "They have not lost—

they have won a country." There was even a reaction from the Aitarak leader, Eurico Guterres. "We are defeated diplomatically," he was quoted as saying. "But we will not give up." Eurico was no longer in Dili, it seemed. He had got on the morning flight to Jakarta, and it was difficult to tell whether this was a good sign or a bad one. "Either he's throwing in the towel," said my British friend Alex, "or he knows that something very nasty's going to happen."

Four planes full of journalists left the next day, and the population of the hotel dwindled to its dregs. Those of us who had decided to stay gathered in the garden and organized ourselves. There were fewer than twenty of us—Alex and I, a handful of other newspaper correspondents, several stringers, a couple of documentary makers, and a single photographer. The Turismo's staff had gone. We began by drawing up a list of our names. Someone volunteered to gather food supplies and look after the cooking. Someone else took responsibility for establishing escape routes from the hotel, in case it should be attacked. *Pop, pop* went the blunderbusses in the background. *Thucka-thucka-thucka* went the AK-47s and the M-16s. Then they fell quiet for an hour or more. Members of the food committee sat in the garden, discussing that night's dinner. I began to think about what I would write.

In the late afternoon I dozed, and when I woke up everything had changed. People were trotting urgently across the garden carrying bags and equipment. A captain in the Indonesian marines was standing at the front of the hotel talking to the few journalists who understood Indonesian. Two dozen armed marines stood at the front of the hotel; they carried automatic rifles and long combat knives and wore flak jackets. And they had bad news. A "warning" had been received that Aitarak was planning an attack on the hotel. Aitarak, with its leather jackets, rusty machetes, and pop guns, was hardly a formidable threat. Nonetheless, the Indonesian marine corps was "unable to guarantee security."

"But why not?" one of the Indonesian speakers asked, pointing to the captain's rifle. "You have this. You are strong. Make the Aitarak go away."

The captain smiled and shrugged and spread the palms of his hands wide.

"'Cannot guarantee security,'" someone else repeated. "'Cannot guarantee security.' Well that's enough for me. I know a death threat when I hear it."

The first of three open-backed police trucks was already pulling up in front of the hotel. I hurried back to my room, shouldered my knapsack, and hesitated over my suitcase before deciding to leave it. I locked the door behind me.

The chairman of the escape committee had elected to stay on with a handful of others, but everyone else was moving to UNAMET. It was becoming impossible to work in the Turismo; in a few days we would return here when everything had calmed down. But once we were in the big truck I felt angry. The policemen laughed as they pushed us over the wooden sides into the truck. The police colonel overseeing the operation barked at us as we heaved up boxes and bags and bottles of water. We were so obviously doing exactly what they wanted.

The trucks started off with deliberate abruptness, and the Indonesians traveling with us guffawed again as the jolt sent us sprawling. I pulled myself off the man from the *Sydney Morning Herald* and looked back toward the hotel to see a militiaman run out from a side street. He brandished a home-made blunderbuss, which he pointed toward us. Soldiers and police watched him with amusement from just feet away. The gun went off with a resonant pop, and we all cringed into the corners of the truck. It had no chance of hitting us. It was more of a two-fingered salute than a genuine attempt on our lives. We picked ourselves up, and the policemen riding with us snickered once again.

At the UN compound, nobody was surprised to see us. The staff were moving in themselves; floor space quickly filled up with folded camp beds and boxes of food. But here at least there were computers and power sockets and satellite telephone connections. I found myself a camp table, a plug, and an ashtray, and sat down to write.

The worst thing happened about an hour later. It began with a new kind of shooting, not pop guns or automatics, but the long, ratcheting bursts of a machine gun, very close, from the other side of the compound. We hurried outside, and now there was a new noise—the screaming of women, close at hand, but muffled, coming in waves from over the wall.

The wall divided the UNAMET compound from an abandoned school next door. The place had completely filled with refugees, who were eating and sleeping on the floors of the classrooms. Now somebody was firing a machine gun over their heads. The rounds were purely for effect. They harmed no one directly, but they didn't need to. There were more than a thousand people in the school, most of them women and children, and now they were all rushing, terrified, for the single door that connected the school to UNAMET. A similar panic had occurred the previous week, and someone in the UN had taken a decision: not only had the door been locked, but the top of the wall had been festooned with bales of bright new razor wire.

The door quickly burst open, and people oozed through it, winded and crushed against the narrow wooden frame. The wall was only seven feet high, and people on the far side were attempting to climb over the wire. They tried to use clothes and bedding to cover its sharp teeth. Parents behind were pushing their children over the top. The children were being forced onto the barbs. Bags were being thrown over and becoming entangled. There were Indonesian policemen in the school, bellowing at the refugees and trying to pull them back. The CivPols in the compound were carrying megaphones and booming uselessly through them in English. The machine gun fire stopped, and then another volley was heard again, followed by a new wave of collective screaming.

I stood close to the gate and thought, what is the best thing to do? I didn't know. No one knew. So I shouted out to the CivPol with the megaphone, "They can't understand you! They don't speak English." Then I just stood and listened to the screaming. I could feel the terror almost physically, like a wind. How strong is the fear that makes a mother lift her baby over her head and push him onto razor wire?

Finally the refugees calmed down. The shooting had stopped, but it was obvious that it could start again at any time. So the door was opened and the refugees came through one by one, calmly now, with sobs instead of cries, some of them gashed and bleeding where they had been bitten by the barbs. That night the man from the UN High Commission for Refugees told me that there were one hundred and fifty thousand people displaced across East Timor. Fifteen hundred of them were here with us now, inside the compound.

The gunfire continued through the evening, sometimes close by, sometimes distant, but by now it was little more than background noise. At 10:37 P.M., there was an intense and prolonged burst. Ten minutes later came a loud, proximate boom that shook the windows and was followed by the shrill sound of more automatic fire.

"Down!" someone shouted. "Off with the lights." Everyone in the press room jumped to the floor and crawled up against the walls and beneath tables.

There was silence. Someone gave a mirthless giggle. A match flared, and soon the only light in the room came from a dozen orange cigarette tips. I thought of the head of the escape committee and the small band that had remained in the Turismo, and wondered how they were.

On the tops of the desks, UNAMET walkie-talkies sat in their rechargers, crackling out conversations between the CivPols and MLOs, as they peered out into the darkness.

*There's the glow of a fire on the horizon.* Crackle, crackle.

*We have a group of men, possibly military, possibly militia, moving away from the west wall of the compound.* Crackle. Silence.

*The weapon has been identified. A grenade, a military issue grenade.*

Ten minutes later, the alarm was over and the lights were back on.

Who threw that grenade? It hardly mattered. The only difference between the militias and the Indonesian security forces was the uniform. I carried the camp table outside and finished writing my story in the open air. The satellite lines were congested, so I called London on my mobile phone and dictated the story, reading it out word by word. Afterward, I drank whisky with my friends, nibbled at the unappetizing rations, and smoked and smoked. When it was very late, we helped one another erect the clumsy camp beds. There was no space left in the press office, so I placed my bed outside, under the eaves of an old classroom. I fell asleep without difficulty. And I dreamed.

It was dusk on Sunday when I had arrived at the UN compound; I would leave on Tuesday afternoon. I doubt that I will ever experience another forty-eight hours so fearful and intense. At other times and places in Indonesia, I had seen violence and cruelty. But even at the worst, I had watched them on my own terms; at any point I chose, I could step away from it to food, company, and a peaceful bed. In Dili, all of these were gone. Law, reason, pity, civilization itself had shrunk to the breadth of the UN compound, to the few hundred square yards between the crumbling walls of the old teacher training college. When I slept on my camp bed outside the press room, I didn't dream only conventional nightmares of pursuit and violence. I dreamed of being a small child: of going to church with my grandparents, of holding the hands of my mother and father. I dreamed of all the certainties that had gone from Timor: the child's trust in the parents, the parents' promise that everything will be all right. They were the saddest dreams possible in such a place, and I woke with tears in my eyes.

I dreamed, too, of being a diver inside a shark cage. I wore an old-fashioned diving suit; the walls and floor of the cage were thin aluminum bars. The water all around was murky and cold, and there was a rushing noise in my ears. Without warning giant shapes emerged out of the dimness: sharks. They swam around the cage with terrible speed, and their noses clanged against the bars, which bent and snapped and fell away. Soon there were no bars at all, just me suspended alone in the current with the sharks swimming around me, brushing my diving suit, circling me over and again, as I waited for the parting of the jaws and the lunge that would end it all. I could feel tugs on the tube that connected me to the surface and I knew that it was a message in a code that I had once understood but that had become meaningless to me.

Even now it is difficult to understand the violence, instigated and overseen by the Indonesian Army, that followed the referendum. No outside agency had forced the popular consultation on Indonesia. President Habibie himself had suggested it. The Indonesian government had freely signed the agreement with Portugal and the United Nations that brought UNAMET into being. And the violence we witnessed was so messy, indecisive, and ugly. Burned houses, terrified mothers and children, frightened UN workers—it seemed almost calculated to make the worst possible impression on international opinion.

But among army and police officers in East Timor itself, and at least among their immediate superiors in the regional command, there was a remarkable degree of planning, coordination, and control. Like all war zones, East Timor occupied an emotional place in the military psyche. Plenty of senior Indonesian officers had served their time there, and for many of them, East Timor was the formative experience of their lives. They had killed there, and seen their friends killed; for the first time, they had been afraid. East Timor was a proving ground and a symbol of the proud unity of the Indonesian state. Now the bug-eyed, lickspittle Habibie was giving it away.

Habibie's announcement appalled and affronted the armed forces, and the violence and intimidation they fomented had several goals. The most obvious was to reduce the number of ballots cast for independence by terrifying voters into supporting the other side or by driving people out of their villages so that they could not register and vote. The terror also served as a goad to Falintil. If the guerrillas could be provoked to fight back, then the army would have the excuse it needed to call off the ballot and resume its operations.

But why go to such trouble after the referendum? The battle was lost; the cause was hopeless. And it was not as if the violence was an instinctive reaction. How remarkable, for example, that, despite the close shaves, none of the "internationals"—no journalist, observer, or foreign UN worker—had been killed. The intention was to terrify but always, at the last moment, to turn the flat of the blade.

One theory had it that the violence was not principally aimed at the East Timorese, but at other rebellious provinces of Indonesia—at Aceh and at West Papua. "You want independence?" the army was asking. "This is what you will get." Before the referendum there was also an idea, popular among militia leaders, that having been cheated of their rightful victory, the pro-Indonesian forces would retreat to West Timor and take with them the four westernmost provinces, which would secede to Indonesia. But the plan came to nothing. It was a fantasy—indeed, beyond the menace and violence, there was a childish quality to the whole undertaking: the oily alienated youths in their fighting fantasy militia uniforms, the drugs and the motorbikes, the toy blunderbusses. What made it unbearably frightening was the presence of efficient and grown-up killers in army uniforms, egging them on, giving them guns and bullets, and joining in themselves.

There may indeed have been orders from the top, but when the time came nothing so direct as an order was necessary. Everything had been laid carefully in place, responsibility had already been dispersed across so many different departments, commands, and individuals, that no words were necessary. Jakarta's silence was the command. In East Timor, the army knew what to do, and once the violence started it gathered speed and power and continued until it had exhausted itself. This was the strangest and most fearful aspect of the violence in East Timor: it could be meticulous and methodical and at the same time so completely out of control.

The UNAMET walkie-talkie on the desk where I wrote crackled out the conversations of the CivPols as they warily patrolled the compound. For most of Monday, these exchanges were technical and uninteresting reports on the movement of troops, the direction of gunfire, and the movement of staff. But by the evening—my second in the compound— the character of the reports changed, and as I reviewed the events of the day, turning over in my mind what had happened and what might come, the little black radio began to give me the spooks.

*Repeated gunfire on the way to the airport.*

*Numerous militias on street. Streets are impassable without armed escort.*

*Smoke rising from the second floor of the electoral commission building. Houses of the Portuguese mission burning.*

The shooting started up outside again. The phones were ringing with requests for interviews. I spoke with an Austrian news agency and the BBC. The act of articulating the situation to an interviewer thousands of miles away made it appear far worse than I had previously imagined it. The thrust of the questions seemed to be, do you expect to be killed tonight?

That night, September 7, at a quarter to four in the morning, a child was born in the small clinic at the back of the compound. The mother was a refugee named Joanna Rodriguez; the child, a boy, was baptized immediately by a member of the UN mission who happened to be a Jesuit priest. He was christened Pedro Rodriguez, and his middle name was given as UNAMET. Later I would hear this described as a gesture of "gratitude" to the United Nations for "protecting" Joanna Rodriguez and her family. But I liked to think of it as something more ambiguous and ironic: a reproach, as well as a plea; a challenge to UNAMET, a direct look into Kofi Annan's eyes.

It was quiet compared to other nights: one burst of concentrated automatic fire at midnight and a second one a few hours later. Two hours after that the cockerels started crowing and with them began another distinctive sound, the low, whispering bustle of the waking refugees. There were two thousand now, but their presence could not have been more discreet or unobtrusive. Without fuss or supervision, they had filled the space between the buildings with colored blankets and faded sheets. After dark, they sat in family groups, whispering to one another or singing prayers and hymns *pianissimo*.

In the two days I spent among them, I saw no fights and no fits of temper, no thievery or truculence. Even the babies hardly cried, and despite the uncertainty, the rumors, and the shooting all around, there was no pleading or begging, no ranting or ill-temper or threats.

I began to dread the sight of the refugees, for I was becoming pre-occupied by a single question: should I stay or run away?

The choice was held out to me, for more evacuation flights were scheduled today. No one could say whether there would be any tomorrow. Outside the press room a list was being drawn up of those intending to evacuate, and my friends were discussing what to do. I marked my name down on the list, then took it off, and then marked it down again.

I paced around the compound, seeking out corners that I had not seen before, as if its physical structure, the condition of the paths and roofs and windows, could provide me with an answer to my dilemma. I took many photographs; I felt an urgent need to fix in my mind the appearance of the compound, this mundane, remarkable place. The outer walls were crumbling cement. At the very back was a gap in the wall beneath the steep slope that led up and away to the hills behind Dili. After dark, many of the refugees were slipping through here to spend the night on the summit, rather than in the snare of the compound.

At 8.20 A.M. there was a burst of phosphorescent tracer fire across the slopes of the hill.

It was about this time, mid-morning, that a small new crisis unfolded within the larger one: simultaneously, it seemed, the entire compound was running out of cigarettes. I was down to my last, my very last, packet, and the prospect of being without them made me feel weak. I found a camp chair beneath a wide cool tree on the edge of the yard and smoked three in a row. Soon, my head was beating with exhaustion, nicotine, and lack of food. In front of me was a Land Cruiser that had been shot up the previous day on the way to the airport. Its rear window was a mess of jagged glass pebbles.

Hour by hour, the morale of the mission was fraying, and all morning UNAMET people sidled up with alarming and subversive nuggets of information. The warehouse had been looted. No, the warehouse had been burned. Evacuation was imminent. Evacuation had been postponed. A group of fifty UNAMET staff were preparing to break away from UNAMET and live in the hills with Falintil and the refugees. Have you heard? Are you leaving? Do you have any cigarettes?

My fear needed reasons, and it found them in the idea of evacuation. It seemed inevitable that at some point there would be a general withdrawal to the airport. Whether the East Timorese were flown out or left to their fate, it would be a time of dread and chaos. I imagined the mutinous disgust among the younger UNAMET staff when the order came through, the angry fear of the East Timorese. Would the CivPols follow their orders? Would they make their escape up the hill? I pictured myself squeezed into a Land Cruiser for the procession through the streets, the snarling of the Aitarak motorbikes, the waving of the blunderbusses. A scared, flustered driver taking a wrong turn, the way blocked by militia, Brimobs looking the other way, and the seduction of a trigger, one squeeze, just to see: what would it look like?

The gates of the compound opened and an Indonesian Army truck backed in, the truck that would carry the day's evacuees to the airport. People heaved up bags and boxes. A New Zealand MLO clambered in and took charge of the loading operation. "All aboard, ladies and gentlemen," he piped cheerfully. "Bags on the outside, bodies on the inside."

I stood up and walked toward the truck.

Another of the MLOs, a British colonel, was standing to one side watching.

"Are you going, Richard?"

"I don't know. I don't know."

"You don't want to stay with us, see this through?"

"I don't know."

There was a rattle of automatic fire, and with it a new sound, a migraine whistling that accompanied each report.

"Now *that*," said the colonel, "was close. When they fire into the air you just hear the crack. But when you hear the bullet singing, that means it's directly overhead."

Two Australian radio reporters ran up dressed in helmets and flak jackets and began loading their bags into the truck. The tailgate was being raised, and the colonel was saying good-bye to those on board. I stood there, waiting for somebody to stop me from going, to make me stay.

"Good-bye, Richard. Good luck!" said the colonel. "Don't worry about it. I'll see you in Darwin."

I was inside the back of the truck.

From the truck, the compound suddenly seemed a very safe place to be. The sides were made of wooden slats, with inch-wide gaps between them. Briefcases, suitcases, boxes, and backpacks were stacked up against them to form an unstable inner wall. A tremendous fusillade of automatic fire fetched up from close by as we passed the UNAMET gates.

"Heads down, ladies and gentleman," said the New Zealander. There were about a dozen of us in the back along with eleven Indonesian soldiers. I had no flak jacket; instead, I had a portable computer in a leather bag. I braced it vertically between my head and the wooden sides, and wondered exactly what effect the interposition of a Toshiba laptop would have upon an M-16 round. I looked at the Indonesians who stood above us with smirking expressions. They felt no need to cower in the bottom of the truck—our guards, here to protect us against an attack by their own comrades.

Through the slats, I glimpsed Dili utterly transformed. It felt like a science-fiction film, a journey through a town overtaken by body-snatchers. During the fifteen-minute trip to the airport, I saw not a single ordinary person. The shops were boarded and shut, the houses still. In front of them, milling singly and in groups, were hundreds of soldiers and black-shirted militia.

The streets teemed with them. I felt a wave of nausea, like the shock of opening a neglected cupboard to find it teeming with rats or maggots. I saw one Aitarak man with an AK-47; the rest carried spears or machetes, and the soldiers above us waved and smiled at them. Behind us passed a stolen UNAMET Land Cruiser, driven by a grinning militiaman. Which were genuine East Timorese and which were soldiers in bandannas was difficult to tell. The shooting resumed again in the middle distance. Thick smoke from newly set fires rose close to the road. I had been in the compound for forty-eight hours, and the sudden sensation of being outside and in motion produced a rush of euphoria. The airport was as ghostly as the town. Papery litter drifted around. Someone had removed all the light bulbs from the overhead sockets. At passport control was an unexpected sight: a dozen young Australian soldiers, several of them women. Very formally and politely, they checked our bags and passports and explained the operation of the seat belts. "Just a few quick health questions, sir," said a soldier with a red cross on her armband. "This may sound a bit strange, but have you been scuba-diving at any time in the last week?"

The Hercules could be heard, its engine roaring out on the tarmac. We ran toward its stubby shape, cringing in the noise and heat. The surge of adrenaline was ebbing now, and I began to feel deep weariness and inklings of dread, as if I had done something unforgivable and was only now beginning to remember what it was. The engine pulsed and surged; the wheels rumbled below us and then came that moment of sudden lightness and lift, and we were in the air.

The hold of the plane was dark and windowless, but the cockpit was flooded with light. Spread out below in greens and browns, almost close enough to touch, was Dili. It terrified me to see it still there. I could make out the familiar landmarks: Motael Church and the cathedral, Bishop Belo's house, even the Turismo. But the rest of the town was all fires.

Even from this height, I could see the licking shapes of individual flames in the town center. Two large Indonesian naval ships lay at anchor off shore. The town grew distant as the plane rose, but I felt myself to be the one who was sinking, as if I were looking up at Dili from the bottom of a deep and narrow well.

# 12

# Back Road Reckoning

Erin Trowbridge

August 30, 1999, should have been a day of celebration for the people of East Timor. In a referendum in which more than 98 percent of the eligible voters cast their ballots, 78 percent voted for independence from Indonesia, throwing off twenty-four years of occupation. It was not, however, a decision Jakarta was prepared to accept. Five days later, on September 4, when the results of the election were announced, forces opposed to independence set about delivering a devastating punishment. With the aim of leaving nothing but scorched earth, the pro-Indonesia militias of East Timor, with the support of the Indonesian army, began rampaging across the country.

In the weeks that followed, more than twelve hundred people were massacred and thousands of women were beaten and raped. According to a United Nations assessment, "Building Blocks for a Nation," two hundred thousand people fled or were pushed across the border into refugee camps in West Timor, the Indonesian half of the island. Overall, 75 percent of the population was displaced. At night, observers could see hundreds of small campfires dotting the mountainside where people waited until it was safe to come back down.

"The militia told everyone in town that if we stayed we would be killed," said Rosarinha Munis in Maliana, a town near the border of West Timor. "They killed my husband and two of my children and they burned down my home, then they made me go to West Timor, to Indonesia. We didn't know if they would kill us there, but when they told us to go, they had knives. We knew what would happen if we stayed."

Human rights activists consider the campaign of forced evacuations the clearest sign that the devastation of East Timor was methodical and not the haphazard, spontaneous outrage of a few unorganized militia groups. In late September 1999, Amnesty International reported, "Independence activists are being hunted down at checkpoints, on boats and in house-to-house searches. Militia and members of the Indonesian army (TNI) continue to intimidate, threaten and attack the displaced East Timorese with total impunity." The report called the forced deportations a deliberate policy by the TNI.

"We knew it was coming," said David Savage, a civilian police officer from Australia who was in Maliana with the UN as an electoral monitor at the time of the referendum. "In the days just after the vote, with every hour there was in increase in violence. We heard gunfire, the houses were being burned. The militia had taken over the town and we were unarmed and unprepared. The last night we were there, we were convinced we would die, they were firing on us, they were burning things down. I called my family to say I wasn't sure I'd see them again. The militia wouldn't let the local staff members leave with us when we finally got clearance to retreat to Dili. They told us we could either go alone or stay with them. We knew the implications. We sneaked them into the transports anyway. We weren't going to leave them to be killed."

There were not, however, enough David Savages to go around in 1999. At the time of the referendum there were approximately eighteen thousand militia, most of whom were foot soldiers loyal to Indonesia and prepared to follow whatever orders they were given, regardless of the consequences for the East Timorese. In the weeks after the vote, the black-shirted militia methodically destroyed crops, stole farmers' tools, killed livestock, and set fire to most of the nation's buildings. Once the towns were razed, they worked their way out into the surrounding countryside and mountains. They followed riverbeds and paths cut through the mountainous terrain for the Indonesian army. They burned, raped, displaced, and murdered unchecked until, on September 20, a UN peacekeeping force was finally allowed to go in.

The violence never reached genocidal proportions, but what happened there in the space of twenty-one days was devastating. The physical destruction of the country was immense—70 percent of houses were destroyed, as were 77 percent of all health facilities and 95 percent of the schools. All public services collapsed.

I arrived in East Timor in July 2001, two years after the massacre, and I could still see the devastation. The narrow, pot-holed streets of Dili were lined with the burned-out remnants of homes. Roofs, windows, and doors were gone. Charred black streaks stretching out from the window frames curled up the sides of houses. Traffic lights hung hollow and askew. Some buildings had only the barest reminder of their former infrastructure—a wall here, half a floor there. There was throughout the city the sweet, pulpy stench of garbage, waste, and rot. Free-roaming swayback pigs ate and rested in the town's irrigation canals. Goats, chickens, dogs, sheep and cows were tied with flimsy rope to trees, fences, or whatever was standing.

In one town, invading militiamen had filled an irrigation ditch with concrete. In the countryside and villages, they had torn the roofs off buildings. The idea was to leave no place for people to gather or take refuge.

In Suai, a tropical haven just a few miles away from the southern coast of East Timor, hundreds of people ran to the church, thinking they'd be safe there. For days, militiamen and Kopassos soldiers, the Indonesian Special Security Forces, drove back and forth in front of the church compound firing into the crowds. Finally, they entered and began shooting. More than two hundred people were killed. The ubiquitous yellow Mitsubishi mini-dumptrucks, small enough to manipulate the torn-up roads, were hired out to haul the bodies across the border into West Timor, where they were dumped, most likely, into the sea. They have not been recovered. Throughout East Timor, few bodies have. Today, hundreds of grave markers are piled up as a memorial just a few feet away from the doors of the church.

When the shooting and burning began in Maliana, people were told, as part of UN protocol, to report to the police station. Hundreds did, and most stayed there for days; but even in the station, they were subjected to beatings and rapes. In the killing fields of the countryside, it was worse. People were chased from their houses, children were killed in front of their families. One woman's husband was shot as she stood in the next room asking what was happening. Before the slaughter stopped, more than fifty villagers had been hacked to death.

Today, crosses stand throughout the countryside, testament to the Catholicism left over from centuries of Portuguese rule. They are solemn memorials for those who disappeared or died in 1999. There are black iron crosses, simple wooden ones, crosses made from dried earth. Piles of stones, too, mark the ground where people fell. Everywhere in the mountainous terrain, there are signs of remembrance.

East Timor is a tiny place, half an island at the far eastern end of the Indonesian archipelago. It is home to only eight hundred thousand people. This half of the island was the main Portuguese holdout in Indonesia during the centuries that the vast spray of islands—thirteen thousand in total—was colonized by the Dutch. Even through the Second World War, when Japanese soldiers invaded and occupied the island, which is strategically positioned only a few hundred miles north of Australia, the Portuguese took to the mountains and fought to get their land back.

In April 1974, Portugal's "carnation revolution" caused tremendous political upheaval and the viability of maintaining East Timor as a colony was finally reconsidered. Portugal began the process of decolonization. On November 28, 1975, the Revolutionary Front for an Independent East Timor—known as Fretilin—an anticolonial, Marxist-based nationalist party, declared independence after four hundred years of colonial rule. Nine days later, and only hours after meeting with U. S. President Gerald Ford and U.S. Secretary of State Henry Kissinger, Indonesia's President Suharto authorized Indonesian troops to invade East Timor. The fear of communism in the West and its spread through the East gave Indonesia an excuse to invade the island, annex the territory, and nip in the bud any separatist movements that may have been spawned by East Timor's brief independence. According to the UN country report, in the first month after the invasion, sixty thousand East Timorese were killed, and after that, the death toll continued climbing. All told, the 1975 invasion, annexation, and repression that followed left, directly or indirectly, more than two hundred thousand East Timorese dead.

When it claimed East Timor as its twenty-seventh province, Indonesia assumed control over a severely underdeveloped country. When Portugal pulled out quickly and without looking back, little infrastructure was left behind. Access to clean water was available to only half the households and sanitation to even fewer.

For the next twenty-four years, Indonesia ruled with terror and an iron fist. The East Timorese independence movement retreated back up into the mountains. Although Indonesia's annexation of East Timor was never recognized by the United Nations, the occupation was carried on, and the world seemingly forgot about the people living in this hostile occupied land.

In these decades, though, the independence fighters kept fighting the occupying forces, and by the end of the nineties, international human rights activists and journalists were denouncing the occupation. Desperate to keep its island nation intact, Indonesia had little need to worry about world opinion on the matter, until 1998, when, after the ousting of President Suharto, B. J. Habibie assumed the presidency. Saddled with an economy wrecked by the Asian financial crisis, vast governmental corruption and cronyism, and growing international criticism of the occupation of East Timor, Habibie called for a popular referendum to decide East Timor's fate. The UN, Indonesia, and Portugal, acting on East Timor's behalf, began to hammer out the details of how the referendum would be held, what the process would look like, and who would be responsible for what. In the end, they decided that the UN would monitor the elections and, in a decision that was to end in disaster, the Indonesian military would guarantee East Timor's safety.

On May 5, 1999, when the three parties finally reached an agreement, Kofi Annan, the UN secretary-general, voiced his concern about the increase in violence throughout East Timor. He urged "all elements and political tendencies in East Timor to refrain from any resort to force and to cooperate with the United Nations." At the time, Annan pointedly noted the assurances given by Habibie that his government would fulfill effectively its "responsibility for law and order and the protection of all civilians."

In the weeks that followed, as the UN established its presence in East Timor under the leadership of Ian Martin, the special representative of the secretary-general, it emphasized its neutrality in press releases and speeches. The UN, its officials made clear, was only in East Timor to ensure that people could vote in a secret, free, and fair election. Meanwhile, reports of harassment and beatings were coming from every part of the country. On June 1, 1999, Martin declared, "An end to all violence is essential for a fair campaign and ballot."

On June 11, the UN Security Council established the United Nations Mission in East Timor (UNAMET) to run through the end of August. In a unanimous resolution, the Security Council agreed to send 280 civilian police officers to advise the Indonesian police and fifty military liaison officers to work with the TNI. The resolution stated that the Indonesian government was to be responsible for the "maintenance of peace and security in East Timor, the integrity of the ballot and for the security of international staff and observers." Nonetheless, the violence continued to escalate. On June 18, at a press conference in Dili, Martin said that tens of thousands of East Timorese had already been forced from their homes. He cited evidence that campaigning by pro-autonomy groups had been supported by the TNI.

By July 22, two hundred voter-registration centers had been opened, and within ten days, more than one-fourth of the population had registered. UNAMET was now forced to deal with the chaos caused by pro-autonomy militia and the Indonesian armed forces. Special registration plans had to be developed for the thousands of East Timorese who had already been forced from their homes.

Some East Timorese leaders, including José Ramos Horta, co-recipient of the 1996 Nobel Peace Prize, suggested postponing the elections and waiting until some of the dust had settled. But according to journalists, East Timorese independence activists, and UN officials, the people of East Timor did not want to wait. Fearing that Indonesia might never offer the same opportunity again and having waited so long, the people of East Timor said they were ready for a referendum.

"Everyone involved in the process behind the May 5 agreements knows that had the United Nations demanded that it be allowed to deploy organized military units here, to protect its staff and East Timor's population, Indonesia would have said no and the referendum would have been off," said Sergio Viera De Mello, administrator of the United Nations Transitional Administration for East Timor (UNTAET). "I don't think there was any way the violence of 1999 could have been avoided in these circumstances. I don't think it was possible to do it differently. The people negotiating with Indonesia and with Habibie knew that the offer for a referendum on independence was hanging by a thread. [If] the UN or Portugal pushed it too far, the thread would break and the window of opportunity would close and never open again."

On August 30, the polls opened and the people voted. For a brief moment the militia pulled back and waited. The violence on August 30 was tame compared to all that had come before. Several polling stations were shut down for a few hours, and after the polls had closed a local UN worker was stabbed to death. But that was it. At the end of the day, Annan confidently described the vote as "an expression by the East Timorese of their will as to their future" and urged all East Timorese groups to "exercise the utmost restraint and patience in the post-balloting period."

If the United Nations had any inkling of the bloodbath that was to follow, it never let on. Four days later, the lull of peace was shattered when the results of the referendum were announced. Nearly eighteen thousand black-shirted militia, supported by the TNI, initiated a campaign of terror that would devastate the country three weeks later. On September 16, Indonesia—faced with growing international pressure to stop the butchery that it had unleashed—conceded the necessity of a UN force to restore order in East Timor. Five days later, the first United Nations multinational troops, led by Australian forces, landed in Dili.

On October 25, 1999, the United Nations Security Council established the United Nations Transitional Administration for East Timor (UNTAET) as the "integrated, multi-dimensional peace-keeping operation fully responsible for the administration of East Timor" It marks the first time the UN has ever run an entire country. It also shows how difficult it is, after a disaster such as happened in East Timor, for the United Nations, or any international agency, to pick up the pieces. When I traveled to East Timor in the summer of 2001, the UN presence was visible everywhere. The pale blue UN flag waved in the dry wind in front of Komodo Airport in Dili welcoming international guests. Passports were stamped with a very matter-of-fact "Permission to Enter—UNTAET." In Dili, white Land Cruisers painted with bold UN-blue acronyms were ubiquitous. The long, white, pillared government building that belonged first to Portugal and then to Indonesia now flew a UN flag and boasted an enormous sign reading "UNTAET HQ."

UNTAET's mandate was to help create a government that could be handed over to East Timor and simultaneously to train people by developing an East Timorese professional class that had been willfully neglected for hundreds of years. It was an enormous task. In 1975, when Portugal left, there were only three East Timorese doctors. By 1999, only seven lawyers were indigenous.

"At the end of 1999, East Timor was a strange land," according to a report issued by Timor Aid in 2000. "There was no government, no official language or currency, no system of law, no media, no shops or schools. Not only was the country physically plundered and raped, but also, no former structure existed which could be used as a base for rebuilding."

The UN strategy for East Timor's development has been to build a modest economy—based on rice, coffee, fisheries and oil—supplemented by strategic international aid. The World Bank has pegged the annual budget for East Timor at sixty-five million dollars. Some say that, with the oil prospects in the Timor Sea, this number is too conservative. World Bank officials assert that for the time being it is better to be safe than sorry.

Coffee has already proved to be a money maker. In 1998, the entire crop of East Timorese coffee—which is "organically" grown because of a lack of access to chemicals and fertilizers—went to Starbucks. The land and the crops, which in 1998 garnered nearly twenty million dollars, have not been fully recovered since the burnings of 1999. José Teixeira, from East Timor's Department for Economic Affairs, estimates that with national support the coffee industry can reap fifty million dollars annually. Driving through the mountainous countryside one can see that the industry is still small and family run. Along the beaten roads, young girls sit outside their homes on blankets covered with beans being dried in the sun. On the roadside, groups of men pry the bean from the pulpy fruit, tossing the shells aside.

But when it comes to economic prospects, oil is the pillow on which East Timor's dreams ultimately rest. In the summer of 2001 a team of UN, Australian, and private sector experts determined that offshore oil and gas fields—which until independence were owned by Indonesia and Australia—belong in fact to East Timor. Although most of the fields are not scheduled to produce commercially until 2003, it is expected that the industry will be a three hundred million dollar annual profit maker.

There is, however, no denying the dire poverty East Timor faces for the time being. According to statistics issued by the United Nations Development Program, more than half the population lives on less than one dollar a day, and two-thirds of the women are illiterate. The GDP per capita is $230, less than that of Chad.

But an even bigger problem—and a sadder one in terms of its toll on families—is the refugee crisis. More than two hundred thousand people were displaced in the three weeks that followed the referendum. The UN has not only had to deal with this crisis but do so with very limited access to and no control over the refugee camps in West Timor. In August 2001, nearly sixty thousand people, or 30 percent of those who initially fled East Timor, were still living in the camps.

Initially the United Nations High Commissioner for Refugees (UNHCR) managed the camps throughout the Indonesian half of the island. But in September 2000, three UN workers were killed in Atambua, a border town in West Timor, and since then, West Timor has been declared off-limits for UN staff. UN personnel are not allowed into West Timor without advance security clearance, and then, only for a limited time span. The camps are run by Satuan Tugan (SATGAS), the Indonesian task force assigned to address refugee issues.

UNCHR representatives meet regularly with SATGAS staff to get updates on the status of the people in the camps. There are frequent reports from returning refugees that the East Timorese in the SATGAS-run camps are harassed and intimidated. Indonesia denies this. But, according to the UN, nearly 70 percent of the remaining refugee population is being held hostage as "human shields" by the militia, who are active in the camps.

Muhammed Hussein, who works with UNHCR in Maliana, said that many of the returning refugees have been hesitant to come back because they have heard that there may be more violence in East Timor. Some people have reported that they were told by the Indonesians that they would be beaten by their neighbors if they returned. They were told there is terrible poverty and little chance of getting work. They were also told they might be killed either leaving East Timor or coming into Indonesia.

The militia and Indonesians who intimidate the refugees have plenty of motive for doing so. As long as the refugees are in the camps, the militia and members of the Indonesian Army who carried out the massacre have bargaining chips to negotiate lesser charges and more lenient sentences. Nobody talks about this on the record, least of all the Indonesians, who still insist that the massacre and burning of East Timor were carried out by independent militia groups with no official support from the Indonesian military.

Two days after I arrived in Dili, I was invited to join officials from the International Organization for Migration (IOM) and UNHCR on a trip to pick up a group of about five hundred people who were ready to return to East Timor. I was told that some may have been pro-Indonesian, pro-autonomy supporters. Some, perhaps, were low-level militia. Most would be women and children, though, coming back on their own while the men waited in camps for reports back on whether or not it was safe to return.

The *Patricia Anne Hutong*, an old Australian survey ship rented out to the IOM, sailed all night from Dili to Kupang, the West Timor port on the opposite end of the island. The ship arrived as dawn broke, with a team of transport specialists, field officers, doctors, and translators.

The sun glared down on the vast parking lot at the heart of the Fatuloli registration center outside of Kupang, where the refugees gathered to officially register for return. Fatuloli is a former exhibition center. It boasted a giant Suharto billboard showing the ousted president smiling coolly, his black *bhaji* hat carefully perched atop his head. In the course of the day, the parking lot filled with dozens of buses and trucks, dumptrucks, and flatbeds stacked precariously high with plastic chairs, mattresses, bicycles, sacks of rice, and batik-covered bundles of clothing. People scrambled off their transports and then watched and shouted out as their goods were tossed off the backs of the trucks.

In the registration center, their names were checked against the list of people pre-registered with SATGAS. They were asked by East Timorese UNHCR officers speaking in Tetum, the national language, if they expected any difficulties upon arrival in East Timor. They were reminded that UNHCR was there to help them, not prosecute them. If they had any fears, if they were former militia who might face retribution back home, they were urged to be up-front. They were told they would be looked out for.

After the registration room, the people moved on to sit momentarily with Dr. Domingos Da Silva, who did a quick oral medical check-up. Once they were cleared for travel by the doctor, they were handed small cups of fresh water and lunches of *nasi goring*, a popular rice dish, wrapped in paper.

As soon as they had run the registration gamut, the refugees milled about the parking lot center, talking and laughing with the family members they would soon leave behind. Later, at the docks, as they boarded the boat, there would be tearful good-byes. In the parking lot, though, the mood was light.

A man played with his toddler son while his wife, who would be going with the child onto the boat, watched quietly. The man was dressed in jeans and a camouflage T-shirt that read "SNIPER—If You Run You'll Only Die Tired." A teenage boy named Hipolito stood away from the crowd. He said he came often to the registration center. He said that in the camp he heard that it is still dangerous to go back to East Timor, that if he were to return after having spent almost two years in West Timor people would suspect that he was with the militia and he would be beaten, perhaps killed. He would like to go back, he said, but he was waiting until it was safe.

A group of men gathered outside of the registration center. They took note of who came out. Young men who had just registered to return shuffled away from the group, heads down. UNHCR officials say that militia frequently show up to keep tabs on who's going back. The men I saw observing the departures sneered when I asked if they spoke English or Portuguese. The Indonesian police insisted all was well. The young men were there as well-wishers, they told me.

IOM officials knew before the ship left Dili that the five hundred refugees they expected might not all show up. Many of the people still maintaining refugee status in West Timor worked with the Indonesians in one way or another. Now, for them, it is a question not only of returning to a land where they may be perceived as collaborators, but also, a matter of money. Many are owed pensions for years of service to Indonesia as policemen, drivers, postal employees, or military personnel. Indonesia, though, is not paying up, and IOM got word that unless the pensions came through, most of the people wouldn't be returning. This turned out to be the case. In total, only 179 people—and their thousands of kilos of belongings—came aboard the *Patricia Anne*.

"In the beginning, when it was more like forty thousand people returning by land and sea each month, the boat was packed," said David John who has been in East Timor with IOM since October 1999. "People ran from their homes, or were forced from their homes, across the border with very little. When the time came and it was safe, people just wanted to get back. These days it's packed with fewer people but with a lot more possessions. At this point they've been away for two years, they've accumulated things. A couple of trips ago, we hauled back an entire restaurant."

The only possessions not allowed on the *Patricia Anne* are cars, cows, and water buffalo. Goats and chicken abound, as do bicycles and furniture, bird cages, and rolls of sheet metal, wicker baskets and plastic tarps, refrigerators and bathtubs, swayback pigs and bony, ragged dogs. Piles of belongings overflowed on the boat's main deck into the cabins and halls below deck. "It's hard to justify running a boat that costs sixty thousand dollars a month to rent and six thousand dollars a day to do these runs, when you've got so few people," said one senior IOM official. "We'd be better off paying for them to return in another manner and concentrating our efforts on other issues."

On August 30, 2001, two years to the date of the last vote, the people again went to the polls. Issues of trade, economics, language, land, law, and governance were all on the table when East Timor held a vote to elect a Constitutional Assembly. Many expected violence, and in the weeks leading up to election day, peacekeeping troops stationed throughout East Timor admitted that they were heightening their patrols, setting up roadblocks, and keeping a close eye on all movement back and forth across the border.

There were rumors that 1999 would be repeated and speculation that everything would again go up in flames. In traditional militia strongholds like Samé, a village in the mountainous western region, one man wore a T-shirt saying "Autonomy Yes," referring to 1999's pro-autonomous movement that advocated allegiance to Indonesia.

But in the end, nobody was killed, nothing was burned, and a Constitutional Assembly was elected and given three months to draw up the Constitution that has become East Timor's blueprint for the future. Representatives of Fretilin, the political party born in the mountains out of rebellion against colonial rule, won fifty-five of the eighty-eight seats in the Assembly, the most for any party. Even more significantly, in the weeks before the election, Fretilin was able to campaign openly and capitalize on the fact that its military arm, Falantil, had waged a successful fight first against the Portuguese, then against the Indonesians. Parades of trucks, cars, buses, and dump trucks, filled with Fretilin supporters flying flags and chanting, passed through town after town, and Xanana Gusmão—currently president of East Timor and a man who, as a result of being held as a political prisoner in a Jakarta jail for nine years, is regarded by East Timorese as their Nelson Mandela—even came out of retirement.

Today, East Timor's troubled past is, however, far from being a distant memory. The greatest challenge facing Gusmão and the country is figuring out how to deal with those who have committed crimes—often heinous ones—against their neighbors. It is an issue on which the UN's mission in East Timor will inevitably be judged, and, in the summer of 2001, things were not going well.

At the village level, in local councils, conditions for return and punishment are meted out for people who did not commit crimes against humanity but who did support, in some way, the destruction wreaked by the militia. East Timor's Truth and Reconciliation Commission, a controversial but popular initiative, has attempted to merge international concepts of justice with local traditions and punitive practices, but it is reserved for smaller crimes, putting the power into the hands of the community, and often into the hands of the very people who were left without homes or family.

The cases most often decided are those of low-level militia, frequently men forced to join the militia under threat, who helped to burn and ransack towns once communities had fled. The punishment, for example, for one man who burned down a house was to rebuild that family's home plus help to build a school in town.

There are, of course, instances in which a man returns, is taken to meet with the village council, sent home, and later that day beaten. Retribution, whether through violence, shunning, or seizing land and livestock, is—despite the UN's best efforts—common. There have been few cases, though, of people who returned and then faced danger so great that they wanted to leave. Most of the men, said one UN source, know they are in for a beating when they return and accept it.

Still, the accused—the ones looking for reconciliation in the communities that they in some way helped destroy—have to answer to the thousands of women and children who have been widowed and orphaned. "They can go ahead and negotiate the return of the men who stood and watched as others killed my husband and burned my house," said Rosarinha Munis. "If they ask me, I say just let me put my hands on them. I lost two children and my husband. I understand the process of reconciliation. I don't know if I can accept it. I ask though that I be given the chance to hit these men. I want to hit them with my own hands. To feel that, I want to use my hands."

Whereas in villages throughout the land the truth commission is helping to mete out ad hoc punishments, a much bigger issue of justice is stalled in Dili and Jakarta, where the UN plays a much bigger role. There, justice for the hundreds of people charged with crimes against humanity is coming about at a much slower pace, if at all, and raising enormous doubts among those who believe true independence can only be realized when the men who organized and led the killings in 1999 are punished.

"On September 8, at night, after they killed my husband," said Filomena Fereira da Silva, "after they killed many and hauled the bodies away, Ernesto Metan [a known militia member] came in and said, 'Now the law is in Indonesia, not East Timor. Now go report to your beloved Xanana, report to your UN, report to Bishop Belo. Call your Xanana. Tell him he can be president for dirt and stones. That is all that will be left in East Timor.' I want them to know they were wrong. The law is here. They will have to answer for what they did. There must be justice. After what happened in 1999, there cannot be independence without justice."

"Serious crimes" have been defined by the UN as those crimes against humanity committed between January 1999 and October 25, 1999. The Serious Crimes Unit of the Office of the Prosecutor General was established to oversee the investigation and prosecution of these crimes. The unit has come under fire for being severely understaffed and for not providing the sort of training, facilities, and technical expertise that ensures that the cases that do make it to trial are fair and need not be retried at a later date.

A scathing Amnesty International report called "East Timor: Justice Past, Present and Future" was issued in August 2001. The report said that "the necessary measures have not been taken with the result that law and order is now barely being maintained, justice is not being administered effectively and the human rights of the East Timorese people cannot be guaranteed. The judicial system is only partially established and what does exist is fragile. Members of the fledgling judiciary lack the necessary training and support and are vulnerable to political pressure, including through threats and intimidation. . . . In addition, the laws that are being applied in East Timor are not always consistent with international human rights standards."

"We've had to learn to deal with what we have here," said Oyvind Olsen, chief of the Special Crimes Investigation Unit, who formerly worked for the International Tribunal in Rwanda. "We planned on having forty investigators. We have sixteen. In Rwanda and Yugoslavia, they have fifty people investigating each crime. It takes years to get to trial. Our critics say we are taking too much time, but we cannot be directed by public demand. I am happy with the way things are going in that they are going."

Others say that there must be more than a laissez-faire approach to justice if UNTAET is to consider its mission here a success. "The Special Crimes Unit isn't looking at that period in 1999 for what it was—a systematic massacre," said Joaquim Fonseca of Yayasan Hak, the East Timorese Foundation for Law Human Rights and Justice. "In the courtroom, there are very few questions asked about who planned, who orchestrated. At this rate and with this mediocrity, it is impossible to reach the high level officials. The people heading the unit worked in Rwanda and Yugoslavia, but they don't understand East Timor. They don't understand that we're a small country. Everyone knew who did what. I don't think that community knowledge is being used."

In Maliana, Filomena Feirera da Silva calmly lists the names of the men who came to her house, the men who threatened her husband in prison, the men who watched as he was killed, the men and women who burned the houses around Maliana. She says she has given all this information to the investigators. She says nothing has come of it. She says she doesn't have faith that justice will come from the current proceedings. There must be justice, she says, but this is not it.

Many are waiting for Indonesia to make good on its promise to prosecute the perpetrators of crimes against humanity living and working there. But to date it has done nothing. Reports from journalists and UNHCR officials working around the ports of West Timor and in Jakarta are that men with indictments against them in East Timor's Serious Crimes Court walk about freely. Eurrico Guterres, the man who ran the militia in East Timor, is rumored to be living well in Jakarta.

"We are having a difficult time in Indonesia," Chalief Akbar, Head of Political Affairs for the Indonesian Mission in East Timor, has acknowledged. "In Indonesia, human rights [violations] are not punishable under our Constitution. We have to develop the legal framework and train judges to prosecute what have been deemed 'crimes against humanity.' It could take years."

A senior UN official, willing to speak only on condition of anonymity, said he has very little faith that Indonesia will follow through on its promise to bring the Indonesian and East Timorese accused to trial. "Indonesia backed the militia, supplied them with guns, trained them, prepared a systematic strategy for leaving East Timor burned to the ground," he said. "This goes right up to the top." Indonesia, he pointed out, "is not going to commit hari-kari here. The only other way to get these criminals is for the United Nations Security Council to call for an International Tribunal. As with Russia's Chechnya and China's Tibet, I'm skeptical."

I saw even greater reason for skepticism just off a dirty, Dili road, where East Timor's first trial for crimes against humanity was taking place. Everyone who entered the courtroom did so as I did, in a whirl of dust that settled thickly on the chairs and desks. Only a handful of spectators even bothered coming to the trial, although it was open to the public.

Few sensations are as unsettling as sitting inches behind a murderer. Joni Marques, the leader of a Los Palos–based militia group called Team Alfa, had already confessed his guilt to charges of crimes against humanity. I studied his back as he listened to a witness described the moments before the witness's friend was killed. Marques and the nine men sitting with him, the other men from Team Alfa, were being tried together for the crimes they committed between April 21 and September 27, 1999. The crimes included murder and torture as crimes against humanity and the forced deportation and persecution of population.

They were charged with killing thirteen people, including nine clergy who were traveling outside of Los Palos. A nun who climbed out of the bus after it had been shot up with twenty-one bullets was killed as she knelt in prayer.

The ten men faced the three judges. They wore dirty jeans and T-shirts and sat on black, metal-framed, vinyl-backed chairs. The court was not air-conditioned, and in the afternoons, the fans did little to break the dry, tropical heat. The trial was conducted in English. The judges—an East Timorese, a Brazilian, and a Burundian—spoke in English to the witnesses and defendants, then waited as their questions were translated into Tetum. Responses were given, then translated back into English. The public defenders spoke a combination of English, Portuguese, Tetum, and Bahasa Indonesia. Everyone in the courtroom wore earphones for simultaneous translation. Everyone, that is, except the defendants, who by and large left the earphones dangling around their necks and nudged one another smiling, gesturing back and forth, or simply staring out the windows.

The justice that everyone calls for throughout East Timor was being played out, and it was impossible to feel good about it. A public defender stood and made a speech about Falantil's cold-blooded killers and his client's need to protect himself. The judge reminded the public defender that to rise and raise an objection required him to object to something. He sat down. His client, with the earphones off, missed the entire exchange.

On the day the trial was originally set to end, the court was hearing the testimony of only the third of the scheduled seventy-three witnesses. Virtually every morning began with lawyers having to hammer out exactly how the evidence and testimony introduced was to be handled. It was clear that few, if any, of the people on the witness stand or in the defendants' chairs had ever been in a courtroom before. Witnesses and defendants were unsure where to stand, whom to address, and what "testimony" meant. For the first witness called by the prosecution to testify about the killing of Evaristo Lopes, the translation was such that more often than not, the witness had to ask for the question to be repeated. Often, by the time the answer was given, it was clear that the question or the answer, or both, had been mistranslated.

"Things are going much slower than planned, and to be honest, I think that a lot of the problems we're seeing here are teething problems," said Stuart Alford, the prosecutor. "In terms of a legal system, the skeleton is there but the meat isn't. Because this is the first big trial, we're laying the precedents to be used later. But every little step is a battle, and frankly we're using the only Serious Crimes Court in the country to discuss how evidence will be handled once admitted. This is stuff traditionally laid out well before. We discussed postponing the trial, but the defendants had already been sitting in custody for two years."

In the afternoon session I attended at the Serious Crimes Court, Moses Lopes testified against Joni Marques and several other members of Team Alfa for the murder of Evaristo Lopes, his close friend, on April 21, 1999. Moses was in the car when Team Alfa stopped it and ordered him, Evaristo, and two other friends out. He listened as Team Alfa decided whom to target. Moses said they went after Evaristo because of his long hair, a style associated with Fretilin supporters. He watched for a few minutes as the men beat Evaristo with an iron bar. It was dark, and he could not always see who was wielding the bar. He was told that if he tried to help, he would be killed. He felt powerless and afraid. He said one man told the members of Team Alfa to take Evaristo up to the compound for a "haircut."

Evaristo Lopes's body was found soon after in a paddy field. His throat had been cut, his hands and legs tied, his body beaten. His hair was unevenly cut.

For Moses, testifying was exhausting. He did not, he told the judges, realize he would have to stand all day. Later, as the session was about to end, he asked if he could be heard again. He wanted the judges to know that he was being threatened back in Los Palos. There he was seen as a traitor. He wanted to join the local police force, but the families of the defendants were making that hard for him. He asked the judges if they could write a letter on his behalf. As the session ended, the prosecutor promised to look into his allegations.

It was not an answer that sounded very convincing to me, and I could not help thinking how slight the rewards for his testimony against men accused of brutal murders had been. Moses said he was worried about going home, he was worried East Timor might be forgotten, and that somehow the fighting would come again. He said he was scared. Leaving the back road court house that day, leaving behind the frustrated judges, ambivalent defendants, and tentative witnesses, it seemed to me that justice, if it comes at all, will come fitfully to the people of East Timor.

# PART FIVE

# No Longer Bystanders

# 13

# Intervention and State Failure

MICHAEL IGNATIEFF

A s we begin a new century, what is most striking about the human rights challenges we face is how different they are from those of the cold war era. Whereas the abuses of the cold war period came from strong tyrannical states, the ones in the post–cold war world chiefly originate in weak or collapsing states. We have not come to terms with this changed situation. Our current debate about humanitarian intervention continues to construe intervening as an act of conscience, when in fact, since the 1990s began, intervening has also become an urgent state interest: to rebuild failed states so that they cease to be national security threats.

To understand how the human rights situation has changed, we need to go back to the end of the Second World War. From 1945 until the end of the cold war, human rights remained subordinate to state sovereignty within the framework of the United Nations Charter. Articles 2.1 and 2.7 of the charter define sovereignty in terms of inviolability and non-interference. The prohibition on internal interference is peremptory, while the language that urges states to promote human rights is permissive. States are encouraged to promote human rights, not commanded to do so.

The UN Charter's bias against intervention reflects the chapter of European history the drafting powers believed they had been lucky to escape. Even in death and defeat, Adolf Hitler remained the ghost at the drafters' feast. Yet it was Hitler the warmonger, not Hitler the architect of European extermination, who preoccupied the drafters. For them, aggressive war across national frontiers was a more salient risk than the extermination of peoples within states. This fact illuminates the degree to which both the Holocaust and the Red Terror existed in suspended animation during the cold war. They were not the all-defining crimes they were to become in the modern moral imagination of the 1970s.

The central problem of the cold war world, from the Western point of view, was to consolidate state order and guarantee that these new states remained in the Western camp. Accordingly, the human rights performance of states mattered much less to the West than their allegiance to the Western camp. Human rights was also given a subordinate place in the UN system. UN bodies, such as the Human Rights Commission, for example, had no power to investigate member states, and after the successful passage of the Universal Declaration of the Rights of Man in 1948, no formal human rights conventions were ratified until the 1970s.

The marginal place of human rights in the institutional order of the cold war also related to the ambiguous light that human rights standards cast on the behavior of superpowers. Universal commitments, even if only rhetorical, can be embarrassing. The Americans had Jim Crow to hide. The Russians' dirty secret was the Gulag. When the Americans and the Russians used the universalistic creed to lecture developing nations, they discovered how easily their own language could be turned against them. Newly emerging nations in Africa and Asia proved adept at using the vocabulary of self-determination to ward off or ignore external scrutiny of their domestic rights records.

What broke this conspiracy of state silence was the emergence of mass-based human rights groups, beginning with Amnesty International in 1961. These organizations transformed human rights into the most powerful critique of the non-interference rule in postwar state relations.

The simultaneous historical rediscovery of the Red Terror and the Holocaust in the 1970s proved important here. The rediscovered memory of these terrible events focused the moral imagination of activists, intellectuals, and foreign policy specialists on sovereignty as an instrument and an alibi for extermination.

Another factor in the renaissance of human rights in the 1970s was the weakening of the Soviet empire. Until 1968, it was able to counter demands for freedom by sending in the tanks. By the mid–1970s, it became dependent for its survival on Western trade and investment. The Helsinki Final Act of 1975, adopted at the Conference on Security and Co-operation in Europe, institutionalized the process by which foreign assistance to an ailing empire was made conditional on human rights concessions. Helsinki marked the moment in which the rulers of the Soviet empire conceded that there were not two human rights languages—one socialist, one capitalist—but one to which all nations, at least in theory, were obliged to conform.

By conceding the right of their own citizens to form human rights organizations—a feature of the Helsinki Act—the Soviets set in train the process that led first to Charter 77 in Prague, Solidarity in Poland, and Memorial in the Soviet Union. The gathering wave of underground civic activism sapped the self-confidence of the Gorbachev-era elite and slowly but surely undermined the empire from within. Andrei Sakharov, Lech Walesa, and Vaclav Havel drew legitimacy away from the regime to the human rights movement, and in doing so, dug the grave of the empire.

With the collapse of the Soviet Union in 1991, human rights ceased to be subordinate to sovereignty. The new nations that emerged after the dissolution of the Soviet empire wrote rights guarantees into their new constitutions and accepted human rights oversight from Western governments as the price of rejoining Europe and the West. As the cold war order disintegrated, human rights became the condition of entry to the emerging security architecture of NATO and the European Union. Turkey, for example, discovered that it could not hope to gain entry to the EU unless it abolished the death penalty. Peace, combined with the emergence of the EU, diluted the exercise of Westphalian sovereignty in the continent that had been its home. With peace at home, European powers found a new overseas role for themselves promoting human rights abroad. Western aid agencies, international banks, and UN organizations increasingly "mainstreamed" human rights in their aid and lending packages for developing nations. These nations, some of which had depended entirely on Soviet support, now felt obliged to comply.

As this summary suggests, the ascendancy of human rights in the post–cold war world has complex causes. Those who see its rise as the simple story of progress, of an idea whose time finally came, are missing the key political dimensions: the weakness and collapse of the Soviet Union, the emerging salience of governance—and therefore of human rights—as development issues in the states of Africa and Asia, and finally, the pacification of Europe and its search for a new legitimizing ideology. A final feature was the coming to power of the sixties generation, nurtured in anti–Vietnam War politics, disillusioned with socialism and Marxism, awakening to the moral reality of the Holocaust and the Red Terror, and discovering in human rights a redemptive cause.

Yet, for all this change, states do not accept that their legitimacy—internal or external—is conditional on their human rights performance. The greatest champion of human rights overseas, the United States, is simultaneously an uncompromising defender of a unilateralist definition of its own sovereignty. American leaders of all political stripes regard foreign criticism of its domestic human rights norms—the persistence of capital punishment, for example—as either irrelevant or impudent.

At this point, we are in a halfway house, no longer in the world of 1945, where sovereignty was clearly privileged over human rights, and yet nowhere near the world desired by human rights activists, in which sovereignty is conditional on being good international citizens. We are somewhere in between, negotiating the conflicts between state sovereignty and international human rights as they arise, case by case.

For all their new prestige and power, human rights concerns have not essentially changed the international law governing recognition between states. In the customary practice that governs recognition of new regimes, legitimacy continues to be defined by whether a particular regime has effective control over a given territory. All states have an interest in ensuring that territories remain under the effective control of a government, regardless of its human rights record. Indeed, some states perceive that the promotion of democracy and human rights, especially in fragile, newly emerging states with complex mixtures of minorities and religions, may actually promote secession, fragmenting the international state system still further. This preference for order has been reinforced by the disintegration of multi-ethnic states like the former Yugoslavia. When democracy came to the Balkans, it came in the form of demands for self-determination on ethnic lines, with catastrophic consequences for the state order left behind by Marshal Tito. Wherever democracy means self-determination for the ethnic majority, state formation all too often means "ethnic cleansing" and massacre for the minority.

Mention of Yugoslavia brings into focus the chief reason why the conflict between sovereignty and human rights came into the open in the 1990s: the process of state fragmentation convulsed the international system. Triumphant apologists for globalization are usually also prophets of an age beyond sovereignty. These fantasies can be indulged in Europe or in the North American free trade area, but they ring especially hollow in Africa and Asia. There effective sovereignty—defined as a monopoly over the means of violence and as the capacity to deliver basic needs to a population—is the precondition for any kind of successful entry into the world economy. It is also the precondition for any kind of human rights observance.

Calling the international order of the post–cold-war era a "system" obscures the reality that it has broken down altogether in the poorer parts of the world. States that are fighting losing battles against insurgents, states where civil wars have become endemic, or where state authority has broken down altogether, radiate instability around them. Failing states are more than problems for themselves. They create what Myron Weiner memorably called "bad neighborhoods." These bad neighborhoods include

Latin America: Colombia, Ecuador, and Peru
South Balkans: Macedonia, Montenegro, and Kosovo
South Caucasus: Georgia, Ossetia, Azerbaijan, Nagorno, and Karabakh
West Africa: Liberia and Sierra Leone

Central Africa: Congo
Southern Africa: Angola
East Africa: Sudan and Somalia
South Asia: Sri Lanka
Central Asia: Pakistan, Afghanistan, Uzbekistan, and Tajikistan

Some of these—Colombia and Sri Lanka—are capable states that are fighting a losing battle against insurgents and terror. Others—Congo, Angola, and Sudan—are resource-rich states whose elites are incapable or unwilling to use resource revenue to develop their countries and end civil wars. Still others—Afghanistan, Somalia, and Sierra Leone—are weak states, with poor resource endowments, and have proved incapable of providing effective governance at all. What all of these states have in common, though, is an inability to maintain a monopoly of the internal means of violence. Violence is eating away these societies from within. It would be impossible to assemble all the reasons why this convulsion is underway, but it represents a widening tear in the system of state order, analogous to the tear in the global ozone layer. Historically, this episode of state fragmentation recalls at least four previous periods:

- 1919: The dismantling of the European empires after Versailles
- 1945: The creation of the so-called people's democracies in Eastern Europe
- 1947–1960: The decolonization of Africa and Asia
- 1989–1991: The independence of former Soviet satellites

In these four periods, the dominant process was state formation and the dismantling of defeated empires. In the fifth and current wave, processes of disintegration predominate. In part, these processes represent an attempt to correct the failure of the previous episodes of state formation. Yugoslavia, for example, figures in three of these four previous episodes of state formation. It was a Versailles state after 1919. It re-emerged as a people's democracy after 1945. In the wake of 1991, it was a satellite of the Soviet system whose component parts set out to create a nation on the basis of popular sovereignty. Each time, these efforts failed. Once democracy returned, each dominant ethnic majority set itself the task of abolishing both the Versailles and the Titoist versions of the federal state. Doing so led them to expel, terrorize, and massacre their minorities. This process is still not completed.

Many of the disintegrative state conflicts in Africa—Congo and Angola, for example—represent the continuing struggle of competing tribal and regional groups to consolidate state authority on the ruins of colonial regimes. Scholars remain divided as to whether state failure is to be blamed on the colonial legacy or on what successor regimes did with that legacy. The Portuguese left behind a weak colonial inheritance, but the Angolan civil war has destroyed what was left of it. In Congo, Belgium left behind little that independent regimes could build upon. In Sierra Leone, however, it could be argued that the British left a decent colonial inheritance, which was then squandered by successor elites. What these examples have in common is state failure, although the extent of the failure differs in each case. Sometimes the state is struggling; sometimes disintegrating; in a few cases—Somalia, for instance—it has collapsed altogether. Sometimes the cause is the colonial legacy; sometimes it is maladministration by an indigenous elite; sometimes, failure is a legacy first of interference by outside powers, and then abandonment. Afghanistan has been devastated both by interference—first by the Soviets, then by the Americans—and then by neglect—the American withdrawal and strategic disinterest after the defeat of the Soviets. Finally, and most important, many failed or failing states are poor and have suffered from the steadily more adverse terms of trade in a globalized economy. An adverse situation is then made worse by corruption, bad planning choices, or ideological dogma. As the developed world has accelerated into the fourth industrial revolution of computers and information technology, sub-Saharan Africa, for example, remains stuck at the bottom of the international division of labor as primary producers.

Given the unrelenting pressure of poverty—made worse by mismanagement—it is unsurprising that state institutions begin to break down. As the tax revenue base shrinks, ruling elites lose their capacity to buy off or conciliate marginal regions or minorities. When these minorities pass from disobedience to rebellion, the elites lack the resources to quell revolts. As these revolts spread, the central government loses the monopoly of the means of violence. Where state order disintegrates, basic economic infrastructure also begins to collapse and a new economic order begins to take root. Armed ethnic groups, bandits, and guerilla forces take over, using violence to secure the forced allegiance of the local population and to extract the remaining surplus. As the weakening government struggles to regain control, it engages in more and more egregious attempts to terrorize the population into obedience, and rebel groups use more and more drastic forms of counter-terror to demoralize government forces. This process of fission may then spread beyond the borders of the state itself, as refugee populations flee across the border, and as insurgent groups use frontier zones for their base camps. A collapsing state thus has the capacity to metastasize and to spread its problems through the region. These poor neighborhoods present a cluster of human rights catastrophes: forced population displacement, ethnic or religious massacre, genocide, endemic banditry, enslavement, and forced recruitment of child soldiers. All these proceed from the incapacity of a state to secure and maintain order.

This is a different profile of human rights abuse from the ones in the cold war. These were not caused by weak or collapsing states, but by strong, intolerant, and oppressive ones. To be sure, the problem of tyranny remains: China, North Korea, Iraq, and Libya are strong states, not weak ones, and their human rights abuses fit into a more classical pattern: arrest of activists, detention without trial, extra-judicial murder, torture, and disappearances. The Rwandan genocide could not have occurred without the existence of a strong and effective administrative structure—the burgomaster system—left over from the colonial period. Yet even if some strong states remain a menace to their own people, the worst abuse now occurs not where there is too much state power, but too little. The human rights dilemmas of the twenty-first century derive more from anarchy than tyranny.

If chaos rather than tyranny is the chief cause of human rights abuse, then activists will have to rethink their traditional suspicion of the state and of the exercise of sovereignty. In the Balkans, as well as west, central, and southwestern Africa, the chief prerequisite for the creation of a basic rights regime for ordinary people is the re-creation of a stable national state capable of giving orders and seeing them carried out throughout the territory, a state with a classic Weberian monopoly on the legitimate means of force. Without the basic institutions of a state, no basic human rights protection is possible. As long as populations are menaced by banditry, civil war, guerrilla campaigns, and counter-insurgency by beleaguered governments, they cannot be secure. In such conditions, international human rights and humanitarian organizations can do no more than bind up the wounded and protect the most vulnerable. These Hobbesian situations teach the message of the Leviathan itself: that consolidated state power is the very condition for any regime of rights whatever. In this sense, state sovereignty, instead of being the enemy of human rights, has to be seen as their basic precondition. Protecting human rights in zones where state order is embattled or had collapsed has to mean consolidating or re-creating a legitimate state. Nation building thus becomes, for the first time since the Allied occupation of Germany and Japan, a critical instrument for the creation of rights regimes. In Japan and Germany, however, total defeat and unconditional surrender gave the Allies the authority to create new democratic institutions from scratch, while the conditions for modern nation building in states recovering from civil war are much less auspicious.

If state fragmentation and collapse are the chief sources of human rights abuse, the debate over humanitarian intervention needs to be rethought. This debate conceives the challenge of intervention as a response to a series of essentially unrelated moral crises, in which differing populations of civilians in desperate need appeal to us for rescue. But the crises themselves are not unrelated, and they are not just humanitarian or moral in their claim on our attention. A crisis of order in a single state risks creating "bad neighborhoods" in a whole region. Pakistan, for example, has been "Talibanized" by nearby Afghanistan. These bad neighborhoods in turn present direct threats to the national interest of states. For bad neighborhoods harbor terrorists, produce drugs, and generate destabilizing refugee flows. Afghanistan is the best example of a failing state that was perceived as a distant humanitarian crisis, when it ought to have been seen as a clear and present national security threat.

As long as the chief motive for intervention is conscience alone, we can only expect sporadic action from a few responsible actors. Once it is realized that we are looking at a crisis in the international order, a tear in the ozone layer of global governance, states that would otherwise remain uninvolved might understand that their long-term interest in stability and order compel them to commit resources to the problem. Putting national interest criteria into the debate also helps with the problem of triage. There are many failed and failing states. The ones that will actually receive sustained international attention will be those that directly threaten the national interest and national security of powerful states.

The debate about humanitarian intervention strikes many people from poorer countries as a lurid exercise in emotional self-gratification— an attempt to demonstrate the power of conscience when the real tasks that rich Western nations need to address are much harder: helping states regain a monopoly over the means of violence, increasing the competence of local institutions, conciliating ethnic conflict, and building up a functioning economy.

The way the academy divides up the debate also enfeebles it. The international lawyers who dominate the humanitarian intervention debate spend more time thinking about intervention criteria than how to rebuild failed states once intervention has occurred. The development strategists who do know something about how to set off self-sustaining paths to growth and institutional competence have no place in the debate. The human rights activists who document the increasingly catastrophic rights abuses in failing states often have no strategy other than denunciation and a perfectionist reluctance to use force to end these abuses. All of these divisions further fragment our capacity to craft strategies of intervention that actually succeed.

Another problem is the way humanitarian intervention is actually done. Most strategies of humanitarian rescue, particularly UN peacekeeping and conflict mediation, are premised on staying neutral in zones of conflict. In reality, as Bosnia cruelly showed, neutrality can become discreditable as well as counterproductive. Once the decision is taken to introduce humanitarian aid into a war zone, backed up with peacekeepers to aid in its delivery, the aid itself becomes a focus of combat, and its provision—even to unarmed combatants—becomes a way not to damp down the fighting but to keep it going. Neutral humanitarian assistance can have the perverse effect of sustaining the fighting it seeks to reduce.

All victims have some claim to mercy, assistance, and aid from those bystanders who can provide it. But if that is all that bystanders do, they may help to keep civil wars going, by sustaining the capacity of a civilian population to absorb still more punishment. Moreover, when neutralist mediators impose a cease-fire in an ongoing civil war, they invariably draw the line in such a way as to reward the side that has waged the conflict with the most aggression and the most success. That is why, when peacekeepers are deployed to enforce the cease-fire, they are usually viewed by the party that has lost most in the conflict as colluders in aggression. Such cease-fires rarely hold.

Neutral humanitarianism, when viewed more cynically, is a kind of hedged bet, in which intervening parties salve their consciences while avoiding the difficult political commitments that might actually stop civil war. The key dilemma in civil wars is which side to back. Unless one side is helped to win, and win quickly, nothing serious can be done to reduce the violence. The basic choice is whether external intervention should be aimed at preserving the existing state or at helping a self-determination claim succeed. In Bosnia, Western interveners thought they were intervening to keep warring parties apart. They failed to understand that a recognized member of the UN—Bosnia Herzegovina—was being torn apart by a self-determination claim, aided and abetted by outside powers, chiefly Serbia, but also Croatia. The crisis was seen as an internal affair, when in fact its chief determinants were illicit foreign subversion: the arming and training of insurgents and the provision of safe bases of operation in both Serbia and Croatia. The war within Bosnia was brought to an end only when foreign intervention was directed not at the internal combatants but at the chief external instigator, Serbia. It was only when outside interveners took sides and bombed Serbian installations, forcing the Serb government to exert pressure on its internal proxies, that the civil war stopped. In other words, the international community finally intervened to sustain the unity of a state and to *defeat* a self-determination claim by the Bosnian Serbs.

The case of Afghanistan illustrates the dilemmas of taking sides. Prior to September 11, the dilemma was this: if Western powers recognized the Taliban, they would help consolidate Taliban rule over the entire territory and thus help bring an end to a devastating civil war. Order would prevail, but it would be the despotism of rural Islam at its most obscurantist. In such a situation, Afghan women would pay the price of a Western preference for order over justice. If, on the other hand, Western support continued to reach the Taliban's opponents, the civil war would continue, and Afghanistan would continue to bleed to death.

Until September 11, Western powers placed a two-way bet, supporting the Northern Alliance just enough to keep it in business, while refusing to normalize relations with the Taliban. The United States allowed the Pakistani secret service to funnel support to the Taliban, while at the same time American officials denounced the regime for its treatment of women and the destruction of religious monuments. This double game has now come apart, and in the wake of September 11, it is apparent that it was bound to. Having washed its hands of Afghanistan after the Soviet departure, the United States spent the 1990s conceiving of Afghanistan as a humanitarian or human rights disaster zone, failing to notice that it was rapidly becoming a national security nightmare, a training ground for terror. Nothing enfeebled American policy more in the 1990s than the refusal to notice that untended human rights and humanitarian crises have a way of becoming national security threats. Afghanistan is the most dramatic example of this tendency. Now, finally, the United States and its allies will take sides, but once they defeat the Taliban, the same problem they have avoided—namely how to rebuild a nation state there—will recur.

Taking sides is not the only dilemma. There is also the problem of triage. Given the fact that resources of willpower, diplomatic skill, and economic aid are always finite, there have to be criteria to determine which conflicts to take on and which ones to ignore. Intervention occurs, in general, where states are too weak, too friendless, to resist. The Chinese occupation of Tibet goes unsanctioned. The Russians reduce Grozny to rubble with impunity. Yet the Serbs are bombed for seventy-eight days. These inconsistencies mean that intervention in the domestic affairs of states will never rest on unassailable grounds. Yet the fact that we cannot intervene everywhere is not a justification for not intervening where we can.

Nor is the experience of intervention as nation building entirely negative. The UN Mission in Cambodia managed to oversee peaceful elections and the creation of democratic rule in a country ravaged by genocide. NATO, the UN, and the EU have joined forces to put Bosnia into a transitional trusteeship. It is a state in which internal peace and security are guaranteed by foreign troops. Resettling of refugees and rebuilding are both funded from the outside. The process is costly, but violence has not returned, and peace in Bosnia has hastened democratic transitions in Croatia and Serbia next door. Further south in Kosovo, another trusteeship experiment is underway. A former province of a state is being prepared for substantial autonomy and self-government. The UN administration has written the constitutional rules for a gradual handover of power to elected local elites, and there is even a chance that eventually the Serb minority will take their places at the table. Finally, in East Timor, a transitional UN administration is handing a new country over to its elected leaders. All of these experiences are fraught with difficulty, but all indicate that an inchoate practice of state building, under UN auspices, is emerging. The next obvious candidate for treatment is Afghanistan.

An intervention strategy that takes sides, that uses force, and that sticks around to rebuild is very different from one premised on neutrality, casualty-avoidance, and exit strategies. It is also based on different premises. These premises have been outlined recently in "The Responsibility to Protect," a report sponsored by the Canadian government and delivered to the UN secretary-general in December 2001. Building on ideas of good citizenship and human security, the commission has argued that all states have a responsibility to protect their citizens. In certain limited cases, where states are unwilling or unable to do that, and where the resulting human rights situation is catastrophic, other states have a responsibility to step in and provide the protection instead. The international responsibility to protect is a residual obligation that comes into play only when a domestic state proves incapable or unwilling to act and where the resulting situation is genuinely catastrophic.

The idea of a responsibility to protect also implies a responsibility to prevent and a responsibility to follow through. Action, especially of a coercive kind, lacks legitimacy unless every effort has been made to avert the catastrophe; once action is taken, its legitimacy depends on staying the course until the situation is on the mend. Thus the responsibility to protect is intended to provide a rationale for constructive engagement by rich countries through an intervention continuum that begins with prevention and ends with sustained follow-up.

All of these exercises in nation building represent attempts to invent, for a postimperial, postcolonial era, a form of temporary rule that reproduces the best effects of empire (inward investment, pacification, and impartial administration), without reproducing the worst features (corruption, repression, confiscation of local capacity). Unlike the empires of the past, these UN administrations are designed to serve and enhance the ideal of self-determination rather than suppress it.

Taking responsibility without confiscating it is the balance international administrators have to strike. The trick in nation building is to force responsibility—for security, for co-existence—back to local elites. This is not easy. The spectacle of disgruntled locals, sitting in cafes, watching earnest young internationals speeding around to important meetings in Toyota Land Cruisers has been repeated in every nation-building experiment of the 1990s. The most successful transitional administrations are ones that try to do themselves out of a job. This is not always possible. The legacy of bitterness in places like Kosovo and Bosnia is so intense that international administration has to remain in place, simply in order to protect minorities from vengeance by the victorious yet previously victimized majority. Controlling the culture of vengeance usually takes longer than the time frame dictated by most modern exit strategies. Once Western forces intervene they are usually committed to rebuild or at least patrol post-conflict societies for a long period of time. It takes time to create responsible political dialogue in shattered communities, still longer to create shared institutions of police and justice, and longest of all to create the molecular social trust between warring communities necessary for economic development and community co-existence. The initiative for these developments has to come from the local people. Internationals can provide impartial administration, some inward investment, and some basic security protection, but the work has to be done by the political elites who inherit the intervention. Nation building takes time, and it is not an exercise in social work. Its ultimate purpose is to create the state order that is the precondition for any defensible system of human rights and to create the stability that turns bad neighborhoods into good ones.

This survey of what has happened to the interaction between sovereignty and human rights since 1945, and how the theory and practice of humanitarian intervention has developed in response to the epidemic of state failure since the end of the cold war, necessarily ends with skeptical conclusions. If we survey the interventions of the recent past, the story is decidedly mixed. In Bosnia, intervention prevented the full realization of Serbian war aims, but it did not prevent the deaths of more than three hundred thousand people and the expulsion of nearly a million from their homes. In Kosovo, intervention put a stop to a civil war that, had intervention not occurred, might still be claiming lives. In East Timor, intervention delivered self-determination to the people, but not before more than a thousand people were massacred for seeking their rights. In Iraq, Kurds remain under the protection of Allied air power, but they do not have the resources to become genuinely self-governing. In places like Cambodia and Haiti, democracy has been restored, but power remains in the hands of corrupt elites. In other places, such as Angola, where the UN intervened with high hopes of moving the society out of a civil war, it has now withdrawn altogether. In still other places, ranging from Chechnya to Tibet, no intervention took place, and the failure showed that universal principles still lack consistent enforcement. Worst of all, eight hundred thousand dead Rwandans remain testimony to our incapacity—even when no insurmountable obstacle exists, either in state sovereignty or Security Council veto—to do the right thing. The most that can be said about the emerging practice of intervention is that at its best it prevents the worst from happening; at its worst, it compromises and betrays the very values it purports to defend.

Yet through it all, an inchoate practice of nation building—in Kosovo, Bosnia, East Timor, and Cambodia—is showing that state order can be successfully rebuilt if wealthy and powerful states are prepared to invest the time and money. More generally, this survey seems to demonstrate something important about legitimacy itself. Intervening to defend human rights will never have anything more than conditional legitimacy, even when the cause is just and the authority right. We all aspire to perfect legitimacy. We want to live in a world in which we do the right thing, and know we are doing the right thing, and believe that the whole world will accept that we have done the right thing. There is no such possibility. Indeed, it is a dangerous utopia. Moral perfectionism is always the enemy of the possible and the practical. Doing the right thing appears to require the tenacity to do it when half the world thinks you are wrong.

# 14

# Raising the Cost of Genocide

SAMANTHA POWER

Raphael Lemkin, a Polish jurist who lost forty-nine members of his family in the Holocaust, invented the word "genocide" in 1944 because he believed that, in the aftermath of the Turkish "race murder" of the Armenians and Hitler's attempt to exterminate the Jews, the world's "civilized" powers needed to band together to outlaw crimes that were said to "shock the conscience." Prior to Lemkin's coinage, the systematic targeting of national, ethnic, or religious groups was known as "barbarity," a word that Lemkin believed failed to convey the unique horror of the crime. "Genocide," he hoped, would send shudders down the spines of those who heard it and oblige them to prevent, punish, and even suppress the carnage.

An amateur historian of mass slaughter from medieval times to the twentieth century, Lemkin knew that genocide would continue to occur with "biological regularity." Moreover, he knew from reviewing the recent past that if it were left to political leaders to decide how to respond, they would inevitably privilege their short-term interests over both the moral imperative of stopping genocide and the long-term consequences of ignoring it.

In 1948, largely on Lemkin's prodding, the UN General Assembly unanimously passed the United Nations' first-ever human rights treaty, the Genocide Convention, which required signatories "to undertake to prevent and punish" genocide. The Convention's language was vague on precisely how the UN member states would meet their obligations, making no mention of military intervention and trusting that domestic prosecution of future "genocidists" would deter massacres. Still, the lively debates over ratification that occurred in national legislatures testified to the seriousness with which delegates believed they were committing their country's resources and prestige to banning targeted slaughter.

More than a half century has passed since the Genocide Convention came into effect, and genocide has proceeded virtually unabated. Press coverage of the atrocities has generated outrage, but it has generally been insufficient to prompt outsiders to act. As the 1990s showed, particularly in the reactions of the United States and Europe to carnage in Yugoslavia and Rwanda (the scene, in 1994, of the fastest and most efficient genocidal campaign of the twentieth century), Western countries replicated the pattern established in their earlier responses to the rise and domination of Hitler—long after they had supposedly internalized the "lessons of the Holocaust."

In order to understand this pattern—and by extension, put an end to it—we must first confront the grim record of international responses to genocide in the twentieth century. In 1915, the Turkish minister of the interior, Talaat Pasha, and the other Young Turk leaders set out to solve Turkey's "Armenia problem" by murdering leading Armenian intellectuals and deporting the rest of the population into the desert, where many would be killed by local gendarmerie, by starvation, or by disease. Some one million Armenians died. Germany, which was aligned with Turkey in the war, actively covered up eyewitness reports of atrocities. Russia, Britain, and France, fighting against Turkey and Germany in the war, publicized ghastly massacre reports. The Allies also called upon the United States to use its leverage as a neutral power either to convince Turkey to mend its ways or to press Germany to squeeze its ally. Woodrow Wilson's administration carefully guarded its neutrality, which was strongly favored by the American people, and resisted these calls for diplomatic intervention. With the exception of the U.S. ambassador in Constantinople (now Istanbul) Henry Morgenthau, Sr., and other consular officials in the field, U.S. officials remained mute. A nongovernmental organization known as the Armenia Atrocities Committee drew wide public attention to the murder of fellow Christians and even managed to raise money for humanitarian aid. But the group drew the ire of former president Theodore Roosevelt because it simultaneously denounced the Turkish slaughter and argued against U.S. military intervention with pacifist appeals to "put safety first." In the end, despite heavy coverage of the Turkish horrors in *The New York Times* and elsewhere, Wilson took no measures that would have put U.S. neutrality in doubt. When the United States finally entered the war in 1917, it did not declare war on Turkey and did not join the Allies' postwar efforts to prosecute Turkish war criminals.

The Nazi genocide, which followed two decades later, left six million Jews and five million Poles, Roma, homosexuals, and political opponents dead. Before the Holocaust, neither U.S. nor European diplomats uttered much protest when Germany passed the Nuremberg Laws and began destroying Jewish businesses, synagogues, and homes. Britain and France went to war with Germany after Hitler invaded Poland in September 1939. But President Franklin Roosevelt, like Wilson, kept America neutral. Only after the Japanese attack on Pearl Harbor and after Adolf Hitler declared war on the United States did the United States join the European battle. Together, the Allies did nothing directly aimed at impeding the Nazis' extermination of the Jews. They feared that drawing attention to the murder of Jews or admitting additional refugees would undermine domestic public support for the war. Thus, they downplayed the numerous and graphic atrocity reports smuggled out of Nazi-occupied territory or intercepted by Allied intelligence officials. They took shelter in the utter inconceivability of what was being documented. To those who pressed for sterner measures, Western leaders argued that the Allies would achieve more by focusing their military resources on winning battlefield victories than on disrupting concentration camp traffic.

The Nuremberg and Tokyo trials prosecuted the leading perpetrators of crimes against humanity after the Second World War. This represented a major inroad into state sovereignty. But political leaders saw the real crime of the Axis powers as waging a "crime against peace." The wartime perpetrators were not prosecuted for crimes they committed before the Nazi invasion of Poland. The cardinal sin was not seen to be Hitler's "genocide" (a term hardly used at Nuremberg), but his cross-border aggression, which was a permanent threat to international stability and, by inference, the strategic interests of the world's leading powers.

By contrast, the 1948 Genocide Convention, which Raphael Lemkin helped draft, made political leaders liable for genocide committed during peace or wartime, inside a state or outside it. Still, in 1969, Britain maintained active support for the Nigerian government while it starved and murdered the Ibo people of Biafra. Eyeing potentially vast oil reserves in Iboland, the United States and the other European powers followed the British lead, opposing Biafran secession and insisting that food be delivered through Lagos, even though the Nigerian government openly used starvation as a weapon of war. Two years later, the Western powers did not protest when Pakistan responded to a Bengali autonomy movement in East Pakistan by sending in its army and murdering more than a million people. The Nixon administration backed Pakistan, which was its intermediary with the People's Republic of China, and when the U.S. consul-general in Dhaka dissented, the State Department recalled him from his post. In 1972, when the Tutsi government in Burundi killed some hundred thousand Hutu, the Western powers downplayed the atrocities, treating them as an "internal affair." In all three cases of genocide, the economic and strategic interests of the United States and its European allies caused them to side with the genocidal governments and to invoke "sovereignty" as an excuse for refraining even from complaint.

One might have expected a more spirited response to the Cambodian genocide that occurred from 1975 to 1979 because it was communist radicals (known as the Khmer Rouge, or Red Khmer) who murdered nearly two million of the country's seven million people. But in the aftermath of Vietnam, Western governments paid little heed to bloodshed committed in a part of the world they were anxious to leave behind. President Gerald Ford denounced the Khmer Rouge's massacres for a month, but then went completely silent. President Jimmy Carter, the first U.S. president to champion human rights, made no mention of Pol Pot's slaughter for the first two years of his presidency.

Although the United States had recently renewed diplomatic ties with China, U.S. officials did not ask China to use its influence with the Khmer Rouge. Once the Vietnamese had overthrown the genocidal Khmer Rouge regime in January 1979, the Carter administration, Ronald Reagan's administration, and all of the European powers maintained recognition of Pol Pot's bloody government in order to prevent the Vietnamese-installed government from being seated at the United Nations or leave the UN seat empty. Khmer Rouge representatives occupied Cambodia's seat at the UN for another decade.

In 1987–1988, Iraqi dictator Saddam Hussein set out to wipe out the country's rural Kurdish population. Iraqi soldiers and police bulldozed several thousand villages, rounded up and executed men, women, and children who remained in homes that fell within Hussein's "prohibited zones," and turned chemical weapons against the Kurdish people, sending tens of thousands of civilians fleeing into neighboring Turkey and Iran. Several European states armed Hussein in this period, and the Reagan administration provided more than five hundred million dollars worth of annual agricultural and manufacturing credits. For the first year of the campaign, none of the Western powers condemned the atrocities, even privately. When Senators Claiborne Pell (D–R.I.) and Jesse Helms (R–N.C.) introduced sanctions legislation that would have suspended the generous U.S. credit program, the Reagan administration and the farm lobby helped block the sanctions, even though the human toll of Hussein's gas attacks had earned front-page news coverage. The White House took the position it did because it had decided to maintain friendly relations with its Gulf ally (and enemy of its enemy, Iran) and to advance the interests of U.S. farmers and manufacturers. Most lawmakers on Capitol Hill wholeheartedly supported the U.S. policy of aiding Iraq even after the assault against the Kurds.

With the end of the cold war and the apparent rebirth of the UN (aided by the obsolescence of the superpower veto), one might have expected a greater readiness to prevent genocide. But the pattern of nonintervention established in 1915 proved durable. In 1992, when Bosnian Serbs began systematically deporting and murdering Muslims and Croats in Bosnia, the United States and Europe decided not to intervene with air strikes to protect civilians. They also opted not to lift a UN arms embargo against the Muslims, even though they knew the measure froze in place a gross imbalance between the outgunned Muslims and their Serb foes, who had inherited the arsenal of the Yugoslav National Army. Britain, France, and the Netherlands responded to public pressure by contributing peacekeepers, but the United States refused to risk its troops to deliver food or protect people under siege. European and American political leaders were unanimous in their belief that they had "no dog" in the Balkan fight. When Bill Clinton assumed the Oval Office in 1993, he contested his predecessor's tendency to blame "all sides" for the violence, pointing out that the bulk of the atrocities were being committed by the Serbs. But he did not contest the killing itself. Fearing confrontation with his military, unsure of domestic political support, and determined to avoid "Americanizing" the war and endangering U.S. soldiers, Clinton avoided meaningful action. Some two hundred thousand people were killed in a three-and-a-half-year war.

The genocide in Rwanda, which occurred in 1994, two years after the beginning of the Bosnian War, left some eight hundred thousand Tutsi and moderate Hutu murdered in one hundred days. France armed and diplomatically defended the genocidal government. Belgium, which contributed troops to a UN mission meant to help usher in Hutu-Tutsi power-sharing, yanked its troops out of Rwanda despite its detailed understanding of the pace and scope of the early massacres. The Clinton administration, burned by a UN mission gone bad in Somalia, kept U.S. troops far from the scene of the crime. But, more egregiously, despite knowing that Tutsi were being systematically murdered, the Clinton team demanded that the UN peacekeepers in Rwanda be withdrawn and then resisted U.S. involvement of even the mildest form. Senior U.S. officials wanted to reduce the likelihood of eventually being drawn into Africa, and they sought to show a U.S. Congress skeptical of the UN that they had toughened up their approach to peacekeeping and learned, in the president's words, "to say 'no.'" Just as they had done during the Bosnia war, U.S. and European officials went out of their way to avoid branding the carnage "genocide." This decision was made partly out of fear of triggering their obligations under the Genocide

Convention, but mainly it was done to avoid the moral stigma associated with allowing what Lemkin described as "the ultimate crime."

In sum, the United States and its European allies have wholeheartedly endorsed the pledge of "never again," while tolerating unspeakable atrocities that have been committed in clear view. The personalities, ideologies, and geopolitical constraints have shifted with time, but the major powers have consistently refused to take risks to suppress genocide. Whatever the growth in public awareness of the Holocaust and the triumphalism about the ascent of liberal democratic values, the last decade of the twentieth century was one of the most deadly in the grimmest century on record.

Genocide occurred after the cold war, after the growth of human rights groups, after the explosion of instant communications, and after the erection of the Holocaust Museum in Washington, D.C. Perversely, public awareness of the Holocaust often seemed to set the bar for concern so high that citizens and statesmen were able to tell themselves that contemporary genocides were not measuring up. As the writer David Rieff noted, "never again" might best be defined as, "Never again would Germans kill Jews in Europe in the 1940s." Either by averting their eyes or attending to more pressing conventional strategic and political concerns, Western leaders have repeatedly denounced the Holocaust and allowed genocide.

What is most shocking about the reaction of what Lemkin called the "civilized world" to these twentieth-century genocides is not that the Western powers did not deploy their ground forces to combat the atrocities. What is most shocking is that they did virtually nothing along a continuum of intervention—from the merely rhetorical to the aggressively military—to deter the crime. Because their "vital national interests" were not considered imperiled by mere genocide, military intervention was rarely even considered. But because it was not considered, high-level officials in the United States and Europe often were not involved in debating alternate policy options. Instead of giving genocide the moral attention it warranted and at least vigilantly denouncing the perpetrators, Western governments repeatedly trusted in negotiation, clung to diplomatic niceties and neutrality, and shipped humanitarian aid. Genocide was met again and again with a policy of silence.

And the Western powers did not merely do nothing. On occasion, they directly or indirectly aided those committing genocide. Beginning in 1979 and continuing throughout the 1980s, the United States orchestrated the vote at the UN to favor maintaining recognition of the Khmer Rouge. The Western powers sided with and supplied credits, military intelligence, and arms to Iraq while Hussein was attempting to wipe out Kurds in northern Iraq. The major powers used their clout on the UN Security Council to mandate the withdrawal of UN peacekeepers from Rwanda and to block the deployment of reinforcements. They maintained an arms embargo against the Bosnian Muslims even after it was clear that the arms ban prevented the Muslims from defending themselves. And they made promises to the people of Srebrenica and Rwanda they did not intend to keep.

Nearly a century after the "race murder" of the Armenians and more than a half century after the liberation of the Nazi death camps, the crucial question is, why do decent men and women who firmly believe genocide should "never again" be permitted allow it to happen? The most typical response throughout the twentieth century was, "We didn't know." But this is simply untrue. To be sure, the information emanating from countries victimized by genocide was imperfect. Embassy personnel were withdrawn, intelligence assets on the ground were scarce, editors were typically reluctant to assign their reporters to places where neither Western interests nor Western readers were engaged, and journalists who attempted to report the atrocities were limited in their mobility. As a result, refugee claims were difficult to confirm and body counts notoriously hard to establish. Because genocide is usually veiled beneath the cover of war, when the killing began, some Western officials had genuine difficulty initially distinguishing genocide from conventional conflict.

But although Western governments did not know all there was to know about the nature and scale of the violence, they knew plenty. Well-connected ambassadors and junior intelligence analysts pumped a steady stream of information up the chain to senior decision makers—both early warnings ahead of genocide and vivid documentation during it. Much of the best intelligence appeared in the morning papers. Back in 1915, when communications were far more primitive, *The New York Times* managed 145 stories about the Turkish massacre of Armenians. During the Holocaust, though stories on the extermination of the Jews were not given anywhere near the prominence they warranted, they did regularly appear. In 1994, the *Times* reported just four days after the beginning of the Rwanda genocide that "tens of thousands" of Rwandans had already been murdered. It devoted more column inches to the horrors of Bosnia between 1992 and 1995 than it did to any other single foreign story.

With advances in technology and in the monitoring of human rights groups, Western leaders have begun relying on a second claim: "We didn't fully appreciate." This President Clinton said in an apology delivered in Rwanda four years after the genocide: "We did not fully appreciate the depth and the speed of the unimaginable terror which engulfed you." This claim, too, is misleading. It is true that the atrocities that were known remained abstract and remote, rarely acquiring the status of knee-buckling knowledge among ordinary citizens. Because the savagery of genocide so defied our everyday experience, many of us failed to comprehend what we had never experienced first-hand. Armenian, Jewish, Cambodian, Tutsi, Bosnian, and other survivors and witnesses had trouble making "the unbelievable believable." The bystanders were thus able to inhabit what one Protestant theologian in the Second World War called the "twilight between knowing and not knowing."

But we must take responsibility for our incredulity. The Holocaust is too present in Western schoolbooks and culture today for genocide to be "unimaginable." We should have learned far sooner to trust even those accounts that could not be independently verified. The stories that emerge from genocidal societies are, by definition, "incredible." Case after case of wishful thinking debunked should have led us to shift the burden of proof away from the harried refugees and to the doubting skeptics who should be required to offer persuasive reasons for disputing refugee claims. A bias toward belief would do less harm than a bias toward disbelief. Instead of aggressively hunting for knowledge or publicizing what was already known, Western officials took shelter in the fog of plausible deniability. In the face of genocide, the search for certainty frequently became an excuse for paralysis and postponement.

In most cases of genocide, those who "did not know" or "did not appreciate" chose not to do so.

The second consoling response usually offered to the question of why the major powers did so little to stop genocide is that any intervention would have been futile. Each time states began slaughtering and deporting their citizens, Western officials claimed that the proposed measures would do little to stem the horrors, or that they would do more harm than good. Usually the officials cited this lack of capacity to ameliorate suffering as a central reason for staying uninvolved. If the hatreds were "age-old" and "two-sided," as was usually claimed, and if the "parties" had in fact been killing one another "for centuries," the implication was that they would kill one another for centuries more. Thus, there was little a well-meaning band of foreign do-gooders could achieve by meddling.

It is difficult, in retrospect, to ascertain what a determined diplomatic, economic, legal, or military intervention could have achieved or what it would have cost. All we do know is that the perpetrators of genocide were quick studies who were remarkably attuned both to the tactics of their genocidal predecessors and to the world's response. From their brutal forerunners, they picked up lessons in everything from dehumanizing their victims and deploying euphemisms to constructing concentration camps and covering their tracks. And from the outside world, they learned the lesson of impunity.

The Turkish minister of the interior, Talaat Pasha, was aware that Sultan Abdul Hamid II had gotten away with murdering Armenians in 1895. In 1939 Hitler was emboldened by the fact that absolutely nobody "remembered the Armenians." Saddam Hussein noted the international community's relaxed response to his chemical weapons attacks against Iran and his bulldozing of Kurdish villages. He rightly assumed he would not be punished for using poison gases against the Kurds. Rwandan gunmen deliberately targeted the Belgian peacekeepers at the start of their genocide because they knew from the U.S. reaction to the deaths of eighteen U.S. soldiers in Somalia that the murder of Western troops would likely precipitate their withdrawal. The Bosnian Serbs publicly celebrated the Mogadishu casualties, knowing that they would never have to do battle with U.S. ground forces. Slobodan Milosevic saw that he got away with the brutal suppression of independence movements in Slovenia and Croatia and reasoned he would pay no price for doing the same in Bosnia and Kosovo. Because so many individual perpetrators were killing for the first time and deciding daily how far they would go, the United States and its European allies missed critical opportunities to try to deter them. When they ignored genocide around the world, the Western powers were not intending to "green light" the perpetrators. But because the killers told themselves they were doing the world a favor by "cleansing" the "undesirables," some surely interpreted silence as consent or even support.

Although it is impossible to know the impact of steps never taken, the best testament to what the Western powers might have achieved is what they did achieve. For all the talk of the futility of foreign involvement, in the rare instances that the United States and its allies took even small steps, they appear to have saved lives. After Senator Pell's sanctions effort forced a reluctant Reagan White House to condemn Saddam Hussein's gas attacks, the Iraqi dictator did not again use chemical weapons against the Kurds. In 1991, after the appeals of Turkey and the personal encounter of U.S. Secretary of State James Baker with Kurdish refugees, the allies succeeded in creating a safe haven for the Kurds in northern Iraq, enabling more than a million Kurds to return to their homes. On a smaller scale, a Rwandan hotel owner credits the mere phone calls of a U.S. diplomat with deterring militias from attacking Tutsi inhabitants of his hotel during the genocide. The 503 UN peacekeepers who remained in Rwanda throughout the genocide protected some twenty-five thousand Rwandans. NATO bombing in Bosnia, when it finally came, rapidly brought that three-and-a-half-year war to a close. Although imperfect, the NATO bombing campaign in Kosovo in 1999 liberated 1.7 million Albanians from tyrannical Serb rule. And a handful of NATO arrests in the former Yugoslavia has caused dozens of suspected war criminals to turn themselves into the UN war crimes tribunal. One cannot assume that every measure proposed would have been effective, but there is no doubt that even these small and tardy steps saved hundreds of thousands of lives. If the Western powers had made genocide prevention a priority, they could have saved countless more.

The real reason the United States and the European states did not do what they could and should have done to stop genocide was not a lack of knowledge or a lack of capacity, but a lack of will. Simply put, Western leaders did not act because they did not want to. They believed that genocide was wrong, but they were not prepared to invest the military, financial, diplomatic, or domestic political capital needed to stop it. The policies crafted in response to each of the major genocides of the twentieth century were not the accidental products of neglect. They were concrete choices made by the world's most influential decision makers after implicit and explicit weighing of costs and benefits. One of the most important and reluctant conclusions one must reach is that the record of the "civilized" world is not one of failure. It is one of "success." The system worked.

To illuminate this point, let us look specifically at the goals of policy makers in the United States. The European responses have either tended to be driven by similar motivations as those of U.S. decision makers or the European allies have directly followed the U.S. lead. From the Armenia genocide forward, U.S. policy makers in the executive branch (usually with the passive backing of most members of Congress) have had two objectives. First, they wanted to avoid engagement in conflicts that posed little threat to American interests, narrowly defined. Second, they hoped to contain the political costs and avoid the moral stigma associated with allowing genocide. By and large, they achieved both aims. In order to contain the political fallout, U.S. officials over-emphasized the ambiguity of the facts. They played up the likely downsides of any proposed intervention. They steadfastly avoided use of the word "genocide," which they believed carried with it legal and moral (and thus political) imperatives to act. And they took solace in the normal operations of the foreign-policy bureaucracy, which permitted an illusion of continual deliberation, complex activity, and intense concern.

To understand why the United States did not do more to stem genocide, of course, it is not enough to focus on the actions of American presidents or their foreign-policy teams. In a democracy, even an administration disinclined to act can be pressured into doing so. This pressure can come from inside and outside. Bureaucrats within the system who grasp the stakes can patiently lobby or brazenly agitate in the hope of forcing their bosses to entertain a full range of options. Unfortunately, while every genocide generated some activism within the U.S. foreign-policy establishment, U.S. civil and foreign servants typically heeded what they took to be presidential indifference and public apathy. They assumed U.S. policy was immutable, that their concerns were already understood by their bosses, and that speaking (or walking) out would only reduce their capacity to improve the policy.

But the main reason American leaders can persist in turning away is that genocide in distant lands has not captivated American senators, congressional caucuses, Washington lobbyists, elite opinion shapers, grassroots groups, and individual constituents. The battle to stop genocide has thus been repeatedly lost in the realm of domestic politics. Although isolated voices have protested the atrocities, Americans outside the executive branch were largely mute when it mattered. As a result of this society-wide silence, officials at all levels of government calculated that the political costs of getting involved in genocide prevention far exceeded the costs of remaining uninvolved.

Here, the exception that proved the rule was the NATO air campaign in Bosnia. Bosnia was the only genocide of the twentieth century that was eventually met with a military response. The domestic pressure was intense. The U.S. failure to stop the atrocities generated a wave of resignations from the U.S. government. The protests of American officials in the foreign service were legitimated daily by sustained public and press activism outside Foggy Bottom. But NATO only intervened in 1995 with a heavy barrage of bombing when its assessment of the costs of intervening was lowered by the Croatian Army's rout of Serb forces, and when its assessment of the costs of *not* intervening was raised by the U.S. Congress's vote to unilaterally lift the arms embargo against the Bosnian Muslims. The lifting of the embargo embarrassed Clinton at home because foreign policy was being made on Capitol Hill by a future presidential challenger, Senate Majority Leader Bob Dole. It also made it likely that European governments were going to pull their peacekeepers out of the Balkans, which would have required U.S. troop participation in a potentially bloody and certainly humiliating rescue mission. This scenario was one that President Clinton wanted to avoid on the eve of his bid for reelection.

With foreign policy crises all over the world implicating more traditional U.S. interests, the slaughter of civilians will rarely secure top-level attention on its own merits. It takes political pressure to put genocide "on the map" in Washington or in any of the European capitals. When Alison des Forges of Human Rights Watch met with National Security Adviser Anthony Lake two weeks into the Rwanda genocide, he informed her that the phones were not ringing. "Make more noise!" he urged. Because so little noise has been made about genocide, U.S. officials have opposed American intervention, firmly convinced that they were doing all they could—and, most important, all they should—in light of competing American interests and a highly circumscribed understanding of what was domestically "possible."

Although U.S. officials have sometimes expressed remorse after genocide, none fear professional accountability for their sins of omission. In the 1970s, Senate hearings on Capitol Hill documented abuses committed by America and its cold war allies in Latin America, southeast Asia, and elsewhere. As a result of this public reckoning and some of the formal checks instituted in its wake, U.S. foreign policy decision makers now fear repercussions for their sins of commission—for decisions they make and policies they shape that go wrong. But while everyone within the U.S. government has the incentive to avoid "another Somalia" or "another Vietnam," few think twice about playing a role in allowing "another Rwanda."

Other countries and institutions whose personnel were actually present when genocide was committed have been forced to be more introspective. The Netherlands, France, and the UN have each staged inquiries into their responsibility for the fall of Srebrenica and the massacres that followed. The inquiries did not lead to any notable political reforms, but they at least "named names," which might affect the behavior of bureaucrats the next time around. The United States has not looked back. When the UN's Srebrenica investigators approached the U.S. mission in New York for assistance, their phone calls were not returned. In the end, the UN team was forbidden from making any independent contact with U.S. government employees. The investigators were granted access to a group of hand-picked junior and mid-level officials who knew or revealed next to nothing about what the United States knew during the Srebrenica slaughter.

The French, the Belgians, the UN, and the Organization for African Unity have undertaken investigations on the Rwanda genocide. But in the United States, when Cynthia McKinney and Donald Payne, two disgruntled members of the Congressional Black Caucus (which was itself quiet during the 1994 massacres), attempted to stage hearings on the U.S. role, they were rebuffed. Two officials in the Clinton administration, one at the National Security Council, the other at the State Department, conducted internal studies on the administration's response to the Rwanda genocide. But they examined only the paper trail and did not publicly disclose their findings. What is needed are congressional inquiries with the power to subpoena documents and U.S. officials of all ranks and roles in the executive and legislative branches. Without meaningful disclosure, public awareness, and official shame, it is hard to imagine the U.S. response improving the next time around.

The September 11, 2001, attacks on the United States may have permanently altered U.S. foreign policy. The hope is that the attacks will make Americans inside and outside government more capable of imagining evil committed against innocent civilians. The fanatics targeting America resemble the perpetrators of genocide in their espousal of collective responsibility of the most savage kind. They attack civilians not because of anything the unwitting targets do personally, but because of who they are. To earn a death sentence, it was enough in the last century to be an Armenian, a Jew, or a Tutsi. On September 11, it was enough to be an American. Instead of causing Americans to retreat from global humanitarian engagement, the terrorist attacks could cause us to empathize with peoples victimized by genocide. In 1994, Rwanda, a country of eight million, experienced the equivalent of more than two World Trade Center attacks every single day for a hundred days. This was the proportional equivalent of two hundred and thirty thousand Americans killed each day, or twenty-three million Americans murdered in three months. When, on September 12, 2001, the United States turned for help to its allies, Americans were gratified by the overwhelming response. When the Tutsi cried out, by contrast, every country in the world turned away.

The fear, after September 11, is that the United States will view genocide prevention as a luxury it cannot afford as it sets out to better protect Americans. Some are now arguing, understandably, that fighting terrorism requires husbanding America's resources and avoiding "social work" such as humanitarian intervention, which is said to harm U.S. "readiness." Many believe that NATO's 1999 intervention in Kosovo and the current trial of Serbian president Slobodan Milosevic, which were once thought to mark important precedents, will in fact represent highwater marks for genocide prevention and punishment.

Without U.S. leadership, the last century showed, others will be unwilling to step forward to act, and genocide will continue. If the United States treats the war on terrorism as a war that can be prosecuted in a vacuum, with no regard for *genocidal* terror, it will be making a colossal mistake. There are two main reasons that the United States and its European allies should stop genocide. The first and most convincing reason is moral. When innocent life is being taken on such a scale and the United States and its allies have the power to stop the killing at reasonable risk, they have a duty to act. It is this belief that motivates most of those who seek intervention. But foreign policy is not driven by morality; it is driven by interests, narrowly defined. And history has shown that the suffering of victims has rarely been sufficient to spark a Western intervention.

The second reason for acting is the threat genocide in fact poses to Western interests. Allowing genocide undermines regional and international stability, creates militarized refugees, and signals dictators that hate and murder are permissible tools of statecraft. Because these dangers to national interests are long-term dangers and not immediately apparent, however, they have rarely convinced top Western policy makers. Genocide has undermined regional stability, but the regions it destabilized tended also to lie outside the U.S. and European spheres of concern. Refugees have been militarized, but they tended not to wash up on America's shores. A key reason European leaders were more engaged in the Balkans in the 1990s than their American counterparts was that Bosnian refugees did land in Britain, France, and Germany. But generally genocidal regimes recognized that if they limited the spillover costs locally, they could count on Western leaders to stay disengaged. Thus intervention only came about on the rare occasions when the shorter-term political interests of Western policy makers were triggered.

American leadership remains essential for mobilizing local, regional, and international responses to genocide. But if it was difficult before September 11 to get U.S. decision makers to see the long-term costs of allowing genocide, it will be even harder today when U.S. security needs are so acute. Nonetheless, the record shows that trying to build walls around genocidal societies almost guarantees trouble down the road. American security and security for Americans abroad is contingent on international stability, and there is perhaps no greater source of havoc than a group of well-armed extremists bent on wiping out a people on ethnic, national, or religious grounds.

States that murder and torment their own citizens almost inevitably target citizens elsewhere. Their appetites become insatiable. Hitler began by persecuting his own people and then expanded his campaign to the rest of Europe and, in time, the United States. Saddam Hussein wiped out rural Kurdish life and then turned on Kuwait, sending his genocidal henchman Ali Hassan al-Majid to govern the newly occupied country. The United States now has reason to fear that the poisonous potions Hussein tried out on the Kurds will be used next against Americans. Milosevic took his wars from Slovenia and Croatia to Bosnia and then Kosovo. The United States and its European allies are still paying for their earlier neglect of the Balkans by having to grapple with violence in Macedonia that continues to threaten the stability of southeastern Europe.

Citizens victimized by genocide or abandoned by the international community do not make good neighbors, as their thirst for vengeance, their irredentism, and their acceptance of violence as a means of generating change can turn them into future threats. In Bosnia, where the United States and Europe maintained an arms embargo against the Muslims, extremist Islamic fighters and proselytizers eventually turned up to offer succor. Some secular Muslim citizens became radicalized by the partnership, and the failed state of Bosnia became a haven for Islamic terrorists shunned elsewhere in the world. It appears that one of the organizations that infiltrated Bosnia in its hour of need and used it as a training base was Osama bin Laden's Al Qaeda. And however high the number of Islamic radicals that were imported during or created by the Serb slaughter of Bosnia's Muslims, the figure would have been exponentially higher if the United States and its allies had allowed the killing to continue past 1995. The current Bosnian government, one legacy of the U.S.-brokered Dayton Peace Agreement, is far from perfect, but it is at least a strategic partner in the war against terrorism. Without the belated NATO bombing and U.S. diplomatic leadership, that same Bosnian government might today be an American foe.

For the foreseeable future, American leadership will be necessary to stop or punish genocide. Clearly, the United States does not have the resources to simultaneously defend itself from attack and deploy its troops to every trouble spot where the threat of ethnic violence lurks. It must be extremely cautious about deploying U.S. forces abroad. But U.S. policy options should not be framed in terms of doing nothing or sending in the Marines. There will be times when the magnitude of the moral harm will demand risking U.S. military force. There will also be times when, owing to America's past dealings in the region, U.S. intervention will be singularly inappropriate. There will be times when the risk to U.S. soldiers will outweigh the benefits a military intervention would likely bring to the victims. There will be times when even a good-faith presidential effort to convince the American people of the value of intervening will fail to create a political constituency for U.S. military action.

But in such circumstances, just because the United States might not deploy its troops, it does not mean that a U.S. leadership role is not required or that other forms of intervention should not be tried. U.S. officials must focus less on avoiding embarrassing the United States and more on accurately diagnosing and treating the atrocities underway. Deliberately calling genocide something it is not—"civil war" or "tribal violence"—in order to mute public pressure is not only dishonest; it is detrimental to sound policy. Handling atrocity as war has led to the deployment of conflict resolution experts, the misguided pursuit of cease-fires, and the spiraling investment in "peace processes" that too often become stalling devices that shield murder.

Instead of regarding intervention as an all-or-nothing proposition, the United States and its allies should respond to genocide by publicly identifying and threatening its perpetrators with prosecution, demanding the expulsion of representatives of genocidal regimes from international institutions such as the United Nations, closing the perpetrators' embassies in Western capitals, and calling upon countries aligned with the perpetrators to ask them to use their influence. Depending on the circumstances, Western powers might establish economic sanctions or freeze foreign assets, impose an arms embargo, or, if warranted, lift an arms embargo. They might use their technical resources to jam inflammatory radio or television broadcasts that are essential to stirring panic and hate. They might set up safe areas to house refugees and civilians, and enforce them with well-armed and robustly mandated peacekeepers, air power, or both.

Genocide prevention is an immense burden and one that must be shared. But even if U.S. troops stay home, American leadership will be indispensable in assembling "coalitions of the willing" to deploy ground troops, in encouraging U.S. allies to step up their capacities, and in strengthening regional and international institutions that might eventually carry more of the weight.

For most of the second half of the twentieth century, the existence of the Genocide Convention appeared to achieve little. The United States did not ratify the Convention for forty years. Those countries that did ratify it never invoked it to stop or punish genocide. And instead of making Western policy makers more inclined to stop genocide, ratification seemed only to make them more reluctant to use the "g-word." Still, Lemkin's coinage has done more good than harm. The international war crimes tribunals for the former Yugoslavia and Rwanda and the permanent International Criminal Court would have likely not come into existence without the Convention's passage. The punishment that takes place at these courts will help deter genocide in the long term. But more fundamentally, without the existence of the Convention, or

Lemkin's proselytizing around it, the word genocide would not carry the moral stigma it has acquired. Hope for enforcement of the Genocide Convention lies in the stigma associated with committing the crime of genocide. And paradoxically hope also lies in the lengths to which Western policy makers have gone to vow never again to allow genocide and the comparable lengths to which they have gone, while allowing it, to deny its occurrence.

Because it is unlikely that Western leaders will have the vision to recognize that they endanger their countries' long-term vital national interests by allowing genocide, the most realistic hope for combating it lies in the rest of us creating short-term political costs for those who do nothing.

# Acknowledgments

We are especially grateful to the Rockefeller Foundation for a grant that allowed us to undertake this project and center it on firsthand reporting from Yugoslavia, Rwanda, and East Timor. We are also indebted to Vanessa Mobley, our editor at Basic Books, who never doubted that a collective undertaking like ours could succeed.

# Index

# About the Contributors

**Bill Berkeley** is a reporter for *The New York Times* and the author of *The Graves Are Not Yet Full—Race, Tribe, and Power in the Heart of Africa.* His writing has appeared in *The Atlantic Monthly, The Washington Post,* and *The New Republic.* He was a senior fellow at the World Policy Institute and for three years worked for the Lawyers Committee for Human Rights conducting investigative reporting in Africa and the Middle East. He is the author of two human rights reports, *Zimbabwe—Wages of War,* and *Liberia—A Promise Betrayed.*

**Kira Brunner** is a freelance writer living in New York and co-editor of *Radical Society.*

**Michael Ignatieff** is director of the Carr Center for Human Rights Policy, John F. Kennedy School of Government, Harvard University. His books include *The Russian Album; The Warrior's Honor: Ethnic War and the Modern Conscience; Isaiah Berlin: A Life;* and most recently *Virtual War: Kosovo and Beyond.* He is a frequent contributor to *The New York Times, The New Yorker,* and *The New York Review of Books.*

**Darryl Li** works for the Palestinian Centre for Human Rights in the Gaza strip. His essay was adapted from a longer study on the role of radio in the Rwandan genocide.

**Peter Maass** covered the war in Bosnia for *The Washington Post* and is the author of a memoir of the Bosnian conflict, *Love Thy Neighbor: A Story of War,* which won the *Los Angeles Times* Book Prize for nonfiction and the Overseas Press Club's Cornelius Ryan Award. Maass is currently a contributing writer to *The New York Times Magazine.* His articles and extracts from his book are archived at www.petermaass.com.

**Nicolaus Mills**, a member of the *Dissent* editorial board and a senior scholar at the Woodrow Wilson International Center in Washington, is professor of American Studies at Sarah Lawrence College. His books include *The Crowd in American Literature*; *Like a Holy Crusade: Mississippi 1964*; and *The Triumph of Meanness: America's War Against Its Better Self*. His articles have appeared in *The New York Times*, *Los Angeles Times*, *Chicago Tribune*, and *Yale Review*.

**Bernardine Niyirora** is a Rwandan genocide survivor who continues to live in the country of her birth.

**George Packer** was a member of the Peace Corps in Lavie, Togo, from 1982 to 1983. He is the author of two works of fiction, *The Half Man* and *Central Square*, and two works of nonfiction, *The Village of Waiting* and *Blood of the Liberals*, which won the 2001 Robert F. Kennedy Book Award. He is currently working on a book about Americans in Africa.

**Richard Lloyd Parry** is the Asia correspondent of the British newspaper, *The Independent*. His work has appeared in *Granta*, the *London Review of Books*, and *The New York Times Magazine*. He is currently writing a book about Indonesia and East Timor.

**Samantha Power**, the executive director of the Carr Center for Human Rights Policy, John F. Kennedy School of Government, Harvard University, is the author of *"A Problem from Hell": America and the Age of Genocide*. She is a human rights lawyer and former war correspondent, whose writing has appeared in *The Atlantic Monthly*, *The New Republic*, and *The Economist*.

**David Rieff** is the author of *Going to Miami*; *The Exile: Cuba in the Heart of Miami*; *Los Angeles: Capital of the Third World*; *Slaughterhouse: Bosnia and the Failure of the West*; and most recently, *A Bed for the Night: Humanitarianism in Crisis*. He is a frequent contributor to *The New Yorker*, *The New York Times*, *Los Angeles Times*, and *The New Republic*. He lives in New York City.

**Geoffrey Robinson** is an associate professor of history at the University of California Los Angeles, and the author of *The Dark Side of Paradise: Political Violence* *in Bali.* Before coming to UCLA, he worked for six years at the Amnesty International research department in London. From June to November 1999, he served as political affairs officer with the United Nations Mission in East Timor.

**Lejla Sabic** was fourteen years old when the war in Yugoslavia began. She and her family survived the war while living in Sarajevo, first in their own apartment and then in the basement of their apartment building. She immigrated to the United States in 2000 and currently lives in Queens and works in Manhattan.

**William Shawcross** is a British writer, journalist, and broadcaster. His books include *Sideshow: Kissinger, Nixon, and the Destruction of Cambodia; The Quality of Mercy: Cambodia, Holocaust, and Modern Conscience;* and most recently, *Deliver Us from Evil: Peacekeepers, Warlords, and a World of Endless Conflict.* A winner of the 1980 George Polk Book award, he serves on the board of the International Crisis Group.

**Filomenia Suares** lives in Maliana, East Timor, where she works in a women's collective making rugs. Her husband, Francisco Torresao, was brutally murdered by pro-Indonesia militia in 1999. The fragments of his dismembered body were later identified by a UN/Australian forensic team and returned for burial.

**Erin Trowbridge** is a journalist whose work has appeared in the *Los Angeles Times, Earth Times,* and on National Public Radio. She wrote her essay on East Timor while on a leave of absence from the United Nations Development Programme.

**Michael Walzer** is a professor at the School of Social Science, Institute for Advanced Study, Princeton, and co-editor of *Dissent.* His books include *Just and Unjust Wars; Spheres of Justice; Exodus and Revolution; The Company of Critics;* and *On Toleration.* A slightly different version of his essay was given as the 2001 Theodore Mitau Lecture at Macalester College, St. Paul, Minnesota.